DATE DUE

DEMCO 38-296

The New Insecurity

SUNY Series in Social and Political Thought
Kenneth Baynes, Editor

THE
NEW
INSECURITY

The End of the Standard Job and Family

Jerald Wallulis

State University of New York Press

Published by
State University of New York Press, Albany

©1998 State University of New York

For information, address State University of New York
Press, State University Plaza, Albany, NY, 12246

Production by Diane Ganeles
Marketing by Dana Yanulavich

Library of Congress Cataloging-in-Publication Data

Wallulis, Jerald, 1947–
    The new insecurity : the end of the standard job and family /
    Jerald Wallulis.
        p.   cm. — (SUNY series in social and political thought)
        Includes bibliographical references and index.
        ISBN 0-7914-3655-1 (hardcover:alk. paper).—ISBN 0-7914-3656-X
    (pbk. : alk. paper)
        1. Job security.   2. Economic security.   3. Social security.
    4. Michel Foucault
    I. Title   II. Series.
    HD5708.4.W35   1997
    331'.25'96—dc21   97-13598
                                                           CIP

10 9 8 7 6 5 4 3 2 1

This book is dedicated to my daughter, Jeanette, and to all other adolescents who are having to learn to be contemporary "planning offices." I hope that she and they will have at least some of the security in life planning that I have been able to enjoy and managed to take for granted.

Contents

Part III: The Struggle for Employability and the Fear of Inadequacy

B. Seebohm Rowntree, *Poverty: A Study of Town Life*, 1902:

A family living upon the scale allowed for in this estimate ["merely physical efficiency"] must never spend a penny on railway fare or omnibus. They must never go into the country unless they walk. They must never purchase a halfpenny newspaper or spend a penny to buy a ticket for a popular concert. They must write no letters to absent children, for they cannot afford to pay the postage. They must never contribute anything to their church or chapel, or give any help to a neighbour which costs them money. They cannot save, nor can they join sick club or Trade Union, because they cannot pay the necessary subscriptions. The children must have no pocket money for dolls, marbles, or sweets. The father must smoke no tobacco, and must drink no beer. The mother must never buy any pretty clothes for herself or for her children . . . Should a child fall ill, it must be attended by the parish doctor; should it die, it must be buried by the parish. Finally, the wage-earner must never be absent from his work for a single day.

If any of these conditions are broken, the extra expenditure involved is met, **and can only be met**, by limiting the diet; or, in other words, by sacrificing physical efficiency.

Time "Man of the Year," 1966: The man—and woman—of 25 and under

What makes the Man of the Year unique? Cushioned by unprecedented affluence and the welfare state, he has a sense of economic security unmatched in history. Granted an ever-lengthening adolescence and life-span, he no longer feels the cold pressures of hunger and mortality. . . . Science and the knowledge explosion have armed him with more tools to choose his life pattern than he can always use: physical and intellectual mobility, personal and financial opportunity, a vista of change accelerating in every direction.

Untold adventure awaits him. He is the man who will land on the moon, cure cancer and the common cold, lay out blight-proof, smog-free cities, enrich the underdeveloped world, and, no doubt, write finis to poverty and war.

Tracy Chapman song, "Subcity," *Crossroads* 1989:

'What did I do to deserve this
Had my trust in god
Worked everyday of my life
Thought I had some guarantees
That's what I thought
At least that's what I thought

Last night I had another restless sleep
Wondering what tomorrow might bring
Last night I dreamed
A cold blue light was shining down on me
I screamed myself awake
Thought I must be dying
Thought I must be dying'

Acknowledgments

This book emphasizes the importance of economic security in life planning. Crucial to its being written are two forms of economic support for my own academic planning received from the University of South Carolina. My sabbatical study in 1995 was supported by the College of Liberal Arts, and I also received financial assistance from a Research and Productive Scholarship Grant from the University.

The grant allowed me to spend part of the sabbatical period at Northwestern University at the invitation of Tom McCarthy. There I attended classes held by Jürgen Habermas. I wish to thank them both for the opportunity, as well as Oliver Lee, a member of the sociology department, for his suggestions concerning academic resources on the topic of social security. I also want to thank Bill Martin of DePaul University for his hospitality and the many philosophical discussions we had.

I am especially indebted to friends from three other midwestern universities during the same sabbatical period. Bert Kögler, Bill McBride, and Karl Ameriks agreed to read an earlier version of the manuscript. In visits with them at the University of Illinois, Purdue University, and the University of Notre Dame respectively, I profited greatly from their many suggestions for improvement as well as enjoyed their hospitality.

Other suggestions for improvement were made by the reviewers for the State University of New York Press. I especially want to thank an anonymous reviewer and Kenneth Baynes, the editor of the series, for suggestions concerning the final section of the book. Shelley Smith and Larry Glickman of the University of South Carolina also read later versions of the manuscript, made helpful comments, and convinced me of the need to add an appendix.

Finally I wish to thank my wife, Annie Duménil, and daughter, Jeanette, for all the support and encouragement they have given me during this project.

Preface: No Longer Secure

I viewed my favorite Christmas season program some twenty-five years ago, so time has probably added to the favorable impression. "Christmas for Grownups" was a regional production of Southwest German Television for viewers in that region. Because it demonstrated the clear non-inferiority of modest budgeting in comparison to the lavish productions of major or national networks, it may be my favorite program of all.

There are four small segments of the half-hour program that are cherished and enhanced in my memory. The first is perhaps standard fare on the "buying orgies" of the department stores and the declining church attendance for Christmas services. The second involves an interview by a prisoner, eligible for parole after twenty years of incarceration, on the meaning of forgiveness. The fourth is a very moving testimony of a person born blind on the personal meaning of sight and the religious significance of the symbol of light.

The third segment, less moving than the fourth, took advantage of the opening of a new opera house in Saarbrücken, the major industrial center of the Saar region. The new director was asked why he chose to inaugurate the opera house and to mark the Christmas season with the "children's opera," *Hansel and Gretel*. His answer pointed to a scene in the opera where the children are lost in a forest on a stormy night and fall asleep afraid. They awake in the middle of the night, the storm gone. Sensing that it is Christmas, they feel secure and safe.

The director ended the interview with a query as to whether many adults attending the opera could feel Hansel and Gretel's sense of security during the Christmas season. Probably not many then, but twenty five years later with the strong cutbacks in manufacturing in the Saar region, probably even fewer now. And maybe in the United States even fewer yet.

From 1973 to 1995 the median family income remained static in the U.S., a marked contrast to the period between 1947 and 1973 when median family income actually doubled. Similarly, real family income has held steady or declined.[1] Downsizing and corporate restructuring have become common business practices and produced in employees nervous uncertainty about employment possibilities, health care coverage, and pension benefits. Gone are the days of career-long devotion to one employer, with a gold watch and a happy retirement the reward of a worker's continued service. The fabled "American dream" of a high-paying permanent job, upward mobility, secure home ownership, and greater prosperity for one's children appears today less achievable, more remote, even romantic. Perhaps equally romantic—at least in the sense of unrealistic— is the expectation of being able to share the American dream with a permanent partner for all of one's adulthood.[2]

And so American adult Hansels and Gretels find themselves in the midst of a stormy night of economic insecurity, uncertain as to whether their Christmases will keep coming. Instead they wake up insecure about their present and future life situations, the future prospects of their loved ones, and the economic stability of their communities and nation.[3] They/we know someone who has gotten a pink slip, if they/we have not gotten one or several such slips. They/we know someone who is unemployed and they/we fear the threat of at least underemployment. They/we know at least someone who is divorced and not remarried, and their/our children are likely to know more friends who come from single parent families. And the majority of them/us do not believe that their/our children's future will be as good as their/our own.

This book is about the uncertainty being felt in a particularly intense way by individuals in the present as to what to do economically and how to plan the family future. I offer a framework for understanding such individual uncertainty in terms of novel challenges and intensified struggles in life planning. My belief is that the challenges to traditional life planning are not just momentary and will not easily lead to a *Hansel and Gretel* ending where the bitter witch of employment uncertainty is magically turned into a sweet honey cake. Nor are the intensified struggles a result of "free-floating" economic anxiety which will disappear when the next "real" economic recovery finally comes. The sense of economic well being and personal confidence in life planning have been greatly affected by the new and non-disappearing economic realities of global competition, automation, the explosions of communication and information technologies, and business reengineering and reorganization in general. Social well being has similarly been threatened by the possible prospects of prolonged loneliness and the real and at least for now irremovable difficulties of single parenthood.

An integral part of the framework for comprehending this contemporary sense of insecurity is a sense of the loss of security from the immediate past. It is this sense of the **no longer** secure individual which provides the historical context for comprehending how intense the new uncertainty is and how significant the change actually is. There is a sense that the long-term career ladders and well established professional career pathways are no longer there and that loyalty to a company, business, or state organization no longer pays off. Marriage appears to be in a similarly precarious situation, for to expect and plan upon permanency appears tantamount to exposing oneself to disappointment, if not even to danger. Because both employment and marriage are no longer so permanent, decisions made in the past appear to count for less in terms of long-term security. The facts of employment and marriage are superseded in importance as life planning goals, it will be argued, by the struggle to achieve employ**ability** and marriage**ability**[4] in the present and to preserve them in the future.

While the feeling of being no longer secure may and probably does refer first of all to the immediate past, it is a mistake, I contend, to view this change only from a short historical distance. The change in individual planning brought about by such factors as the demand for worker flexibility and the loss of expectation of permanent marriage is best understood in the context of a much longer history of social practices and individual practices of the self. This history begins with an analysis of self-discipline in the period of absolutism by Gerhard Oestreich. The Neo-Stoic ethic of Justus Lipsius counseled soldiers in early modern times to fight, not flee, and workers to work, not be idle. My diagnosis of the present is that such imperatives have been turned around remarkably, if not completely on their heads. This diagnosis relies (1) on a reading of contemporary literature on the effects of business reorganization on career management and (2) on Zygmunt Bauman's analysis of individual identity today as characterized by the strikingly different demands both not to close off options but to keep them open and, at all costs, not to mortgage the future.

Another quite different, but equally crucial part of my larger history is the development of what some social theorists have termed the "insurance state." The emergence of the insurance state has enabled life planning to be carried out with the presumption of having social insurance and with the reliance upon political programs of social assistance. Social insurance has provided security from risks of unemployment, disability, and indigent old age and, at least in many countries, direct support has been offered for full-time female homemaking and mothering.[5] However, while social insurance has played an undeniably important role in the genesis of more secure life planning, the new economic realities threaten to undermine the long-term, full-time employment which has functioned and continues to function as its basis. Moreover, the collective endeavor to protect individual security has also come under fire in the context of a political attack, often termed a tax-payer revolt, against welfare assistance. My book both highlights the historical contribution of the insurance state to the original achievement of individual security and introduces new options showing how income assistance could buffer the most adverse economic and familial effects of the loss of secure employment.

The development and implementation of social insurance is, of course, a story capable of being told of all the "developed" countries of Europe, Asia, and North America. This study, however, pays particular attention to the American tradition of individualism and the liberal implementation of social insurance and social programs. Although social insurance and welfare were first initiated, as will be explained later, for conservative reasons in Bismarckian Germany and are most strongly established in European countries with strong traditions of social democracy, I consider above all the liberal introduction of social security in the United States (and England).[6] This is because the phenomenon most central to the study, the no longer secure **individual**, is most evident, I believe, within the accelerated changes of what Edward Luttwak has dubbed "American-style, turbo-charged capitalism,"[7] even if neither its appearance nor its prevalence is confined to such boundaries. Although the context for the discussion of the threatened loss of individual security is clearly more American and sociological in emphasis, my tools for developing a larger history of life planning are more European and philosophical in origin. Part One of the book outlines a genealogy of the secure individual. Here I am obviously indebted to Michel Foucault and to work on statistics and liberalism accomplished by scholars broadly associated with his thought. This choice of intellectual sources has a great deal to do with the applicability I find in Foucault's later research on governmentality for the present American context. Similar to the content of that low budget television program mentioned above, I am convinced that this research on modernity and on the origins of the subject, when modified to apply more to the economicality (my own term) of practices of the self, pertains in a direct and challenging manner to the life planning and practices of individual Americans who have enjoyed security in the past and find it threatened now. As indicated above, I am particularly influenced by how Foucault's emphasis on social practices of discipline complements Oestreich's history of a Neo-Stoic ethics of constancy as an individual practice of the self, and how this past attitude of constancy contrasts with Bauman's analysis of a new and prevalent attitude of "not mortgaging the future." In no way, however, do I claim that my combination of these resources is the only historical framework suitable for comprehending the new demands of worker flexibility. Indeed I heartily welcome any other interpretive attempt which is equally committed to understanding the impact of the new globalization on individual attitudes and practices as historically momentous.

After the genealogy of the secure individual, I continue my project with a negative diagnosis of the secure individual's present status and a rhetorical argument in favor of its future restoration and preservation. In all of these parts, the book relies on a group of broadly interdisciplinary authors to complement the continental philosophical sources. They include, among others, sociologists of the modern life cycle and of the family, historians of liberalism, social security, and statistics, and economists concerned with modern work and its future transformations. These authors have, in my estimation, made very important contributions to the understanding of their particular subjects. They have not, of course, made exhaustive analyses either of their own fields or of the material relating to my conception of individual security. Hence my references will appear highly selective to specialists in these areas and they undoubtedly are far less than comprehensive. The selectivity is a result of my purposes and intellectual limitations; it is not a fault in the sources themselves.

Finally, there is a third, still different kind of source which influences the analysis of the present and future status of the secure individual in my book. At the conclusion of *Post-Capitalist Society*, Peter Drucker claims that there will have to be a change in the notion of the educated person in accordance with the new type of knowledge society in which we live: "The educated person will . . . have to live and work simultaneously in two cultures—that of the 'intellectual,' who focuses on words and ideas, and that of the 'manager,' who focuses on people and work."[8] This book is, or at least aspires to be, a contribution of the more limited intellectual sort from a leopard who has a great deal of difficulty in changing his spots. However, it also seeks to acknowledge and integrate into its presentation many managerial sources—Drucker and Charles Handy preeminently among them—who have written insightfully and trenchantly about the newest economic transformations. A process of selection is undoubtedly at work and I am certain that some of the most important contributions of this genre have been overlooked.

Most books that can be broadly categorized as of the "managerial" culture affirm or at least accept the economic transformations now taking place and counsel individuals on how to adapt to, if not profit from, the ramifications of the larger changes in the economy and society. My view is a quite different one, a stance of scepticism and anxiety, and the counsel resulting from that view is more of reform than adaptation. These differences may be attributed to a lack of adequate acquaintance or knowledge of the managerial culture on my part, but there may equally well be an important conflict between cultures at work. The issues addressed by the loss of individual security in the senses considered in this book are so important that they cannnot be left to the talented analysts of the managerial culture alone.

Introduction: Destandardized Lives

Not only is there a personal feeling of being no longer secure in comparison to the immediate past; this change also occupies a place in the social scientific literature as well. The modern sense of individual security and the contemporary feeling of loss of security correlate with a large and interesting body of literature on the standardization and destandardization of the modern life cycle. According to social scientists, sociohistorians, and social theorists, a process of standardization of the life cycle began in the modern period and has become more and more established. The high degree of standardization, the topic of the first section of the introduction, has not precluded, however, an equally important process of individualization. In turn, this process has intensified how far in advance the individual plans out her or his life history. Ulrich Beck has captured this aspect of planning in a trenchant metaphor which is explained in the second section of the introduction and will continually reappear throughout this book: we[1] are—and have to be—our own "planning offices."[2]

More recently, sociologists of the life cycle have proposed at least a partial destandardization in life history with particular reference to work histories and family relationships. Important uncertainties have arisen in regard to the stability of what is designated the family cycle, especially in regard to marriage and the care of children. Major changes, if not upheavals, have been brought about by larger economic factors such as computer technology, telecommunications, automation, and organizational

1

reengineering or downsizing. The implementation of what has been called "flexible specialization" on a work force of core and periphery workers has greatly affected the nature, likelihood, and duration of employment.

The third section of the introduction, "Planning without Guarantees," considers the topic of destandardization in life history with specific respect to its impact on individual life planning. The effects of destandardized work and family relationships, which will later be examined in greater detail in Part Two of the book, are introduced and related to the personal confidence with which individuals have planned in advance in the past. This confidence had, and hopefully still has, a crucial role in making individuals secure, especially when the individual has been able to rely upon governmental programs of social insurance and social protection as well. The loss of security threatened by the loss of confidence in individual life planning and by the inadequacy of the present collective endeavors to insure individual security provides both the larger framework of *The New Insecurity* and later the specific subject matters of its final two chapters.

The Standard Life Cycle

The care and nurturing of infancy and early childhood together with the growth and educational training of adolescence, the occupational and probably familial involvements of adulthood, the "third age" of retirement and the "fourth age" of the decline of old age and death—these are the chronological stages of modern life. Many of them—youth, adulthood, and "third age" or "the age of living, as the French would have it, which follows the first age of learning and the second of earning"[3]—are even said to have been "invented"[4] in the modern period (according to the historian Philippe Ariès in his famous study of childhood). They have become parts of what sociologists have termed the "standardized" life cycle.

A standardized life cycle because, according to Martin Kohli, the duration of life has been transformed "from a pattern of relative randomness to a pattern of predictable life span."[5] The decisive feature of this transformation is the extension of the life span from forty-seven years in 1900 to now more than seventy-five years. As John Kotre and Elizabeth Hall explain this change, "The change has not come about because our genetic potential for long life has increased, but rather because improving health conditions have allowed more of us to reach the potential we've had all along."[6] Although there is an initial high rate of infant mortality and a later high rate of old-age mortality, in between lies a fairly constant, lower mortality rate. As Kohli states, "death has almost disappeared from early and even middle adulthood, and tends to strike in old age only."[7]

A standardized life cycle also because of the emergence of what is called the "family cycle." Kohli claims that the concept of a family cycle has "questionable value" in regard to the premodern family.[8] Now, however, sociologists and psychologists refer to or even presuppose a family cycle in the sequence from marriage to birth of the first child to birth of the last child to the last child leaving home and finally widowhood. Although divorce rates have increased and empty nests do not now always remain so, a conclusion of the research is that the historical change up to the most recent times "has not resulted in the dissolution of the family, but rather in the strengthening of the normative pattern."[9]

A standardized life cycle perhaps most importantly because of a modern work cycle of training, career, and retirement as well. A period of work preparation or "First Age" begins with the learning of childhood and extends to the further education and/or apprenticeship for adolescents (and post-adolescents) and the final awarding of appropriate credentials for employment. It is followed by a "Second Age" of earning, a long period of work or career activity that may feature a more orderly and progressive development or be of a spontaneous or even chaotic character. At the conclusion of this activity, the prospects of a "Third Age" of retirement living offer themselves to the majority of the working or the total population in accordance with a sufficient level of public and/or private pension assistance, before a "Fourth Age" of either slow or more rapid decline occurs.

Finally, a standardized life cycle in virtue of the increased welfare role of the modern state. According to Karl Ulrich Mayer and Walter Müller, "general rules" have been developed through wide-ranging social security legislation which "define obligations and legitimate claims" and even regulate "very specific eventualities of daily life." As a consequence, "Life develops into a series of precisely circumscribed events and states with well defined entries and exits" into educational, occupational, and retirement phases. According to their imagery, "the state can be thought as imposing structure on the life course by creating 'welfare tracks' in the course of life."[10]

Individualization and the Modern "Planning Office"

In addition to uniform mortality rates, "normal" family patterns, homogenized educational requirements, standard career "clocks,"[11] and welfare "tracking," most social scientists who study the standardized life cycle speak of a process of individualization which is just as prominent as the standardization of modern life stages. Beck, Kohli, and Marlis Buchmann all view individualization as a general process in which the individual is released from the restrictions of "status, locality, and family," but at the same time exchanges them "for the constraints of existence in the labor market and as a consumer, with the standardizations and controls they contain."[12] Beck adds that "liberated individuals become dependent on the labor market and **because of that**, dependent on education, consumption, welfare state regulations and support, traffic planning, consumer supplies, and on the possibilities and fashions in medical, psychological and pedagogical counseling and care."[13] The consequence of these institutional dependencies, according to Buchmann, is described as follows: "Individuals **can** make life course-related choices, but they also **must** make them in correspondence with the requirements of the standardized life course."[14]

Beck seeks to capture the close interrelationship between standardization and individual project through the concept of "institutionally dependent individual situations" where the "apparent outside of the institutions becomes the inside of individual biography."[15] He also employs the concept of "institutional biographical patterns" and has in mind the "entry into and exit from the educational system, entry into and exit from work, or determinations of the retirement age based on social policy."[16]

The "institutional patterns" in regard to education are dominated by considerations of the transition from the educational system to the labor market. While the patterns of entry into and progress within the educational system are all standardized on an age-graded basis, it is the achievement of certificates at the conclusion of this educational sequence that is of primary individual importance. These certificates grant access to specific occupational positions and so may be said to "sort" individuals in regard to their suitability and potentiality for future work success. At the same time Buchmannn notes: "The transformation of educational certificates into occupational status on the labor market is not an automatic process. It has to be individually realized. It is at that point that the **real** social value of an educational certificate is established on the labor market."[17]

After education, the "point of entry, the sequences of professional development and related transitions, mobility chances and their timing, and the culmination of a (successful) professional career"[18] are all parts of a similarly highly standardized and yet highly individualized institutional pattern regarding occupational entry and exit. Buchmann writes of "socially defined occupational trajectories" which individually define "what is attainable and what is beyond reach in the course of a professional life."[19] Individuals "orient their plans and actions toward the steps and sequences of the professional trajectory, and they reorient themselves each time they complete a step."[20]

An occupational trajectory that is less "well structured" carries with it a high amount of contingency and is consequently less calculable and predictable. It is easy to get "off track" and hard to discern when one is "on track " or maybe even where the track is leading. Because there is no "clear apprehension of occupational attainments" or highly delineated pattern of timing, the accompanying process of individualization is often judged to be "diffuse."

The highly structured occupational trajectory, on the other hand, offers individuals "clear-cut alternatives from which to choose, using their past experiences and their present needs as guides" and "well-defined timetables that function as schedules for the timing of events in the individual life."[21] In "highly sequenced, lifelong professional trajectories," "the biographical time perspective seems to be very long and the present is experienced as an outcome of the past that leads to the future."[22]

Given such secure frameworks afforded by standardized occupational trajectories, Buchmann argues that "individuals tend to internalize and to respect the social limits encoded in the institutionalized trajectories."[23] Beck writes of the same process that "socially prescribed biography is transformed into biography that is self-produced and continues to be produced."[24] He then goes on to describe the consequences of this transformation as follows:

> The institutional conditions that determine individuals are no longer just events and conditions that happen to them, but **also consequences of the decisions they themselves have made**, which they must view and treat as such. . . . What assails them was formerly considered a "blow of fate" sent by God or nature, e.g. war, natural catastrophes, death of a spouse, in short an event for which they bore no responsibility. Today, however, it is much more likely events that are considered "personal failure," from not passing an examination to unemployment or divorce.[25]

Consequently, for Buchmann, Beck, Kohli and for other social theorists of the modern life cycle as well, the individualized "life plan" or "life design" is of an importance at least equal to the high standardization of the modern life and indeed contributes greatly to making the life cycle so standard. Crucial to the modern life plan are both a greater sense of calculablity and predictability in its sequential steps and a greater sense of personal responsibility for the individual sequencing of these steps. Crucial to the nature and configuration of the modern life plan is, above all, the activity of the life planner behind the life design. In Beck's words, the individual is "actor, designer, juggler and stage director of his or her own biography, identity, social networks, commitments and convictions."[26]

Behind and essential to the modern life cycle of childhood, adolescence, adulthood, and old age is the modern life planner of these stages. This life planner recognizes the predictability of educational, career, and retirement pathways in modern life. However she or he also takes personal responsibility for the individual positioning in that sequencing and for the crucial transitions between stages. She or he not only **can** but **must** be a life planner seeking to achieve favorable future outcomes and to avoid crises and catastrophes. She or he must be, in Beck's words, her or his own "planning office": "In the individualized society the individual must therefore learn, on pain of permanent disadvantage, to conceive of himself or herself as the center of action, as the planning office with respect to his/her own biography, abilities, orientations, relationships, and so on."[27]

Planning without Guarantees

The metaphor of the "planning office" conveys in a vivid manner the requirement that "both within and outside the family, the individuals become the agents of their educational and market-mediated subsistence and the related life planning and organization."[28] Yet for this requirement to be at all a viable one, what is demanded, according to Beck, is "a **vigorous model of action in everyday life**, which puts the ego at its center, allots and opens up opportunities for action to it, and permits it in this manner to work through the emerging possibilities of decision and arrangement with respect to one's own biography in a meaningful way."[29] Nevertheless in contrast to this ideal model (ideal in its vigor, if not its egoism), Beck is at least equally aware of the reality which we also may already know to be true from our own life planning. He states, "It is precisely individualized private existence which becomes more and more obviously and emphatically dependent on situations and conditions that completely escape its reach."[30]

Beck, Kohli, and especially Buchmannn have analyzed effects on individualization and life planning which have produced a dramatic, at least partial "destandardization" of life histories. In a similar manner and following their lead, I examine in this book perhaps the most critical situations and conditions that appear to escape the reach of individual privatized existence in today's accelerated (Luttwak's "turbo-charged" capitalism) pace of economic change. By situations I have in mind the end of an era of company loyalty, the disappearance of long and well-defined career pathways or ladders within which the individual can find a place, and the lack of expectation of permanent marriage. Under new conditions, there is the individual struggle to preserve employability in this new situation of job insecurity and heightened job competition, and the shared or lone struggle to preserve marriageability in a time when two salaries are deemed essential. Finally an individualized private existence is described in which, to paraphrase the Red Queen in *Alice in Wonderland*, it really does take all the planning you can do to keep in the same place, and twice as much planning to get you somewhere else.

The modern planning office "we are" is, it will be argued, put in a most ambivalent position regarding the planning of destandardized lives. On the one hand, there are possibilities of new and highly individualized job and family biographies.

These biographies are no longer standard, but rather contain a greater variety of work and non-work experiences and the prospects of material returns at least equal to the past. These possibilities are combinable with the chances for a comfortable and stable dual-earner marriage (maybe even with a home in the suburbs not far from either workplace). Thus it is conceivable for some to plan so well and be so fortunate that the dreams, promises, and predictions of the *Time* "Man of the Year" in the opening quotation may persist and even continue to ring true thirty years after 1966.

For the many, on the other hand, there are the real risks of short or menacingly long periods of unemployment—or at least underemployment—due to company and organizational reengineering, global competition, and business mergers. Because there is the real possibility that the gaps in work histories may become themselves permanent, there is increased pressure placed upon life planning and the individual fears of making mistakes are heightened. These uncertainties about the future are of course not the sole ones. There is also the threat of gaps—if not long periods—of loneliness outside relationships or of a perhaps equally unsatisfying seriality of superficial relationships of a short and unpredictable kind.

Given the very title, *The New Insecurity* obviously emphasizes the instability caused by the destandardization of the modern life cycle and the new uncertainties in life planning and dangers to privatized existence which it brings.[31] The dangers are considered in their relationship to a more stable period of employment when jobs appeared so permanent that workers worried about being caught in "ruts" and the apparent danger in marriage was to choose the wrong partner and then be stuck for life. Now, it is argued, employability and marriageability gain in priority over actual employment and marriage, and the responsibility falls upon the individual not to lose either. With specific reference to work, the individual now struggles to preserve employability both lacking any of the earlier company promises of continued employment and uncertain of the future value of her or his abilities, credentials, and past experience.

The new difficulties in planning work and family relationships may also give rise either to a fear of being an inadequate or even inept life planner or maybe even to a sense of futility that life planning does not pay off at all. Any of these three difficulties—the struggle for employability, the fear of inadequacy, and the frustration of futility—is so powerful in its effects that it is capable of undermining the confidence with which the modern planning office has planned in advance. The penultimate chapter of the book will argue for such a "new insecurity" in the planning of destandardized lives.

The thesis of a new insecurity has, of course, very immediate and pressing ramifications with regard to individual life planning. Nevertheless the immediate perspective toward the radical change in economic insecurity, as important as it is, is supplemented by two much longer historical perspectives which I find to be even more instructive and perhaps more ominous. The first of these perspectives traces the planning strategies of the modern secure individual back to their early modern roots. These roots are found first of all in an attitude of constancy promoted by the Neo-stoic ethics of Justus Lipsius for commanders in the religious wars. This ethic is evidenced and, if anything, extended in the efforts to maintain financial sufficiency by the prototypical working family at the turn of this century described in the opening quotation from B.S. Rowntree. This family faces a roller coaster ride of alternating periods between want and comparative plenty. In between periods of relative sufficiency in early and in later adulthood, each parent and every child must survive three periods of poverty:

(a) In childhood—when his constitution is being built up.
(b) In early middle life—when he should be in his prime.
(c) In old age.[32]

Thus Lipsius's self-disciplinary imperative to the commander to fight not flee is matched if not exceeded by the extreme thrift and mutual help required of the laborer family to endure the uncertainties of their periods of poverty.

The second larger historical perspective concerns the development of governmental programs of social security. Such programs were introduced originally with families like Rowntree's in mind in order to help them both to survive the periods of want and to deal with the misfortunes of unemployment and emergency. Indeed part of the very design of the program was to smooth out the reversals between want and plenty, in addition to addressing the interruption or loss of earning power and the impact of large families. Influenced by Rowntree's study, William Beveridge would write of the famous report of 1942 which bore his name: "The Plan for Social Security is a plan for dealing with these two causes of want, by a double redistribution of income—between times of earning and not earning (by social insurance) and between times of large and small family responsibilities (by family allowances)."[33]

As Howard Glennerster comments on the contemporary challenges of social insurance and social assistance, "Modern life cycles are not any less, and are probably more, variable and vulnerable than the one Rowntree described."[34] The variability of modern life is expressed in the destandardization of the standard life cycle introduced above and the challenges such destandardization presents for the modern planning offices we are. The vulnerability, on the other hand, appears to be a function of the inadequacies of the promises of both social insurance and assistance to address directly "the new economic realities" with which we have to deal. Both the variability and the vulnerability come together in the song from Tracy Chapman at the book's beginning. The frustration of un- or underemployment and the fear of future inadequacy are expressed by Chapman when she both writes and sings: "Worked everyday of my life / Thought I had some guarantees / That's what I thought / At least that's what I thought."

The fear expressed in Chapman's song is, it will be contended, a fear in no way confined to the Subcity resident from whose perspective the song is sung. The immense value of security in life planning is something we are all threatening to learn about in a retrospective manner. The fear of insecurity is a widespread, indeed population wide reaction to the threat of at least underemployability if not worse. Yet if that fear can be admitted for what it truly is, then a population wide solution can also be sought in the same way that earlier programs of social insurance were developed for the fears of physical disability, premature spousal death, and indigent old age. As will be argued in the concluding chapter, the individual life planner aware of today's "new economic realities" and fearful of their consequences should explore the possibility of an income assistance program to buffer the impact of income swings of want and plenty characteristic of work life today.

The book as a whole has three sections: "A Genealogy of the Secure Individual," "'The New Realities': Economic and Social Impermanence," and "The Struggle for Employability and the Fear of Inadequacy." The first section contains four chapters and introduces both of the larger historical perspectives described above. It will be of interest to the reader who wishes to see the impacts of the destandardization of life history and of the new economic realities from the context of a much longer historical viewpoint. The first two chapters, "Docile Bodies and Constant Minds" and "Disciplinary Police and Liberal 'Governing Better,'" examine the disciplinary techniques of modern military training and reason of state governmentality, as well as the critique of this governmentality by liberalism. The next two chapters, "The Interweaving of Social Insurance and Social Protection" and "The Secure Individual," provide the background for the liberal development of governmental programs of social insurance and social protection which helped originally produce the now threatened secure individual.

For the reader who wishes to proceed directly to the immediate historical context for understanding the new insecurity, Part Two describes the "Economic and Social Impermanence" which is produced by "The New 'Economic Realities.'" The first three chapters of the section, "The Death of Company Loyalty and the Birth of Corporate Support," "Functional Flexibility and Job Compression," and "Flexibility on the Margins and the Destandardization of Work," describe the large-scale impermanence of employment in light of downsizing, mergers, and global competition, the individual struggle to preserve employability in core economic positions, and the flexibility or adaptability to present circumstances required by the new "economic realities." The fourth chapter, "Intimacy, Independence, and Insecurity," deals in less detail with the effects of the loss of the expectation of permanent marriage on life planning.

Part Three, "The Struggle for Employability and the Fear of Inadequacy," concentrates still more on the effects of destandardization on both individual planning and the collective effort to provide security. The first chapter, "The Planning Office As Opportunity and As Self Expression," explores the managerial literature for individual strategies for achieving employment continuity in a period of discontinuous economic change. "Work As Chapter and As Episode" describes how an attitude of "until-further-noticeness" comes to pervade the struggle for employability and cause deep-seated fears of inadequacy. The title chapter explains how insecurity may come to characterize individual life planning in any or all of three ways: (1) through a priority given to the struggle for preserving employability over the present employment which is actually held, (2) in a personal fear of being an inadequate or inept life planner, and (3) in a deep frustration and dissatisfaction as to the futility of life planning at all. The final chapter, "The Prospects of the Secure Individual" (together with an appendix on income assistance programs), opens ground for the consideration of extending and modifying the social security mechanisms to provide protection against the strong fluctuations of income in destandardized work lives.

Detailed Chapter Overview and Indication of Sources

For the reader who is interested in the intellectual resources and influences on this work and who does not wish to proceed directly to either the longer or the more immediate historical perspectives, the following broader outline and indication of sources is offered. The primary intellectual resource for the first major section of this study will be Michel Foucault. As in any enterprise with a genealogical aspect, such a selection is hardly surprising. What may be surprising is the more positive use that is made of Foucauldian genealogy. In his interview on the subject of social security, Foucault speaks of both its "perverse effect" and "positive demand." The emphasis here will not be on the "perverse effects" of social security, the "increasing rigidity of certain mechanisms and a growth in dependence."[35] Rather the genealogy is much more about the "positive demand" for "a security that opens the way to richer, more numerous, more diverse, and more flexible relations with oneself and with one's environment, while guaranteeing to each individual a real autonomy."[36]

Foucault's great relevance for my project comes from both his general predilection for "how" approaches to the understanding of social practices and from the specific fruitfulness of his conception of governmentality for the historical understanding of subjects such as liberal governmentality, modern statistics, and the rationality and importance of social insurance. This fruitfulness is evidenced not only in his own writings but perhaps even more by the importance of other researchers in the same Foucauldian vein who have written in *The Foucault Effect* and elsewhere—above all Colin Gordon, Ian Hacking, François Ewald, and Daniel Defert.[37] Moreover Foucault's work also relates closely to the work of Gerhard Oestreich, another historian of early governmentality, whose work complements and perhaps supplements the famous treatment of docile bodies with an important discussion of miltary self-discipline and the ethics of constancy of Justus Lipsius. Indeed it is only the combination of **all** these scholarly resources, together with the historical perspectives toward social security of Theda Skocpol, Michael Freeden, and others as well as the sociological insights of Beck, Giddens, Buchmannn, Zygmunt Bauman, and others, which affords the potential for a genealogical form of inquiry into the modern life planner parallel to the famous genealogical inquiries of Foucault into madness, delinquency, medicine, and other subjects.

The first section of the book, "A Genealogy of the Secure Individual," will introduce technologies of domination and technologies of the self operative in the military and bureaucratic practices of the absolute state. It also will offer a more detailed description of Foucault's genealogy of the liberal state, directing particular attention to the concept of political security mechanisms. Finally it will conclude with my own genealogical extrapolation of Foucault's writings and the contributions of his associates. A conception of "social security mechanisms" will be introduced and the modern life planner will be interpreted as "the secure individual" who acts according to these mechanisms.

The first chapter, "Docile Bodies and Constant Minds," takes up Foucault's famous discussion of military techniques of discipline in *Discipline and Punish*. However, it also adds to this account and gives equal place to the explication of military ethics that is given in *Neostoicism and the Early Modern State* by Oestreich. The result of the combination of these topics is to provide a contact point between the techniques of discipline described by Foucault and the techniques of self-discipline of Neo-stoicism. This contact point between docility and constancy provides the initial historical baseline for comprehending the quite different "new insecurity" later. It will reappear in subsequent chapters on Foucault's views on governmentality, on the later interpretation of social security, and on the later correlations that are attempted between the most recent business rationality and practice and correlative individual work strategies.

The second chapter concerns Foucault's views on the topic of governmentality and deals with far less familiar matters. In

1978 and 1979, he gave two important series of lectures on "Security, terrritory and population" and "The birth of biopolitics." Of these series, only one of the 1978 lectures, "Governmentality," has been published. Consequently, the major sources for this chapter are the above mentioned essay, the Tanner lectures delivered at Stanford in 1979—"Omnes et Singulatim: Towards a Criticism of Political Reason"—and the authoritative essay by Colin Gordon that introduces *The Foucault Effect.*

According to Gordon's interpretation of Foucault on governmentality, perhaps the most general thesis of this work is that "we live today not so much in a *Rechtstaat* or in a disciplinary society as in a society of security."[38] The first section of chapter 2 will discuss the reason of state governmentality, as described by Foucault and Oestreich, in terms of a "disciplinary society" and as a transition to a "security society." This significant change will be first of all foreshadowed by the similar change in the meaning and practice of statistics explicated in Hacking's *The Taming of Chance.* The statistical introduction of the importance of population will make understandable Foucault's genealogy of the governmentality of the liberal state which emerges from the disciplinary regime of reason of state governmentality. Finally, the important conception of political security mechanisms operative in liberal governmentality will be introduced and explained.

The specific resource of greatest relevance for chapter 3, although very closely related to the conception of political security mechanisms, is one that is not developed systematically in any of Foucault's published writings. Its nature is only able to be developed by means of extrapolation from these writings and by writings from his associates on the theme of social insurance. Chapter 3 surveys the writings of Ewald and Defert on the origins of social insurance, as well as the important aspects of social assistance and protection that were developed by later liberal thinkers as justifications for the introduction of social security programs. Both the statistical rationality of social insurance and the resources provided by social assistance will be seen to be at work in the operations of "social security mechanisms" characteristic of contemporary liberal governmentality.

The conception of mechanisms of social security will also be used in chapter 4 to introduce the "subject" of such mechanisms, what I have termed above as "the secure individual." A "birth" of the proposed secure individual will be proposed in a way similar to the "births" of the disciplined individual in *Discipline and Punish* and the rational economic agent in Foucault's lectures on governmentality. This secure individual will be shown to be the actor in the earlier described modern life cycle, and its—our—close relationship to the modern social security mechanisms of liberalism will be described in detail, above all through an emphasis upon the role that life planning plays in our modern lives.

The second major section of the book, "'The New Realities'": Economic and Social Impermanence," is comprised of four chapters and deals with more contemporary developments in regard to the secure individual and its present prospects. More specifically, it will take up what was earlier described as the standardization of the modern life cycle. This standardization has now been called into question in virtue of quite recent developments in regard to the stability of families, the preparation for employment in the educational system, and above all the demands for employee flexibility. The argument for a "destandardization" of the modern life cycle will be presented in regard to the preservation of employability in the contemporary workplace and of marriageability in familial relationships. Crucial to the statement of this argument will be two additional research sources: more extensively, practical writings on, on the one hand, corporate management strategies, and, on the other, individual work strategies by authors such as Peter Drucker, Jeremy Rifkin, Robert Reich, Charles Handy, and William Bridges; and, less extensively, economic and social theoretical literature on women and the family by Barbara Bergmann, Ruth Sidel, Barbara Ehrenreich, and others.

Chapter 5 deals with an earlier era of company loyalty and the transition to a quite different policy of corporate support. The secure career pathways that won the loyalty of employees and motivated them to be good workers for the company appear to be a thing of the past. This change is viewed as an effect of many important causes: global competition in manufacturing and elsewhere, the advances in automation and telecommunications, and the organizational effects of business reengineering. Companies which have been affected by these major changes no longer appear to guarantee employment but do claim to enhance the worker's employability through programs of corporate support in a new type of "contract" be-tween company and worker.

Chapter 6 initiates the discussion of the core-periphery distinction quite commonly used in discussions concerning the new economic developments, particularly regarding what is called lean production. The focus of the chapter will be upon the core worker and her or his need to demonstrate what is called functional flexibility, the possession of multiple skills rather than a single skill as characteristic of the earlier period of mass production. Beyond being multiskilled in the present, the worker must also possess the ability to improve continually in these skills, and the capability to work together in teams with other core workers with other core skills. Indeed the emphasis upon continual improvement on the part of the individual is essential in a process characterized by the systematic incorporation throughout the whole organization of continual improvement in the whole process of production.

Subcontractors and part-time or temporary workers are not as well placed in the business organization. As peripheral employees, they must demonstrate numerical flexibility to allow the company to react quickly to changes in product or service demand. The required flexible scheduling works to the advantage of many workers who need the flexibility, but the peripheral status is a disadvantage to those workers who wish for more central roles in the organization. The great numbers of such peripheral jobs contribute greatly to the destandardization of work histories in comparison to the well-delineated career ladders of the past. Such destandardization, chapter 7 argues, offers the potential benefits of individualization for those wishing and daring to plan their own sequencing of employment, while at the same time the threat of insecurity looms for those who fear the consequences of underemployment or even joblessness.

The final chapter in the section, chapter 8, takes up the possibility of a destandardization in family history to match the changes in work biography. The great factory layoffs in the 1960s helped undermine the single family wage which the breadwinner garnered in the breadwinner/homemaker marriage. The other foundation to that famous structure of marriage was the expectation of lifelong marriage which made it at all feasible for the homemaker to stay at home. This even more important foundation to the standardization of family life was itself undermined by the large increase in the divorce rate and the "laying off" of lifetime homemakers. The new destandardization of family history exhibits a similar ambivalence to the destandardized job history, offering both for some the opportunities for new and more individualized kinds of family structure and for others the threat of the diminishment of one's marriageability and the prospect of continuous loneliness.

If there has occurred a destandardization of life history, then the implications of such a change upon the subject of this history, the modern "life planner," must certainly be discussed. The next and final major section of the book, "The Struggle for Employability and the Fear of Inadequacy," continues to pursue above all the theme of economic destandardization and does so under the twofold and ambivalent aspects of opportunity and threat. From the point of view of opportunity, it considers the positive potential of the literal advice to be an entrepreneurial planning office and the tools it offers for coping with such profound and discontinuous social change. Under the contrasting aspect of threat, the way employment can take the character of "until further notice" is explained, as well as the strong fear of inadequacy that the individual may feel in the struggle to maintain and enhance employability. This fear of inadequacy is not examined solely for the effects it has as a profound challenge to life planning, but also for the political basis it might provide for the effort to preserve and modify the social security mechanisms which produced the secure individual of Part One.

Chapter 9 discusses two complementary strategies for dealing with the new economic realities as they have been proposed by William Bridges in the book, *Jobshift*, and by Charles Handy in the book, *The Age of Unreason*. This discussion will introduce two new strategies for dealing with the economic destandardization of life history, the composite career "cable" from Bridges and the worker "portfolio" which Handy introduces to, among other things, integrate work history with the other stages of life history. Both of these metaphorical pictures will be presented as strategies for approaching discontinuous change optimistically and preserving at least some of the features of security of the earlier career pathways.

The next chapter presents a quite different assessment of discontinuous change as it impacts upon the secure individual. Zygmunt Bauman's more general discussion of the new changes

in identitity formation in *Life in Fragments* speaks of a transition from lasting frames of reference (such as in the medium
of photography) to disjointed episodes (characteristic of videotape), with an accompanying and even more important change
in goals from the pursuit of future control to not mortgaging
the future and avoiding commitments. Bauman's thought provides the basis for a quite different approach to individual
strategies for dealing with work history under the backdrop of
such large and momentous economic changes. Rather than
the strength of Bridges' cable or the completeness of Handy's
portfolio, what is prominently emphasized is the fear of inadequacy involved in the struggle to preserve employability and
an even deeper-seated fear of personal self-forming ineptitude
altogether.

The struggle for employability and fear of inadequacy are
analyzed in more detail and with broader scope in the
penultimate and title chapter. The struggle for employability
with its emphasis upon maneuverability is contrasted with the
constancy of the original Neostoic ethic of discipline which
prescribed fighting or working rather than escape. The fear of
inadequacy in the present is related to an earlier period of
career planning which starts to receive a more positive social
critical evaluation for its security in comparison to the earlier
critiques of its conformity and assimilation. Finally, a possible
sense of futility regarding the usefulness of life planning is seen
to result from the unpredictable fluctuations and prospects for
turbulence in contemporary work histories. In any or all of
these ways, the individual facing the accelerated changes of a
"turbo-charged" economy becomes no longer secure.

The final chapter returns to the endeavor to preserve collective security described in Part One. It introduces one final
larger business strategy, in this case involving plant and office
closings and reopenings, and finds correlations between it and
the individual politics surrounding the dynamics of taxpayer
opposition. The way that this individual strategy of opposition
"stands by oneself" is then contrasted with the collective endeavor to preserve security. As Theda Skocpol has claimed, this
endeavor to preserve individual security may best be defended
by being changed, in this case in light of the strong fluctuations
in income in destandardized job histories. The argument is
advanced that the fear of individual inadequacy in the struggle
for employability is a legitimate political basis for considering

the modification of social security mechanisms in order to provide more adequate forms of income assistance.

An Appendix to this chapter compares three different alternatives for providing income support: guaranteeing the individual a basic annual income, providing a participation income for individual involvement in a wide range of socially useful activities, or offering a social insurance program of income buffering. No larger public policy recommendation is attempted, but each alternative is examined in two important respects: (1) for its merits in helping with the new insecurities of job and family destandardization and (2) for its ability to answer the main accusation of taxpayer opposition that financial aid will be offered to free-riders or "spongers."

Part I

A Genealogy of the Secure Individual

1

Docile Bodies and Constant Minds

In the twentieth century, the best social theoretical writings on the topic of the modern individual's adaptability to society have provided compelling descriptions of conformity with strong warnings about the dangers of assimilation. Any genealogy of what may be termed the "secure individual" must consequently stand under suspicion of ignoring these descriptions and warnings. However, the main treatment of the topic of individual adaptability in this book will not occur in this section, but rather in Parts Two and Three. Rather than "mass" individuality, "outer directedness," "one dimensionality," or the "decline of the individual," the focus will be precisely on the new lack of longer and broader career pathways to conform to and on the present impossibility of self-assimilation into forms of company loyalty. Adaptability will be criticized not in relation to standardization, but in relation to destandardization and the powerful insecurity that it can bring with it for individuals.

Michel Foucault is of course well known for his own discussion of docility. The famous discussion in *Discipline and Punish* equals, if not surpasses, any analysis of conformity or any genealogy of decline in individuality in this century. While a summary of this discussion is presented in the first section of this chapter, it is not intended as the key to the understanding of adaptability as it is spoken of later. Rather, docility is but a first step on the path which Foucault himself takes towards contemporary forms of self-conduct, or technologies of the self, undertaken in light of larger strategies of governmentality or, as in this study, in response to economic reengineering, downsizing, and lean production.

Foucault's later writings on governmentality are a more important resource than the discussion of docile bodies both for understanding contemporary programs of social security and for grasping the different emphases of adaptability as flexibility in this study. Indeed the first steps of the genealogical path that is traced in Part One are the steps from the treatment of docile bodies in *Discipline and Punish* to the introduction of mechanisms of security in the lectures on governmentality. In these lectures Foucault deals with technologies of the self that contact with the technologies of domination from his earlier work:

> I think that if one wants to analyze the genealogy of the subject in Western civilization, [one] has to take into account . . . the points where the technologies of domination of individuals over one another have recourse to processes by which the individual acts upon himself . . . and conversely, [one] has to take into account the points where the technologies of the self are integrated into structures of coercion or domination. The contact point, where the way individuals are driven by others is tied to the way they conduct themselves, is what we can call, I think, government.[1]

The notion of a "contact point" between technologies of domination and technologies of the self establishes a process of correlation between individual conduct and larger social practices. This process of correlation plays a crucial and determining role in the present section devoted to the genealogical study of the secure individual and also in a later pivotal argument on the best way to interpret the requirement of flexibility on the part of individual employees in the contemporary workplace.

In the second part of this chapter, a contact point is sought for Foucault's emphasis upon military technologies of domination by way of Gerhard Oestreich's treatment of the modern military army and the Neo-stoic attitude of constancy in *Neostoicism and the Early Modern State*. Oestreich claims of the influence of the important Neo-stoic thinker Justus Lipsius upon Maurice of Orange and his cousins John and William Louis that it led to the institution of the standing army. Of this new institution he writes that its "incorporation into the activities of the state was what first created the early modern state with its concentration of power at the centre."[2] Crucial to this development is, according to Oestreich, a twofold achievement of Lipsius encompassing both the technologies of discipline and an individual ethics of constancy: "Lipsius performs two great services for the military: he gives it a comprehensive concept of discipline which can serve as a basis for reform, and he sets up the Roman Stoic ethic as the morality and ideology of the new army."[3]

For Lipsius, "Neostoicism meant the moral and spiritual arming of the individual and the community."[4] Under the conditions of religious confessional warfare immediately surrounding Lipsius, the choices facing the individual are either to fight in the war or to attempt to flee elsewhere. The moral and spiritual arming comes from the strengthening of the inner resolve to fight. As Oestreich explains,

> One must be a different person, not in a different place. Everybody carries the war with him, carries it within him. Constancy is required before all else; only in fight can one be victorious, not in flight. The watchword is "resist," not "yield," "fight," not "flight."[5]

This Neo-stoic ethic of constancy will be presented as a technology of self that contacts with the practices of domination of Foucault's docile bodies. Later on it will also be related to the modern demands for flexibility and the need for a quite different kind of individual technology of the self. An irony of this later argument is that it will call into question whether "fight" is the recipe for victory in the modern workplace and will point instead to the very prominent role that yielding and abandonment play on today's economic "battlefields."

Docile Bodies

Long after the writing of *Discipline and Punish*, Foucault made the retrospective comment, "Perhaps I've insisted too much on the technology of domination and power."[6] Nowhere is this insistance more obvious or more brilliantly executed than in the chapter, "docile bodies." The chapter begins with a historical comparison between the heroic *"homme de guerre"* of the early seventeenth century and a well-trained *militaire* of the late eighteenth century. The obvious difference in the comparison is to be attributed to a "birth" very similar to the "birth of the asylum" in *Madness and Civilization* and itself at work in the "birth of the prison"; namely, "the birth of meticulous military and political tactics by which the control of bodies and individual forces was exercised."[7] Military discipline "is no longer a mere means of preventing looting, desertion or failure to obey orders among the troops; it has become a basic technique to enable the army to exist, not as an assembled crowd, but as a unity that derives from this very unity an increase in its forces."[8]

The anonymous "Ordonnance du 1er janvier 1766" indicates several of the ways in which the traditional actions of the *homme de guerre* are broken down and rearranged. If earlier soldiers marched in file to the beat of the drum, the Ordonnance introduces "a collective and obligatory rhythm, imposed from the outside"[9] in the form of four kinds of steps with correspondingly different rhythms. It then continues this "instrumental coding of the body" (D&P, 153) by specifying the three stages employed by the soldier in raising his rifle. Foucault comments on this coding, which is termed a "*manoeuvre*":

> It consists of a breakdown of the total gesture into two parallel series: that of the parts of the body to be used (right hand, left hand, different fingers of the hand, knee, eye, elbow, etc.) and that of the parts of the object manipulated (barrel, notch, hammer, screw, etc.); then the two sets of parts are correlated together according to a number of simple gestures (rest, bend); lastly, it fixes the canonical succession in which each of these correlations occupies a particular place. . . . Over the whole surface of contact between the body and the object it handles, power is introduced, fastening them to one another. It constitutes a body-weapon, body-tool, body-machine complex.[10]

The Ordonnance directions for raising the rifle were soon outstripped by Prussian regulations that stipulated six stages for bringing the weapon to one's foot, four for extending it and thirteen for raising it to the shoulder. This development shows the "positive economy" of discipline, both its general expansiveness and its particular relationship to time, how it extracts from time ever more available moments and ever more available forces.

The twenty-three "elementary" movements of the Prussian procedure are incorporated into one military exercise. The constant and regular repetition of the exercise produces regular physical movements as long as one does "not pass to another activity until the first has been completely mastered."[11] Exercise is "that technique by which one imposes on the body tasks that are both repetitive and different, but always graduated."[12] The graduated aspect of the exercise can be elegantly achieved through a "disciplinary polyphony of exercises," which begins with the directive to

> lay down for each individual, according to his level, his seniority, his rank, the exercises that are suited to him; common exercises have a differing role and each difference involves specific exercises. At the end of each series others begin, branch off and subdivide in turn. Thus each individual is caught up in a temporal series which specifically defines his level or his rank.[13]

In order to indicate the level or rank of the soldier, space must be used as effectively as the broken down and rearranged employment of time. Rather than a polyphony of movement, what is required, at least initially, is an orderly grid:

> it is necessary to define beforehand the nature of the elements to be used; to find individuals who fit the definition proposed; to place them in the ordered space; to parallel the distribution of functions in the structure of space in which they will operate. Consequently, all the space within a confined area must be ordered; there should be no waste, no gaps, no free margins; nothing should escape.[14]

However, for the space to serve the important disciplinary effect of ranking, it is also necessary for the individuals to be placed in ordered spaces that do not hold them in fixed positions, but allow them to circulate in a network of relations with other individuals. Foucault's primary example here is an educational one, the early Jesuit college, but the example comes replete with military trappings:

> the classes, which might comprise up to two or three hundred pupils, were subdivided into groups of ten; each of these groups, with its "decurion," was placed in a camp, Roman or Carthaginian; each "decury" had its counterpart in the opposing camp. The general form was that of war and rivalry; work, apprenticeship and classification were carried out in the form

of the joust, through the confrontation of two armies; the contribution of each pupil was inscribed in this general duel; it contributed to the victory or the defeat of a whole camp; and the pupils were assigned a place that corresponded to the function of each individual and to his value as a combatant in the unitary group of his "decury." It should be observed moreover that this Roman comedy made it possible to link, to the binary exercises of rivalry, a spatial disposition inspired by the legion, with rank, hierarchy, pyramidal supervision.[15]

Of course, serious military tactics had changed immensely from earlier times of the joust. In fact, they had even changed a great deal from immediately previous times through the invention of the rifle and its superiority over the musket. This invention "made it possible to exploit fire-power at an individual level; and, conversely, it turned every soldier into a possible target, requiring by the same token greater mobility; it involved therefore the disappearance of a technique of masses in favor of an art that distributed units and men along extended, relatively flexible, mobile lines."[16] The military unit became "no longer simply an art of distributing bodies, of extracting time from them and accumulating it,"[17] but "a sort of machine with many parts, moving in relation to one another, in order to arrive at a configuration and to obtain a specific result."[18]

The particular movements of the soldier had to be controlled both in relation to other movements of the soldier and in relation to other particular movements from other members of the unit. This kind of control requires, in the most memorable phrase of this chapter on discipline in *Discipline and Punish*, "docile bodies." The increase in the economy and efficiency of the movements of the soldiers produces an increase in their "aptitude" or "capacity" to do battle, but this increase in aptitude that occurs when aptitudes are combined and coordinated with one another is dissociated from any earlier signification that the bodily movements might have had.[19] As Foucault writes of discipline in general and of military tactics in particular, "In short, it dissociates power from the body; on the one hand, it turns it into an 'aptitude', a 'capacity', which it seeks to increase; on the other hand, it reverses the course of the energy, the power that might result from it, and turns it into a relation of strict subjection."[20] The body accomplished through the techniques of domination military training is the body of a *militaire*, a disciplined soldier, quite different from the earlier *homme de guerre* both in terms of increased military aptitude and equally increased docility.

Constant Minds

One of the main subjects of the essays by Gerhard Oestreich in *Neostoicism and the Early Modern State* is the formation of the first modern army in the Netherlands. In his account of this important new formation, he points toward the presence of an ethics of constancy that accompanies and indeed guides the exercise of military discipline: "At the heart of Dutch thinking on military reorganization is the disciplined professional soldier, led by an equally well trained and ethically sound professional officer."[21] This ethics of constancy is evident in both the commands and actions of the trained and ethical professional officer and, as will be seen later, also in the directives of the trained state official as well.

For Oestreich the development of the modern army begins with the recovery of ancient military procedures by humanistic philologists: the "'politico-technical literature of the humanists was supposed to bring together all the ancient works in a gigantic filing system as it were, so that they might be immediately accessible at any time."[22] However, the truly central figure in advancing this development is Justus Lipsius and, of his many writings, the military treatises rank among the most important. What Lipsius did was to call for a "military ethics" of "action, constancy, self-control and obedience" to be "treated as an equally important ingredient of reform."[23] This military ethic "appealed to the commanders and their officers, for here was an answer to the burning question of the moment—how to establish and maintain good order and military discipline in the unruly armies of the day."[24]

Oestreich writes that Lipsius had a higher aim in mind than the purely military program in writing his treatises. At stake was the "moral regeneration of the rude soldiery" without which "there is no lasting obedience among the troops." Consonant with the treatment of military discipline by Foucault, Lipsius advocates the drill of daily weapon-practice, marching and the digging of fortifications,[25] regulations to order marching, military camp, and battle, and a system of severe punishment for misdeeds and promotion and honors for brav-

ery and good conduct. However, Lipsius also adds a fourth
element, *coerctio* or self-discipline to the other elements of
discipline: exercise *(exercitium)*, order *(ordo)*, and example
(exemplum).[26]

According to this further element, obedience is not merely
a requirement of military discipline, but also something "that
befits a man, a virtue."[27] It is demanded by Lipsius from within
the context of civil unrest and the very real and immediate
danger of religious war. The Neo-stoicism of Lipsius is developed from the standpoint of a non-confessional mode of individual ethic in the face of this religiously charged and perilous
situation. He carries over the art of living of the Greek and
Roman Stoa from the *vita civilis* to the *vita militaris*. The most
central virtue, from a triad including patience and firmness, is
that of constancy.

The choices of the individual are, according to Lipsius's
dialogue on constancy, to flee from the danger of bloody combat or to endure it and fight. What constancy requires is not
to flee one's country but rather one's emotions of fear and
danger. The crucial virtue of constancy is defined as "the proper
and immovable strength of the mind that is neither elated nor
downcast by outward or fortuitous circumstances."[28]

Lipsius poses the questions: "Should one not let one's
hands rest in one's lap if the *mala publica* [poverty, exile, death]
are determined by an ineluctable fate? Should one exert oneself
in any way for the community?"[29] However, the wise interlocu-
tor in the dialogue responds that if

> something is to happen in the world, man must first fulfill
> certain conditions. . . . If fate wants the unstable, sinking ship
> of state to be saved, it also wants men to fight for it and
> defend it. . . . Whether the country totters or falls, decays or
> perishes, the good citizen *(bonus civis)* must retain his
> *constantia*.[30]

Oestreich writes of this "exceedingly severe, controlled
manliness in the Stoic mould" that it "was not for nothing that
this philosophy appealed to men who were determined on resistance in the religious wars, and especially to soldiers."[31] The
"famous Lipsian style, with its terse, laconic, peremptory language and its abundance of military similes and metaphors,
was bound to captivate the select circle of officers educated in

the classics, a class which was so important in this warlike age."[32] Lipsius

> revives the classical picture of the ideal commander. He should carry the lance at the head of his men and share in all their tribulations. He should set an example and not simply issue orders. The ideal commander is tireless in making his dispositions, controlled in danger, wise and swift in execution, blameless and irreproachable, moderate in all things, of proven loyalty and faith, favoured by fortune, and amiable towards everyone.[33]

The ideal officer fulfills Lipsius' new casting of the Promethean myth by breaking through the chains of his fear and the fear of his unit. As Oestreich explains, "The allusion to the freeing of Prometheus bound to the rock incorporates the two elements which together consitute the aim of the *Constantia*—the renewal of the self by self-liberation and active participation in political society."[34] Indeed such self-liberation and active participation were not limited to Promethean achievements on the battlefield, but extended to inside state offices as well. State bureaucrats were "the servants of the state in the broadest sense of the work, the absolutist society, rational in conduct, disiplined and accustomed to commanding and obeying." This absolutist society "supplied the personnel for the proliferating state bodies and the ever-increasing army—both under the leadership of the monarch." The upper bureaucracy educated in the law" and "the upper ranks of the officer corps, scienti-fically trained to arms" constituted, together with their rank and file, "the sitting army of officials and the standing army of soldiers."[35]

Oestreich writes of Lipsius' ideal of Neostoic constancy that it "was so in tune with the political spirit of the age that agreement was soon achieved between his anthropology and the form of the state."[36] It "was not just the army that was put through its paces on the parade ground: the same rigour prevailed in administrative, economic, moral and spiritual spheres as well."[37] The modern state, according to Oestreich, "emerged based on order, power, unity, authority, discipline and obedience."[38]

In Part Two of this study, a quite different form of economic "spirit of the age" will be interrogated in regard to a possibly quite different anthropology. Rather than the "public evils" of "poverty, exile, and death," a quite different assemblage of apparently "lesser" and "private" evils will come to the fore. Rather than poverty, permanent or semi-permanent un- or underemployment will loom as the evil to be avoided at all costs. The modern "planning office" must also deal if not with exile, then with unstable childrearing and financial conditions including the possibilities of absent fathering and the lack of child support. Finally, rather than the tragedy of an early death, the miseries of a prolonged, underfunded, and lonely retirement must be avoided by prudential action in the present.

An analysis of these "evils" in Part Three will even go so far as to call into question the Neo-stoic ethic of **constancy** which not only was valid for Lipsius' time but remains familiar to us up to the present day. A modern "ethics" of **flexibility**, it will be argued, may require above all an inner resolve not to fight and continue, but rather to abandon and flee. If this argument is at all persuasive, we will be faced with options for which there is no Stoic or Neo-stoic ethic to draw upon and with even lesser prospects for developing a "Post-stoic" ethic to cope with our predicament.

2

Disciplinary Police and Liberal "Governing Better"

This chapter begins with the governmental practices of Oestreich's bureaucrats in the absolute state and outlines how they imposed the rigor of discipline in all the spheres of its subjects' lives. Crucial to these practices is, according to both Foucault and Oestreich, the new science of police with its very detailed forms of disciplinary control. Foucault also introduces a personage quite different from the courageous Neostoic commander, but one who plays at least as prominent a role in the exercise of this police science.

Foucault claims that the Christian practice of the pastor, operative in his care for assigned souls, marks the point of departure for a political technology which is crucial for the understanding of government from the time of absolutism to the present day. This Christian conception of pastoral power traces its history back to the Hebrew ideal of the shepherd who gathers together and leads his flock. Already in the Hebrew ideal, the "shepherd's power implies individual attention paid to each member of the flock."[1] The Christian pastoral technique takes over this ideal, but also amplifies it in three ways:

> "the shepherd must be informed as to the material needs of each member of the flock and provide for them when necessary. He must know what is going on, what each of them does—his public sins. Last and not least, he must know what goes on in the soul of each one, that is, his secret sins, his progress on the road to sainthood."[2]

Foucault's estimate of the general effects of pastoral technology upon both the past and the present is well known and clear. Christian pastorship is

> [a] strange game . . . which seems to have nothing to do with the game of the city surviving through the sacrifice of the citizens. Our societies proved to be really demonic since they happened to combine those two games—the city-citizen game and the shepherd-flock game—in what we call the modern states.[3]

However, the governmentality of reason of state not only receives such harsh appraisal by Foucault in the present; during its own time it of course occasioned both critique and the call for reform. Liberalism is well known as a **critique** of reason of state political theory and practice as "an earlier functioning of government from which one tries to escape."[4] Liberalism seeks to reform past absolutism by renouncing its totalizing ambitions in favor of a more minimal and efficient way of governing.

Yet if liberalism is undeniably a critique of the excesses of reason of state, Foucault's interpretation of its form of governmentality exactly parallels, it will be argued, his earlier treatment of the liberal reformers of punishment in *Discipline and Punish*. Foucault describes the objective of the humanistic reformers of punishment as "not to punish less, but to punish better; to punish with an attenuated severity perhaps, but in order to punish with more universality and necessity."[5] Even though Foucault to some extent considers the reforms of liberal politicians and thinkers to be a transition from discipline as well as sovereignty, these reforms are similarly conceived with a similar objective: not so much to govern the population "less"—in terms of social discipline—but rather to govern it "better"—in terms of the contact point between technologies of domination and technologies of the self.

Rather than being simply a critique of governmental power, liberalism is also the practice of government with its own particular governmental technology. This technology is influenced both by the economic management of people and things in the family and by the displacement of this model to the level of population through a monumental change in the practice of statistics. Laissez faire governmentality is not simply one of nonintervention with members of the population, but rather involves the employment of "mechanisms of security." If, according to Oestreich, absolutist society seeks through social disciplining to bring about the systematic raising of levels of achievement of individuals, it will be argued that liberal security mechanisms bring about this same goal without all of the severity of meticulous police surveillance yet perhaps with even greater universality and necessity.

Reason of State and the Christian Pastorate

"Government" has both a very broad and a more specific meaning in Foucault's lectures on the topic. According to the broad meaning, government "could concern the relation between self and self, private interpersonal relations involving some form of control or guidance, relations within social institutions and communities, and, finally, relations concerned with the exercise of political sovereignty."[6] While the broad meaning of government could be seen to apply in reference to the discussion of military discipline above, the specific meaning of government is of course conveyed by the final of these concerns, political sovereignty. However, Foucault is not interested in it alone, but rather in its interconnections with other forms of governing. Indeed the continuity between the different forms of self-governing, the governing of the family, and the government of a people proves crucial in the identification of an "art of governing" or governmental rationality, which emerges in the practices of reason of state and is later modified by liberal reformers. Modern pre-liberal governmentality is the invention of a form of "secular political pastorate," which couples the "individualization" of the Christian pastoral technique with the "totalization" of the strong modern state.

Foucault traces the totalizing of the "city-game" through the emergence of doctrines of reason of state (*raison d'état*) in sixteenth-century Europe. Machiavelli is often taken as an exponent of the reason of state doctrine, but Foucault emphasizes that the realism of *The Prince* is confined to the seizing and maintaining of power by the ruler. The shift of focus from the prince to the state allows reason of state theorists such as Botero, Palazzo, and Chemnitz to introduce secular perpetuity as a goal in regard to the state itself: "Rational government is this, so to speak: given the nature of the state, it can hold down its enemies for an indeterminate length of time. It can only do so if it increases its own strength."[7]

With much the same eagerness that Foucault searched anonymous military manuals in Part Three of *Discipline and Punish*, he turns his attention to a new discipline, the science of the police, from the period after the Thirty Years War and uncovers obscure Italian, French, and German authors of *Polizeiwissenschaft*. For Turquet de Mayenne, for example, the goal is not to choose the most ideal type of constitution, as the title of his main work, *AristoDemocratic Monarchy*, well indicates. Rather his primary interest is devoted to a fourth "grand official" who stands next to the Officers of Justice, the Army, and the Exchequer. This official oversees the police, but in the sense noted by Foucault in the essay, "The Politics of Health in the Eighteenth Century": "Down to the end of the *ancien régime*, the term 'police' does not dignify, at least not exclusively, the institution of police in the modern sense; 'police' is the ensemble of mechanisms serving to ensure order, the properly channelled growth of wealth and the conditions of preservation of health 'in general.'"[8]

The major concern of *Polizeiwissenschaft* is the increase of strength of the state demanded by the new reason of state doctrine. But the strength that must be increased requires bringing the economy into the management of the state as well. The "art of government" involved in this introduction involves the establishment of continuity between the governing or managing of the household and the management of the economy as a whole by the state. Upwards continuity from the family to the state "means that a person who wishes to govern the state well must first learn how to govern himself, his goods and his patrimony, after which he will be successful in governing the state."[9] Downwards continuity to the family, on the other hand, ensures that "when a state is well run, the head of the family will know how to look after his goods and his patrimony, which means that individuals will, in turn, behave as they should."[10] If the prince's "pedagogical formation" should provide the required upward continuity, it falls to the province of the **police** to insure the downward continuity to individual behavior and the running of the family.

The way the family "runs" provides a conception for the "art of governing" that allows a new form of governmentality or practical governmental rationality to emerge:

> Governing a household, a family, does not essentially mean safeguarding the family property; what concerns it is the individuals that compose the family, their wealth and prosper-

ity. It means to reckon with all the possible events that may intervene, such as births and deaths, and with all the things that can be done, such as possible alliances with other families; it is this general form of management that is characteristic of government . . . [11]

The primary object of this new governmental rationality is not the exercise of sovereignty over territory, but rather the productive reckoning of people and things evidenced by the efficient family head:

> To govern a state will therefore mean to apply economy, to set up an economy at the level of the entire state, which means exercising towards its inhabitants, and the wealth and behaviour of each and all, a form of surveillance and control as attentive as that of the head of a family over his household and his goods.[12]

The achievement of this efficient and productive management involves a "central paradox" perhaps best expressed by another classical police theorist, Von Justi: The state can achieve its increase of strength only by fostering the individual lives of the state's population in such a way that the total strength of the state is also improved. Police theory recognizes, consequently, how the totalization of the strong modern state is intimately linked to the individualization of its citizens. As Foucault expresses the linkage, "As a form of rational intervention wielding political power over men, the role of the police is to supply them with a little extra life; and by so doing, supply the state with a little extra strength."[13]

Modern police practices continue the earlier Christian pastoral technology, only in a political context. They both aim for detailed knowledge of the state's population and direct particular attention toward material concerns. Concerning the knowledge required by the new science, Gordon writes:

> Police is a science of endless lists and classifications; there is a police of religion, of customs, of health, of foods, of highways, of public order, of sciences, commerce, manufactures, servants, poverty . . . Police science seems to aspire to constitute a kind of omnivorous espousal of governed reality, the sensorium of a Leviathan. It is also (again in aspiration) a knowledge of inexhaustibly detailed and continuous control.[14]

Concerning the attention directed at material concerns, Gordon writes: "Police government is also an oeconomy, through its way of equating the happiness of its individual subjects with the state's strength. Police is therefore a kind of **economic pastorate** . . . or a secular hierocracy, albeit somewhat different in its regime from the Catholic pastorate which had placed its obstacles in the path of the early capitalists."[15] As Lois McNay expresses the nature of this economic pastorate, "It is no longer a question of ensuring the salvation of individuals in the next world, but rather of augmenting their existence in this world."[16] The previous political concern for religious salvation "takes on different meanings: health, well-being (that is sufficient wealth, standard of living), security, protection against accidents"[17]—all the same concerns that the prudent family must also reckon with as well as manage efficiently.

The police successor to the Christian pastoral technique "disciplines, compartmentalizes, fixes."[18] Foucault calls the Cameralist (*Polizei*) political technique "an *étatisation*, a taking into state control, of discipline"; that is, "a continuous network of power connecting the vigilance of the sovereign to the minute regulation and supervision of individual conduct."[19]

This new perspective toward police technology is elaborated upon with important and necessary detail by Oestreich who writes that this "conception of 'police' soon gave rise to the claim on the part of the ruling authorities to a general competence in the combating of all social disorders for which law and custom did not provide a remedy."[20] One reason for this claim of omnicompetence lay in the "increased density of population" which "led to stresses which had not been felt hitherto and which lowered the threshhold of tolerance towards the unrestricted development of personal life-styles and towards diversity and deviation from a certain norm."[21] There resulted new norms concerning "hygiene, social ethics and conduct in the economic sphere." Another cause lay in "the failure of ecclesiastical jurisdiction," which promoted the formulation of public "edicts concerning blasphemy, adultery, seduction, gaming, excessive drinking, ostentatious expenditure, and so forth."[22] In either case, "[g]reater social complexity brought a greater deployment of authority."[23] Oestreich writes of the "disciplining" of society as "a fundamental process which affected every possible sphere of life and virtually all classes, groups and professions."[24]

In the same way that Foucault stresses the downward continuity of police operations on the population, Oestreich writes, "People had to be 'coached,' as it were, for the tasks created by the more populous society and the claims which it made on its citizens."[25] He claims that the "attitudes and the conduct of even the simple subject were shaped, controlled, and regulated by the process of disciplining."[26] Moreover, "[t]hese changes were far more fundamental, far more enduring, than the institutional changes in politics and administration."[27] Foucault and Oestreich thus concur that the "establishment of social discipline was the effective achievement of absolutism.[28] The "tone" of such "absolutist society at large" is one "characterized by authority, discipline, and the systematic raising of levels of achievement."[29]

An Excursion into Statistics

In the "Governmentality" essay, Foucault narrates an interesting transition in the meaning and effects of the discipline of statistics in its early history that is indicative of concurrent changes in the practices of governing from absolute governmental rationality to liberal laissez faire. With its first emergence in the sixteenth century, statistics literally meant "the science of the state," and was directly linked to the pastoral goals of *Polizeiwissenschaft* that emphasized knowledge for the sake of disciplinary control. Foucault describes the change in the meaning of statistics as follows: "Whereas statistics had previously worked within the administrative frame and thus in terms of the functioning of sovereignty, it now gradually reveals that population has its own regularities, its own rate of deaths and diseases, its cycles of scarcity, etc. . . . " Because these aggregate effects of population are irreducible to those of the family, "population comes to appear above all else as the ultimate end of government."[30]

The change in the role and meaning of statistics is a momentous one that is analyzed in much greater detail by Ian Hacking in *The Taming of Chance*. As he explains, the change depends upon a new understanding—indeed even the "making"—of population: "Take so seemingly unproblematic a notion as population. We have become used to a picture: the number of people in a city or in a nation is determinate, like the number of people in a room at noon, and not like the number of people in a riot, or the number of suicides in the world last year. But even the very notion of an exact population is one which has little sense until there are institutions for establishing and defining what 'population' means."[31]

The establishment and the definition of national "populations" was made possible through the work of amateur statisticians and, above all, through the institution of governmental bureaus which claimed "a special type of knowledge, and a new kind of skill, the ability to collect, organize and digest numerical information about any subject whatsoever."[32] These amateurs and professionals produced, in Hacking's colorful phrase, "an avalanche of printed numbers." This avalanche could be employed by a statistical style of reasoning "involving collective regularities and frequencies rather than close attention to the causes of individual events."[33]

A most important early example, in Hacking's terms, a "powerhouse of the statistical movement," was Adolphe Quetelet. Quetelet made extensive use of the "avalanche" of numbers by appealing to the "law of large numbers" which "referred simply to the tendency for events frequently repeated and not too closely dependent on one another—that is to say, virtually everything counted by government statistical agencies—to occur in approximately constant numbers from year to year."[34] The stability of such statistical aggregates ensured stable mean values within the aggregates, and Quetelet made use of this fact in bequeathing upon humankind the famous "average man." This is an obviously mathematical construction that correlates to a mathematically defined population, but the actual use that Quetelet makes of the construct is a highly bio-political one. As Hacking explains,

> . . . Quetelet was not talking about an average for the human species. He was talking about the characteristics of a people or a nation, as a racial type. Where before one thought of a people in terms of its culture or its geography or its language or its rulers or its religion, Quetelet introduced a new objective measurable conception of a people. A race would be characterized by its measurements of physical and moral qualities, summed up in the average man of that race. This is half of the beginning of eugenics, the other half being the reflection that one can introduce social policies that will either preserve or alter the average qualities of a race. In short,

the average man led to both a new kind of information about populations and a new conception of how to control them.[35]

As important as the concept of the "average man" was (and is), Quetelet initiated a further step in social statistical reasoning with even greater repercussions. It can be observed from the above quotation that he sought to measure physical and moral qualities of the average man. In appraising these measurements, he made use of the "curve of error," the famous bell-shaped curve of "normal" distribution. Hacking comments: "Now whether we think of the Normal distribution as an error curve or as the limit of a binomial coin-tossing game, we are concerned with what we think of as real quantities. . . . Quetelet changed the game. He applied the same curve to biological and social phenomena where the mean is not a real quantity at all, or rather: **he transformed the mean into a real quantity**."[36]

The story of this transformation is a complicated and important one that Hacking describes in detail in chapter 13 of *The Taming of Chance*. It depends on an analogy between multiple measurements of the same physical attribute of one individual, in this case the size of the chest, and measurements of the same physical attribute of multiple individuals, in this case 5,738 Scottish soldiers. Quetelet claimed that the distribution of measurements of the 5,738 soldiers are distributed around a mean in the familiar bell-shaped fashion in the same way that 5,738 measurements of the one individual, allowing for errors of measurement, are distributed. This proved to him that human traits—not only physical attributes but moral attributes as well—are "normally distributed" within a population.

Quetelet's primary interest in social statistical data concerned data about criminals. His motivation in this respect, as well as the motivation of the Englishman William Farr, is explained by Hacking as follows:

> Quetelet and Farr alike represent the philanthropic and utilitarian aspect of nineteenth-century statistics. That is its dominant side. Both men appear to have had the most worthy of instincts. They wanted to improve the lot of the laboring classes, and they thought that they could do so by exercising a new kind of control. Discover what are the statistical laws that govern crime, disease, vice, unrest. Then find ways to alter the conditions under which those laws apply.[37]

The "new kind of control" of Quetelet and Farr is something that will be much in evidence in the later discussion of security mechanisms. These mechanisms will be interpreted as attempts to alter conditions only not with the negative goals of removing crime or disease but rather with the positive aims of increasing wealth and individual security. However, Hacking points out the great degree to which the avalanche of printed numbers in the nineteenth century—and not only Quetelet's and Farr's—dealt with crime, disease, vice, and suicide. This was especially true of the French who "were obsessed by the declining birth rate, and connected this with deviancy, be it madness, vagrancy, crime, drunkenness, prostitution or suicide."[38]

Consequently there is a strong historical linkage between the social category of deviancy and the statistical concept of deviation from the normal distribution. This linkage has important consequences, especially when the pre-statistical history of the concept "normal" is brought into play. Hacking comments: "The normal was one of a pair. Its opposite was the pathological and for a short time its domain was chiefly medical."[39] The meaning of normal in the medical context itself underwent a change shortly before 1800, when the normal becomes the right or proper biological state from which the "pathological" state deviates. The meaning of "normal" with its medical connotation moves, according to Hacking, into the sphere of "almost everything": "People, behavior, states of affairs, diplomatic relations, molecules: all these may be normal or abnormal. The word became indispensable because it created a way to be 'objective' about human beings."[40]

However, the word "normal" is employed in statistical laws not only because of its appearance of objectivity, but also for its prescriptive effectiveness. Hacking makes the following important argument concerning the non-overtly disciplinary ways that statistical laws "work" on people: "People are normal if they conform to the central tendency of such laws, while those at the extremes are pathological. Few of us fancy being pathological, so 'most of us' try to make ourselves normal, which in turn affects what is normal."[41] If the "cardinal concept of the psychology" of the earlier Enlightenment had been "human nature," it was now replaced by "normal people."[42]

Hacking's history of statistics illustrates how Quetelet's "average man" becomes a social reality susceptible to legal definition and how new, less disciplinary forms of administrative control cluster around "normality." The optimal mean is taken not only as a mathematical construction, but also as a social reality as well, because variations from the tolerable bandwidth in statistics are interpreted as deviations from "normal" distribution of behavior where "normal" still has the historical connotations of medicine which distinguishes the normal state from "pathological." However, even this wide range of effects may be of a too limited scope to capture the effects of statistical thinking. For Hacking also uncovers another important meaning of normal that is both statistically and behaviorally important.

This new meaning is termed by Hacking "Galton" in distinction to the emphasis on the pathological of "Durkheim." The quite differing range of effects take their inspiration from "the idea that the normal is only average, and so is something to be improved upon."[43] For Galton, the goal is not to fall within the mean, but rather to surpass its mediocrity in the same way as, according to Foucault in *The History of Sexuality*, the bourgeois sought out and embraced new family practices to distinguish themselves from the laboring masses. For Galton as for them, "the abnormal is exceptional, and may be the healthiest stock of the race."[44]

Thus there are "two visions of the normal."[45] Moreover, the same group of us who do not fancy being pathological do not much like being mediocre either. Consequently there are also two quite different prescriptive effects of the statistical norm of distribution, insofar as whether we judge the norm to be the "right" and the "proper" or the scarcely acceptable minimum of "mere" averageness. In either case the "avalanche of numbers" could and did and does have great behavioral effects both individually and on the population as a whole.

Active, Non-active Liberalism

Foucault's description of a transition in the meaning and import of statistics is confirmed by a January 1, 1798 diary entry by John Sinclair, which is quoted by Ian Hacking in a footnote to *The Taming of Chance*:

> "Many people were at first surprised at my using the words, *Statistics* and *Statistical*. . . . By statistical is meant in Germany an inquiry for the purpose of ascertaining the political strength of a country, or questions concerning matters of

state; whereas the idea I annexed to the term is an inquiry into the state of a country, for the purpose of ascertaining **the quantum of happiness enjoyed by its inhabitants and the means of its future improvement.**"[46]

However, Sinclair's citation does far more than attest to a change in the meaning of statistics. The specific emphasis given by the author at the conclusion of his entry is also evidence of an equally important transition in regard to the practices of governmentality. For Italian and German police science, the purpose of strengthening the state was achieved through strengthening the lives of its individual citizens. Sinclair, on the other hand, distinguishes between improving the happiness of the inhabitants and strengthening the state, precisely because he believes the former goal to be quite different from the latter. Sinclair's diary entry is not one of a reason of state theorist but rather of a liberal.[47]

The transition in meaning of "statistics" is crucial, according to Foucault, in understanding the "transition which takes place in the eighteenth century from an art of government to a political science, from a regime dominated by structures of sovereignty to one ruled by techniques of government."[48] The first effect of the introduction of the perspective of population was, as has already been alluded to earlier, to eliminate the model of family reckoning and efficient home economic management in government. When it is seen that considerations of the population as a whole are irreducible to the family, the "family becomes an instrument rather than a model: the privileged instrument for the government of the population and not the chimerical model of good government."[49]

A second, even more important effect of population was to displace sovereignty itself as the end of government. Rather than the reason of state emphasis on strengthening government, focus shifted, as seen earlier, to the welfare of the population, the improvement of its condition by increasing its wealth, longevity, and health. Eighteenth century French and English economists found there to be "an incompatibility of principle between the optimal development of the economic process and the maximizing of governmental procedures."[50] Hence they "wanted to free reflection on economic practice from the hegemony of reason of state and from saturation by governmental intervention."[51]

Liberalism, as summarized by Gordon, "undertakes to determine how government is possible, what it can do, and what ambitions it must needs renounce to be able to accomplish what lies within its powers."[52] The aspect of renunciation is of course captured in the "slogan-formula" laissez faire. However, Foucault makes the important claim as a third effect of the introduction of population into politics that laissez faire is "a way of acting, as well as a way of not acting."[53]

Gordon illustrates this most important feature of Foucault's conception of liberalism by citing Albert Hirschman's discussion of James Steuart, a contemporary to Adam Smith with his own conception of liberalism:

> The basic consistency of Steuart's thinking is best understood through his metaphor of the watch to which he likens the "modern oeconomy." He uses it on two different occasions to illustrate in turn . . . two aspects of state intervention. . . . On the one hand, the watch is so delicate that it "is immediately destroyed if . . . touched with any but the gentlest hand"; this means that the penalty for old-fashioned arbitrary *coups d'autorité* is so stiff that they will simply have to cease. On the other hand, these same watches are continually going wrong; sometimes the spring is found too weak, at other times too strong for the machine . . . and the workman's hand becomes necessary to set it right"; hence well-intentioned, delicate interventions are frequently required.[54]

For Foucault, as for Steuart, liberalism is not only the critique of government but also a new practice of government, "entailing an order of skill more exacting than that of government by police."[55] The skill of government by police involves the "idea of a police that would manage to penetrate, to stimulate, to regulate, and to render almost automatic all the mechanisms of society."[56] Liberalism, by contrast, arises "at the very moment it became apparent that if one governed too much, one did not govern at all—that one provoked results contrary to those one desired."[57] The new kind of governmentality comes about with the realization that from

> the moment that one is to manipulate a society, one cannot consider it completely penetrable by police. One must take into account what it is. It becomes necessary to reflect upon it, upon its specific characteristics, its constants and its variables. . . .[58]

Population as an object of governmental manipulation is "aware, vis-à-vis the government, of what it wants, but ignorant of what is being done to it."[59] The "new target and fundamental instrument of the government of population" becomes interest both at the individual level and at the level of the population "regardless of what the particular interests and aspirations may be of the individuals who compose it."[60] The new tactics and techniques of liberalism involve an injunction "not to impede the course of things, but to ensure the play of natural and necessary modes of regulation."[61] However, they also entail the discovery and the promotion of the conditions under which these "natural" modes of regulation can operate optimally as well. Therefore, Foucault attributes to liberal governmentality a wide range of active, non-active techniques of management: "manipuler, susciter, faciliter, laissez-faire." (FE, 17)[62]

In order to capture the active, non-active character of liberal governmentality, a specific kind of political technology is introduced that is distinct from both the purely economic and the purely legal. The active meaning of laissez faire entails for Foucault

> the setting in place of mechanisms of security . . . mechanisms or modes of state intervention whose function is to assure the security of those natural phenomena, economic processes and the intrinsic processes of population; this is what becomes the basic objective of governmental rationality.[63]

Liberalism opposes the police gridwork of disciplinary order, although Gordon is careful to insist that the "contrast between this new figure of liberty-security and the security of police is not an absolute one."[64] What liberalism affirms in its place is "the necessarily opaque, dense autonomous character of the processes of population."[65] Population is "a variable based upon a certain number of factors . . . far from all being natural factors (the tax system, the activity of circulation, the distribution of profit are the essential determinants of the rates of population)."[66] Nevertheless, the dependence on these factors can "be rationally analyzed in such a way that the population appears as 'naturally' dependent upon many factors which can be artificially modified."[67] "Mechanisms of security" carry out these artificial modifications in light of the vulnerability of the health, wealth, and other economic considerations of the state's population. They do so by making the "natural" regulations of the economy **secure** in the face of these vulnerabilities.

Foucault offers three characteristics to account for how security mechanisms can "function by playing on forces operative within the reality to be controlled, rather than by trying to impose an order on it." First they deal "in series of possible and probable events," when, for example they are directed towards the prevention of events which constitute a threat to the social order (such as grain shortages), rather than to the policing of dangerous situations. Second, they evaluate "through calculations of comparative cost." As Gordon elucidates, "The idea of an 'economic government' has, as Foucault points out, a double meaning for liberalism: that of a government informed by the precepts of political economy, but also that of a government which economizes on its own costs."[68] Finally they prescribe "not by absolute binary demarcation between the permitted and the forbidden, but by the specification of an optimal mean within a tolerable bandwidth of variation,"[69] a feature which Foucault does not explain in detail, but has been earlier taken up in Hacking's discussion of Quetelet and other of the first statisticians as well as of the two "visions" of the normal. All three of these features together allow liberalism to be conceived of as a practice or a set of practices to govern through "a greater effort of technique aimed at accomplishing more through a lesser exertion of force and authority."[70]

Gordon judges Foucault's discussion of security to be "one of his most important subsequent extensions to the framework of analysis he uses in *Discipline and Punish.*"[71] It plays a crucial role in the history of transition from an art of governing to a science of politics and in the concomitant rise of the individual reckonings and efficient management of *homo oeconomicus.* However, it also has obvious applications to the discussion and understanding of the development of political thought and practice beyond classical liberal governmentality. In particular, it points to the possibility of conceiving a specific form of social practice, the social security mechanism, a conception which Foucault himself did not develop, but which some of his closest associates and collaborators, Daniel Defert and François Ewald, have helped clarify in their analyses of risk and insurance technology. In the next chapter their work and other historical studies of the new liberalism will be discussed, with special emphasis both on another role for modern statistical thinking operative in social insurance and on the development of public assistance to deal with insecurity. The result of these discussions will be another "birth" to compare with the earlier appearances of the disciplined individual and rational economic man; namely, that of the secure individual.

3

The Interweaving of Social Insurance and Social Protection

In the previous chapter, liberal governmentality was described in terms of the maintenance of a delicate watch mechanism, a metaphor for the "modern oeconomy." The two aspects of non-active noninterference and active, but delicate intervention indicated how society "was discovered to be in a complex relationship of exteriority and interiority to the state."[1] The exteriority of society, stemming from the independence of considerations of population, had to be acknowledged so that the clear message of liberalism as critique was to "govern less." The interior way that the political economy also conditions the state led to the quite different requirement to "govern better" through the implementation of appropriate security mechanisms that would allow society to prosper.

This combination of the critical imperative "to govern less" and the governmental rationality "to govern better" was both powerful and attractive. However, its stability was threatened by the source of what was initially its greatest strength, the reliance on laissez faire in regard to the political economy. As Gordon explains, "The most obvious limitation of this system was that the governmental virtues it invested in the economy were, at best, constrained in their effectiveness by the performance of the economy itself; but that economy, by accelerating the formation of a precarious mass population of the urban poor, could be seen to provide neither for the political security of the state, nor for the material security of the population."[2]

In the transition to more modern forms of liberalism, another form of security, the **social security** of the population, comes to play a role equally vital to that of the political security of the state. Gordon writes that "our government involves a distinctive circuit of interdependence between **political security** and **social security**" and immediately adds that it "is misleading to envisage the dimension of the social as the state's antagonist or its prey."[3] J. Douglas Brown, "one of the outstanding authorities in the United States in the field of social security" in the late 1940s, obviously concurs, when he listed at that time three "ingredients" that needed to be "combined" in order to insure "the survival of democratic capitalism"—"individual incentive, mutual responsibility, and an effective framework of protection against the corroding fear of insecurity."[4]

In a certain sense, the fear of insecurity has already been discussed in the previous chapter with the initial formulation of the reason of state doctrine and its emphasis upon the indefinite survival of the state. However, the focus of Brown is not upon the imposed discipline of reason of state, but on the "modern state of security, guaranteeing the citizen against old age and misfortune, redistributing resources, where security comes to signify not the old military notion which referred to the occupation of a territory, but that modern idea which enfolds in itself the lives of each and all."[5] There is a new form of liberal governmental rationality embodied in the very terms that Brown chooses to pose his critical question: "How can we establish an effective framework against the fear of insecurity in order to sustain individual incentive and to assure mutual responsibility . . . ?"[6]

The primary subject of this chapter will be the liberal (as distinct from conservative or social democratic) manner of interweaving the rationality of social insurance and the resources of public assistance that characterizes so many of the social security programs of the Western industrialized nations. The first section of the chapter will discuss the innovations brought about by social insurance as explicated by François Ewald and Daniel Defert. The next section will then take up the various legal measures of social protection that were proposed by modern liberals in the pre-World War I period as illustrated by Michael Freeden's history of English liberalism. Then an explanation of social security mechanisms, parallel to political security mechanisms, will ᴅe offered in terms of the necessary interrelationship in modern social politics between social insurance and social assistance.

The "Birth" of Social Insurance

In conscious imitation of Foucault's birth of the asylum and birth of the prison, François Ewald writes of a momentous "birth" of social insurance at the end of the nineteenth century. Ewald is similarly interested in the "how" of insurance practice and conceives of it as a technology of risk. He distinguishes between an everyday meaning of risk and the insurance meaning that relates to a collectivity of individuals or a population:

> In everyday language the term 'risk' is understood as a synonym for danger or peril, for some unhappy event which may happen to someone it designates an objective threat. In insurance, the term designates neither an event nor a general kind of event occurring in reality (the unfortunate kind), but a specific mode of treatment of certain events capable of happening to a group of individuals—or, more exactly, to values or capitals possessed or represented by a collectivity of individuals: that is to say, a population.[7]

The conception of risk involved in insurance is one of "chance, hazard, probability, eventuality or randomness on the one hand" and of "loss or damage on the other"—the two aspects coming together in the notion of "accident."[8] The technology of insurance objectifies every event as a potential accident and the accident is insured against as though one is betting in a high-stakes game of chance. Ewald makes the important claim of such "gaming" that it "is the practice of a type of rationality potentially capable of transforming the life of individuals and that of a population."[9]

The first of Ewald's three "great characteristics" of risk is that it is calculable. At the basis of insurance is a calculus of probabilities, indeed a "sister activity" to the "social physics" of Quetelet as earlier described by Hacking. At the heart of the calculation is the same "law of large numbers." As the first statistical study on industrial accidents in mining demonstrated in the mid-nineteenth century, when "put in the context of a population, the accident which taken on its own seems both random and avoidable (given a little prudence) can be treated as predictable and calculable."[10] The stability of such statistical aggregates ensures stable mean values within the aggregates. This feature was exploited by early forms of private insurance in regard to industrial accidents and also, as is shown by Daniel Defert, Ewald's fellow researcher on social insurance, in regard to the calculation of average life expectancy for the purposes of life insurance. The constancy of the large numbers means that the only unknown is "who will have the accident, who will draw one of existence's unlucky numbers."[11]

Risk's second crucial feature, according to Ewald, is that it is collective:

> Strictly speaking, there is no such thing as an individual risk; otherwise insurance would be no more than a wager. Risk only becomes something calculable when it is spread over a population. The work of the insurer is, precisely, to constitute that population by selecting and dividing risks. Insurance can only cover groups; it works by socializing risks. It makes each person a part of the whole.[12]

If each person is a part of the larger group, each person is at the same time individualized by her or his probability of risk relative to the population of which she or he is a member. Insurance deals with unacceptably high risk by exclusion, but it also incorporates supplementary practices to accomplish a more individualized inclusion, as Defert explains:

> The target population for insurance is precisely that population which conforms to the general laws of mortality, it is the true, regular plenitude of biological life that here becomes the object of observation. Yet even what falls outside this model can become the object of a specific form of insurance by adding a supplement to the premium. You aren't inoculated for smallpox? A supplement. You travel? A classification of countries is drawn up according to their dangerousness, to fix your additional premium. And so on.[13]

Defert concludes: "Insuring a population means classifying it, subdividing it in line with a scale of degrees of risk and with an analysis of behaviours, thresholds, marginal categories which are first excluded, then treated as special sub-classes while excluding still more marginal groups, and so on."[14]

Ewald's third characteristic of risk concerns the object of the insurance practice: "What is insured is not the injury that is actually lived, suffered and resented by the person it happens to, but a capital against whose loss the insurer offers a guarantee."[15] Insurance involves a "dualization" between "the injury as lived by the victim" and "the fixed indemnity paid out by the insurer," a dualization which first began in regard to shipping goods but then extends to life itself. Chauffon describes the process by which this dualization expands in his 1884 book on insurance:

> Man first thought of insuring his shipping against the risks of navigation. Then he insured his houses, his harvests, and his goods of all kinds against risk of fire. Then, as the idea of capital, and consequently also that of insurable interest, gradually emerged in a clear form out of the confused notions that previously obscured them, man understood that he himself was a capital which death could prematurely destroy, that in himself he embodied an insurable interest. He then devised life insurance, insurance that is to say against the premature destruction of human capital. Next he realized that if human capital can be destroyed, it can also be condemned to disuse through illness, infirmity and old age, and so he devised accident, sickness and pension insurance. Insurance against the unemployment or premature destruction of human capital is the true popular form of insurance.[16]

Chauffon describes an evolution of insurance practices that can be explained entirely in terms of private insurance practices. **Social insurance** as a governmental policy was, of course, a major expansion and modification of earlier practices of private insurance. Employers initially contracted for private insurance which they paid for through payroll deductions. However, it "is the imperative of **guaranteed** security in workers' insurance that leads to the debate over state insurance."[17] Furthermore, behind "this problem lies another, profounder one, namely the problem of the permanence of insurance institutions."[18] The solution for these problems occurred in France "by nationalizing the industrial accident departments of the private insurance companies."[19] This nationalization of insurance by, to use Ewald's phrase, the "provident state" is understood by both him and Defert as "a new, statistical mode of management of populations."[20]

Ewald claims that "without insurance everything is uncertain for the worker: the present lacks confidence, the future hope and consolation."[21] On the other hand, as a political technology of risk undertaken by the provident state, "insurance makes it possible to envisage a solution to the problem of poverty and working-class insecurity."[22] In his 1916 book on social insurance, I.M. Rubinow comments on the threat of poverty: "Absence of a wage-earner in the family (premature death by accident or any other cause, or desertion), disability to work (accident, sickness, motherhood, invalidity, old age), or inability to obtain a living (unemployment), these three causes practically cover all causes of poverty."[23] And earlier in the introduction, Rowntree's description of the typical working family of his time had emphasized the insecurity caused by the many transitions that family members made between want and comparative plenty. With social insurance to cover the three causes of poverty delineated by Rubinow and allay the insecurities of Rowntree's family, the working class could become confident citizens in the newly developing provident or insurance state, just like the middle class who were able to afford most, if not all, of Chauffon's forms of private insurance.

The Social Protection of the Citizen

The social assistance that was to be offered to citizens in the changing liberal state at the beginning of the twentieth century had to be, according to John Myles in his book, *Old Age and the Welfare State*, "reinvented." This is because the earlier welfare policy had not been for the purpose of assistance itself, but rather "to mobilize an unwilling population to enter the nascent industrial labor force."[24] The relief that was provided "was to be such that the recipient's position would always be less 'eligible' (desirable) than that of the poorest worker in the labor force."[25] Receipt of poor relief entailed confinement in poorhouses "designed less for the relief of poverty than for the deterrence of relief."[26] Indeed Maurice Stack writes of earlier systems of public assistance that "the indigent were regarded as quasi-criminals by the State, which treated them repressively."[27]

The technology of social insurance was first introduced in Germany through the work of mutual assistance societies and later, under the leadership of Bismarck, enacted into law in the form of national accident insurance and pension legislation. As described by Gerhard Ritter, the technology depended on a threefold system of contribution:

> Based on contributions from the employers and the employees and subsidies from the state, social insurance borrowed essential elements from three earlier forms of collective subsistence: the system of mutual benefit societies as practised by the guilds, corporations and journeymen associations, the employer's obligation to provide his servants and clerical workers with protection as laid down in the Prussian General Law Code . . . of 1794 and the provision of poor relief by the state and local authorities.[28]

As Ritter further explains,

> Unlike the traditional system of poor relief, which stressed the individual's personal blame for his hardship, it placed firmly in the foreground those general factors which produced crises in the life of the individual, for which he himself could not be held responsible. It differed from earlier forms of private insurance in that it provided security, not against predicaments arising from "natural" causes but against those resulting from "social" factors. . . . it helped promote the view that poverty and the accompanying de facto loss of citizen's rights were no longer a stroke of fate which the individual and his family had to suffer helplessly.[29]

Hence the German social insurance legislation accomplished all the features of risk sharing described by Ewald. However, the grounds for the nationalized initiation of such social insurance lay under the suspicion of being motivated far more by concerns of state security still committed to reason of state authoritarianism than by any immediate concern for the security of workers and their families. In Ritter's judgment, "The main impetus behind Germany's social insurance legislation before 1914 was the attempt to combat the danger to the political and social order from a socialist workers' movement which was widely regarded by contemporaries as a revolutionary threat."[30] Martin Kohli points to Bismarck in particular as an example par excellence of the state interest in security: "As is well known, Bismarck repeatedly asserted that nothing would reconcile the workers better with the state, and thus lower the risk of a proletarian revolution, than the perspective of a stable life course with a public guarantee of material security."[31]

When national social insurance programs were introduced in countries such as England some twenty-five years later, liberal thinkers oriented themselves to the problem of mass poverty[32] and sought after less state-centered justifications for the legislation. S. A. Barnett, for example, distinguished among the unemployed between the unable and the unwilling to work and advocated non-disciplinary forms of relief for the former group.[33] For him and many others, the emphasis fell upon the development of a system of social protection wherein government contributions became essential to the program. The development of this system is detailed by Michael Freeden in the chapter "The Social Policy of New Liberalism" in his book, *The New Liberalism.*

According to an editorial in *The Nation*, almost universal assent was given in England to three propositions in regard to the National Insurance Act of 1911: "first, that private machinery of self-help is unequal to the full task of making adequate provision for invalidity and unemployment; secondly, that compulsion may properly be employed to stimulate provision by workers and employers; thirdly, that the public interest in the achievement of these purposes warrants public expenditure on their behalf."[34] Concerning the first of these propositions, it was clear that the "normal" working family, described in the Rowntree quote at the beginning of the book, lacked the economic means both to take care of its present economic needs and to save for future needs and possible dangers at the same time. Concerning the second, the contribution of the worker to the social insurance program was viewed as an essential means for stimulating social responsibility, while the contribution of the employer expressed an immediate responsibility toward the worker. At the same time, the amount of the contribution could not be so severe as to impede either the efficiency and the contentment of the labor force or the willingness and the profitability of the employer, so the third proposition points to the political need for state assistance. The consequence of all these three factors was the development of a tripartite system of contributions similar to the German system, with the employer, worker, and state all playing instrumental roles.

The tripartite system was not only required by reasons of economic efficiency but also by a more positive concern for social solidarity and a sense of state citizenship on the part of the employed. As Freeden explains, the employer did have a certain responsibility towards his workers. But it was not, nor did any liberal expect it to be, one that considered the welfare and interests of the worker as a prime concern. That over-all view was supplied by the state. The state, then, had to manipulate the situation in a manner which Utilitarians would have approved of: to make the protagonists, while pursuing their own interests, contribute towards the general welfare. But unlike the Utilitarians, new liberals saw the community and state as directly motivated by ethical values and ends which could only be perceived by the comprehensive outlook of the whole social body.[35]

In order to achieve this comprehensive outlook, national insurance was only one of the important new social policies that the new liberalism advocated. Freeden lists as the other most essential social policies the initiation and implementation of old-age pensions, the discussion of "right to work" in the context of unemployment, and the feeding of school children.

The initiation of old-age pensions is considered as a social program different in nature from social insurance, insofar as the discussions surrounding these reforms involve a new and further principle: "the recognition of social service." The state had earlier recognized a social duty to care for certain of its citizens—its soldiers and sailors, postmen and policemen—in view of their important service to the country. Chiozza Money argued that such a viewpoint of service extended not only to these important civil and defense responsibilities but to all forms of employment:

> . . . a labourer, whether he worked mentally or physically, worked not only for his employer, but for the nation at large, and . . . the nation as a conscious entity was coming increasingly to regard itself as an organisation. When that was once realized it was seen that the worker . . . was in a very real sense a contributor to the greatness and wealth of his country, and, therefore, it became the duty of the State to assert itself consciously on his behalf.[36]

Under the very considerable assumption of the time that old-age pensions "were a distant and often doubtful benefit, whereas the rewards of insurance were much more likely to be reaped at an earlier stage,"[37] citizens were not required to contribute to pensions in the same way as national insurance. Hence, "pensions were regarded as a reward for what citizens had already done for society, whereas insurance was mainly a means to enable them to perform their role as citizens in the future."[38]

The liberal advocacy of free meals for schoolchildren also involved further principles of social protection. Two motives for this advocacy were considerations of humanitarianism and national self-preservation, which could indeed be interlinked in the manner of the following *Nation* editorial: "To secure the proper nurture for children is a matter of the highest importance, not merely from the point of view of the suffering child, but of the society into which the child is born."[39] A third motivation lay in the opportunity for an "education in citizenship" that the child could receive from its recognitions of the benefit from state nourishment. In any of these instances, the

> significance of the shift in ideas was that the state often assumed direct and always ultimate responsibility for the welfare of children. Its assistance could indeed be interpreted as of prime educational value in demonstrating to the parents their duties. The concept of welfare had once more been expanded under the impact of a new appreciation of the "natural resources" indispensable to the well-being of the community. Children had become too valuable to be left entirely to the responsibility of individuals, though they be the parents themselves.[40]

Hence the complete array of liberal legislation in England at the beginning of the century was indeed deeply influenced by the principles of social insurance but was arguably also motivated to an even greater degree by social protection. In Money's words, "the first duty of a civilization is so to pool its resources and its risks that no man, or set of men, shall be made to endure the consequences of an irregularity which civilization cannot prevent."[41]

Social Security—Program and Mechanism

If, according to new liberal thought, society has a duty to protect the life of the individual, individual life, beginning with children and their school lunches, is also more closely tied to the organization of the state. Not only should individual security be at least minimally guaranteed, a solidarity of the citizenry is expressed in such policy. The proposal and initiation of new social programs means that "the activities of government themselves begin to acquire something of the density and complexity formerly attributed by liberal thinkers to the object of government, namely commercial society or the market."[42] The social is being consituted as a sphere with its own dynamics of population, and social security is thereby coming to have a role at least equal in importance to that of political security. Gordon argues that what "entitles us to think of this as a transmutation, rather than a liquidation or betrayal, of liberal government is that it proceeds not by the institution of a new reason of state but by the invention, out of a range of extraneous sources, of a set of new roles **for** the state."[43]

Of course the new social programs were not immune from considerations of reason of state, even if that was not the primary purpose from the new liberal perspective. As Ewald notes in historical detail in *L'Etat providence*, consideration for state survival could interject itself not only into the concern for political security, but also into the social realm as well. Crucial to this aspect of social security were the fear of "social evils" and the biopolitical steps that could be taken to prevent or correct them. Social security understood primarily as prevention or correction has already been encountered in the earlier discussion of Quételet and his manner of employment of statistics. Examples of social security measures mentioned by Ewald in conjunction with the eradication of social evils include: (1) intelligence testing—introduced in France at the same time as the first forms of social insurance, it seeks to make Quételet's "average man" a normative reality through the prevention of mental retardation; (2) handicapped legislation—handicapped are defined as "abnormally feeble" and are identified, recorded, and in cases isolated from the "normally skilled"; (3) "dangerousness"—is introduced as a category in criminal behavior and personality to be analyzed by criminal penology and psychology and as an identifiable subpopulation to be incapacitated through legal measures. In all these instances, "risk factors" are identified with respect to the population at large and preventive measures of social control are undertaken to combat the perceived social "dangers."[44]

If such disciplinary effects of social security were and are undeniably present, another aspect of social security plays a more prominent role in the proposal of programs of social assistance to advance the security of the people as a whole. While earlier liberal governmentality distinguished between and perhaps even opposed security and liberty, the new programs of social security sought to produce, in the words of Abraham

Epstein, "continuance of an income to working-class families during sickness, accident, unemployment, death and old age,"[45] but in ways that mutually reinforced individual liberty. The goal was—and is—in Ewald's phrase, "a politics of social foresight" which did not subsume individual life into collective existence, but rather frees people to live their own lives.[46]

In the previous chapter, the political security mechanisms of liberalism were interpreted by Foucault as active, non-active mechanisms for securing the economy. Social security can similarly be examined not primarily as a political program, but rather as a form of governmentalilty which seeks to produce social security through active, non-active interventions of the rationalilty of social insurance together with the resources of social assistance. In other words, I propose in the remaining part of this chapter to interpret the program of social security in terms of the employment of effective **social security mechanisms**, analogous to the political security mechanisms of the previous chapter, which have "been instrumental in prolonging life, improving national health, increasing industrial efficiency, stimulating patriotic idealism, and securing greater national stability."[47]

The interpretation of social security as a security mechanism does not award a priority to either social insurance or social assistance but rather emphasizes their necessary interrelation in the modern insurance state. According to Maurice Stack's characterizations of social insurance and social assistance in an article of 1941, they are both "intermediate forms between the extremes of private insurance and poor relief."[48] Although each begins according to Stack from an "opposite starting point," each also assumes features "proper to the other."

The "grand advantage" of social insurance is, according to Stack, "that it is financially feasible where assistance is not."[49] By a "fortunate coincidence," "the bulk of the low income group is comprised within the class of wage-earners, from whom contributions can easily be collected through the employer, while the latter can be made to contribute as well."[50] However, social insurance also has a corresponding limitation "in the restriction of its scope to employed persons and in the more or less close dependence of the benefits of an individual upon the contributions credited to him."[51] The former restriction is addressable by extension of social insurance to independent workers. However, the more important restriction on the proportionality of benefits has been mitigated from the outset "by consideration for the family responsibilities of insured persons and by the principle that the cash benefits of insurance should, as far as possible, be sufficient in themselves for maintenance."[52]

Such mitigating factors of proportionality obviously go beyond the requirements of social insurance and "are clearly in the nature of assistance." Moreover, concerns for maintenance clearly increase in importance as "family medical benefit, dependants' supplements added to periodical payments in respect of sickness, invalidity, old age, accident and unemployment, not to speak of the purely family nature of maternity benefits, survivors' pensions and, finally, of family allowances"[53] are included. Nevertheless, the standard liberal reflection "shows that the ability of a nation to bear increasing pension charges depends solely on its increasing productivity."[54] Hence, Stack argues that "uniform pensions can at best guarantee a minimum of subsistence, and take no account of the differences in standards of living which will always persist in some degree."[55] While "scientific progress" may help increase productivity in the future, the largest consequence of such growth can be "modest growth of the average pension over a long period of years."[56]

Stack concludes that the principles of social insurance and the policies of social assistance "meet, as it were in the centre and merge": "A pension insurance scheme which approaches universality in its scope, whose essential benefit is on a subsistence level, which is largely financed by a State subsidy, and which may even require a means test for certain supplements, comes to resemble very closely a social assistance scheme."[57] The conclusion of the 1941 article was highly contestable as to the necessity of a **central** meeting point. But as an argument for the necessity of "blending" social assistance with social insurance, the argument is much less debatable.

The calculations of social insurance allow for, in Churchill's memorable phrase, "bringing in the magic of averages to the aid of millions."[58] Moreover, the contributions required provide for "a sure sense of revenue" and at the same time their compulsory nature can serve "as a public lesson of responsibility." But considerations of social assistance are needed to provide for the full amount of individual security. A criterion of "social adequacy" allows for the return from the participation of the poorest contributors in the program to exceed the level of their contributions and thereby achieve a socially more sufficient level. Thus it is the blending of social adequacy with the calculations of social insurance rationality that characterizes a social security mechanism for a contemporary liberal governmentality concerned with and actively, nonactively planning the social welfare of its population.

The Bifurcation of Social Security and Welfare

The liberal history of the implementation of social security mechanisms has undergone its own splits and divergences since the first programs of social insurance and assistance were adopted. The major source of difference has been mainly in regard to the last feature of Stack's proposed synthesis of social insurance and social assistance; namely, the use of means testing. According to some historians of social programs, the splits and divergences may have a great deal to do with how comprehensive the implementation of social security mechanisms was in the first place.

A comprehensive employment of such blending social security mechanisms in liberal governmentality is more characteristic of the English history of social security than the American. In the same year that Stack's article appeared, William Beveridge was chosen to lead an English commission to study and make recommendations concerning the earlier Liberal social legislation. This commission responded to "growing public pressure for a guarantee that there would never be a return to the poverty and inequalities of pre-war Britain."[59] The main recommendations from the commission's report were for the reform and for the more comprehensive extension of the social insurance programs. Under the impetus of this report, the post-war government revamped old-age insurance, unemployment insurance, disability insurance, and workers' compensation, as well as extended social insurance coverage to family allowances and created a national health service. The "sum of these innovations was called 'the welfare state,' a phrase coined to contrast the aspirations of Britain with the horrors of the Nazi 'warfare state.'"[60] According to the Beveridge report, this welfare state was universal in its scope, with each English citizen contributing and each benefitting as well.

In contrast with England, the implementation of social security mechanisms in the United States has been much more restricted and incomplete. In the original Social Security Act of

1935, only social insurance programs for unemployment and old age and public assistance for the elderly poor and for dependent children were included. Only the social insurance program for old age was national in scope, and it won for itself the honorific appellation of "social security" which had actually been intended for a comprehensive program of social insurance and protection.

After 1935, additional social insurance programs were added to the original "Social Security" to cover surviving dependents (1939), disabled workers (1956), and retirees in need of medical care (1965). At the same time, the financial support provided by Social Security to the elderly population also began to eclipse in importance the financial aid provided to them by the program of public assistance. What began to occur, unlike in England's case, was a process of bifurcation between Social Security, especially in regard to the aged, and "welfare," especially in regard to dependent children: "'social security' for the stably employed majority of citizens had become by the 1960s institutionally and symbolically bifurcated from 'welfare' for the barely deserving poor."[61] Social security became associated with universal programs of social insurance, while welfare bore the stigma of means-tested public assistance.

The concluding questions from Roy Lubove's *The Struggle for Social Security* attest to the process of bifurcation and at the same time pinpoint the specific concerns of this study on the secure individual. An important treatment of the beginnings of welfare programs in the United States, Lubove ends his history with two questions which, although formulated in the 1960s, presaged both the present "welfare" crisis and the threatening situation to the secure individual as well:

> Must economic security remain so closely tied to stable, long-term labor force participation? Must the unemployable—dependent children, blind, handicapped, aged, able-bodied but unskilled—who compose the overwhelming percentage of the assistance rolls be penalized for the incapacity to compete in the labor market?[62]

The second question foreshadows of course the present "crisis" of welfare. Even as formulated twenty-five years ago, it indicates already the stigma of being non-participators or non-contributors which is borne by the "unemployable." This stigma relates most directly to the social problems and political challenges facing modern welfare programs designed to assist restricted groups by means testing. Indeed, American conservatives and "new democrats" alike appear to agree on the need to end "welfare as we know it" and differ only on the measures to be taken and the swiftness with which to begin (and take credit for) combatting welfare "dependency."[63]

However, the primary focus of the following chapter on the secure individual and for the extended discussions on economic employment in Part Two is upon Lubove's **first** question. For those who have been fortunate enough to have "long-term" (and full-time) employment, the birth of the **secure** individual— not the dependent individual—is an indeed appropriate appellation. The next chapter will explain how the universal protection of Social Security has promoted the future "planning with" of social insurance and "planning upon" of public assistance that has produced such secure individuals.

Before beginning this discussion, however, I wish to point toward Theda Skocpol's strategy for opposing the American historical process of bifurcation between social insurance and welfare[64] and show how it later influences the discussion of income assistance programs in this book. In *Social Policy in the United States*, Skocpol has attested to the interweaving of social insurance and social assistance with regard to the original program of Social Security. According to her, administrators of this program worked **both** "to make benefits higher for everyone, and relatively better for the less privileged, so that benefits could be closer to a sufficient retirement income."[65] In its original inception and following its social insurance aspects, "social security has always disproportionally favored not the neediest Americans but the stably employed and the middle class."[66] However, "benefits were gradually redistributed toward poorer elderly people and were larger than they would have received from a mere proportional return on their own payroll taxes collected at their preretirement wage levels."[67]

The conclusion of Skocpol's historical assessment of the implementation of the Social Security system is that "Today Social Security is not only the most politically unassailable part of U.S. public social provision, but also America's most effective anti-poverty program."[68] In accordance with this conclusion, she argues not for fewer but for more universal programs of social insurance which would also disproportionately protect the neediest. In the final chapter of this book, Skocpol's general strategy will be emulated and a similar program of interweaving insurance and protection will be examined which buffers strong fluctuations in income in a world no longer promising stable employment.

4

The Secure Individual

Modern social security is not solely a product of a liberal (or conservative or social democratic) social politics and the techniques of social insurance applied on the level of population. Rather it is at least just as much a result of the individual planning for security. While the individual technologies of the self have often been mentioned and detailed in previous chapters, they have never been the primary focal point for discussion. However, the emphasis of this chapter will be explicitly upon the "subject" of the social security mechanisms that interweave social insurance and public assistance.

The technology of the self associated with this subject begins with the head of the family whose prudent reckoning and efficient management of the family economy provides the initial model of governmental rationality for the absolutist state. While operations of the police attempt to ensure the prudent economic strengthening downwards by surveillance and meticulous recordkeeping of the family, liberal governmentality seeks the same end only through less disciplinary means and in regard to the population as a whole. Already in the conception of political security, an obligation to plan is apparent in terms of an originally bourgeois ethic, later more generalized imperative, to plan out one's interests economically, to be a *homo oeconomicus* in an economy of similar economic agents who would not then require direct governmental control. In the case of social security, Gordon writes that the "rhetoric of daring modernity and its risk-pledged souls seems . . . to have been mobilized in the nineteenth century largely for the purpose of exhorting the working class to adopt the bourgeois ethic of individual life, conceived as an enterprise which providently reckons with its chances of death and disablement as 'professional risks' of human existence."[1]

The bourgeois ethic regarding individual life required and promoted planning, since to plan rationally would secure what was reasonably expectable from future social living. Even more importantly, such planning was advantageous precisely because of the promise of individual security. Insofar as social security mechanisms could make individual security more generally attainable, they could even be said to promote the emergence of a *homo securus* analogous to the much more celebrated counterpart. From this admittedly less established perspective, to be a rational self-planning individual in the modern state is to be a rational and secure individual in a larger population of secure individuals.

Modern individuals are—we are—life planners. We plan perhaps and hopefully out of a sense of mutual obligation, but certainly out of a sense of obligation to ourselves. Furthermore, we plan our lives in order not to have them pre-planned by liberal governmentality. The rational, active life planner is the correlate and presupposition of the actively non-active, social politics of the liberal state. It also will be the subject of examination of this chapter.

Planning With and Planning Upon

The parallel between political and social security mechanisms can be pursued more closely in order to articulate a common structure of individual conduct promoted by their implementation. Gordon introduced the discussion of the workings of political security mechanisms through a comparison by the classical political economist Steuart between the economy and a watch. The mechanism of the watch—understood as a metaphor for the economy of a population—was delicate and cannot be interfered with save for by the "gentlest hand." Yet the same watch continually goes wrong so that the same gentle hand is a requirement for also setting it right. Hence what are needed, as has been explained above, are political mechanisms that can accomplish more "through a lesser exertion of force and authority."

What is the individual conduct that is the correlate to political mechanisms of security? It is a conduct as complicated as the active, non-active governmental technology itself. On the one hand, it is the conduct of the famed rational economic actor who both possesses a rational understanding of economic principles and is secure in the knowledge that the government will not interfere in the pursuit of such rationally guided and rationally understood self-interest. At the same time, it is the conduct of a political citizen who expects the government to enact the general environmental and population policies to promote her or his individual economic advancement without the infringement upon any individual right. The individual may "both revile and invoke the power of the state,"[2] but more crucial to the understanding of the subject of political security mechanisms is the fact that she or he both **plans with** rational economic principles and **plans upon** prudent governmental intervention to order to advance economically.

Concerning social mechanisms of security, the individual conduct is no different either in regard to its complexity or, I would argue, in regard to its basic structure. As Graham Burchell has stated in regard to our modern complexity, we oscillate "between a suspicious fear and criticism of the state's impertinent interventions in detailed aspects of our lives, and an expectation that government will, and/or a demand that it should, respect our rights while taking responsibility for improvements in the conditions and quality of our individual lives, for sheltering us from insecurities and dangers, for providing the conditions and opportunities for individual advancement, for meeting our individual health needs, for protecting the local community and natural environment in which we live, and so on."[3] Concerning the structure, that is also a combination of "planning with" and "planning upon" in accordance with the dual nature of the social security mechanism that has already been explained.

If the bourgeois individual could become secure in accordance with the new principles of private insurance outlined by Chauffon, the general citizen can now reckon with social insurance as described by Ewald and Defert. Therefore, potentially all members of society can now **plan with** the calculus of probabilities of the whole population and correspondingly "dualize" their actions or misfortunes as both lived experiences and financially indemnified events. They can and do undertake a new statistical mode of individual foresight correlative to the statistical mode of social foresight of social insurance.

Ewald interprets this probabilistic mode of individual foresight as a "moral technology" or technology of the self. He
describes it as follows:

> To calculate a risk is to master time, to discipline the future.
> To conduct one's life in the manner of an enterprise indeed
> begins in the eighteenth century to be a definition of a moral-
> ity whose cardinal virtue is providence. To provide for the
> future does not just mean not living from day to day and
> arming oneself against ill fortune, but also mathematizing one's
> commitments. Above all, it means no longer resigning oneself
> to the decrees of providence and the blows of fate, but instead
> transforming one's relationships with nature, the world and
> God so that, even in misfortune, one retains responsibility for
> one's affair by possessing the means to repair its effects.[4]

The ambitious goal and desired outcome of planning with
is to seek "to master time, to discipline the future." This involves for modern individuals, to return to the theme of life
planning from chapter 1, no longer viewing events as primarily
external happenings, but rather as "consequences of the decisions that they themselves have made, which they must view
and treat as such." To plan with in regard to these personal
decisions is to "conduct one's life in the manner of an enterprise." This is to require that life be viewed as an enterprise
whose survival depends upon prudent and self-interestedly
rational planning into the future or, as Anthony Giddens expresses it, "living with a calculative attitude to the open possibilities of action, positive and negative, with which, as individuals
and globally, we are confronted in a continuous way in our
contemporary social existence."[5] To plan with in this prudently
and self-interested way is to "mathematize one's commitments"
in accordance with Ewald's principles of insurance rationality.
Since social insurance allows one to minimize the bad financial
effects of a maximally bad outcome and thus "repair its effect"
as much as possible, the planning with of this rationality indeed helps to secure an uncertain future and perhaps even
discipline it.

In a similar manner, the modern individual also **plans upon**
social protection against the "risks" of life. As Freeden summa-
rizes all the legislation of "the Social Programme of Liberalism"
in England, he claims that it was aimed "at the protection of the
mass of the population against the 'risks' of life—childhood, sick-

ness, unemployment, invalidity, and old age."[6] In his words, it was "a complete transformation of the idea of social reform"; it was "a claim for a share in life."[7] And what was claimed then for the first time has now become an array of resources to be taken for granted by contemporary individuals.

The protection that is planned upon takes the form of assistance programs such as public pensions and social security, public hygiene and health assistance programs, and public education and children assistance programs as well. In the terminology of social scientists in the introductory chapter, such programs offer welfare tracks that make a stable future plan a reasonable and predictable expectancy. This stability is above all enhanced by the feature of social assistance that the outlay from the welfare tracking may indeed exceed the amount of individual contribution in reflection of particular need. Given this possible excess, individual security no longer appears to be a dream beyond the reach of the individual, but rather offers itself as an achievable goal made possible by the security mechanisms of the insurance state.

Therefore, to be a self-planning individual of the modern state is not only to be an enterprise-planning economic agent. Rather it is to be, perhaps even more centrally, a life-planning "secure individual." Secure individuals are—we are or aspire to be—life planners. We "plan with" potentially even Ewald's and Hacking's mathematical sophistication of statistical probability in reducing the effects of accident or misfortune; and, should misfortune still occur, we "plan upon" assistance from the state to help us live adequately. The "secure individual" is both the product and, more interestingly, the self-product of the merging of the rationality of social insurance and the resources of social assistance as these are operative in the social security mechanisms of modern governmentality.

The Standardized Life Cycle

If these representations of the activities of the "secure individual" are at all accurate, they are pertinent above all in relation to the standardized life cycle. No longer is it a cycle that is viewed primarily in terms of happening to us, but rather it is viewed as a sequence of our own personal decisions for which we take ultimate responsibility. As Anthony Giddens expresses the point forcefully in his important book, *Modernity and Self-Identity*, "We are not what we are, but what we make of ourselves."[8] So we plan our education and training (and the childhood and education of our children), our occupational trajectories (perhaps in great detail), and our retirements (with perhaps equal diligence). As Giddens elaborates,

> The trajectory of the self has a coherence that derives from a cognitive awareness of the various phases of the lifespan. The lifespan, rather than events in the outside world, becomes the dominant "foreground figure" in the **Gestalt** sense. It is not quite the case that all outside events or institutions are a "blur," against which only the lifespan has form and is picked out in clear relief; yet such events only intrude in so far as they provide supports for self-development, throw up barriers to be overcome or are a source of uncertainties to be faced.[9]

Giddens argues that in "a world of alternative lifestyle options, strategic **life-planning** becomes of special importance."[10] My contention is that this argument can be strongly supported by the prominent roles of what I have termed "planning with" and "planning upon" regarding life-planning strategies.

Concerning the standardized life cycle introduced in chapter 1, the individual becomes "secure" by being able to predict and plan out a safe future in the coming stages of life. The extension of a future until a period lasting beyond work into retirement and old age allows for the entire series of distinct stages of the modern life cycle to come to completion. The modern individual, in a truly actuarial sense, "plans with" a completed future in a way that was not possible in earlier historical periods when death or an age of weakness, not any "third age" of living and fourth age of medical assistance, marked the concluding point of work activity.

To plan with in regard to a Third Age of retirement is of course not merely to rely on living into retirement age. Rather it is to plan out in detail the attainment of a financially secure retirement for at least oneself, if not in conjunction with a life partner in a process of mutual life-planning. Planning backwards from this desired goal requires that attention be paid to the securing of an adequate pension and the completion of its funding at the same time that other, more immediately pressing financial necessities are also to be taken care of. In this way, the future is a constant factor in the present planning of the modern individual who would be secure later in life.

Planning with is probably even more prominent in the movement from present to future than it is in planning backwards from retirement. Such planning with may of course not take the explicitly statistical form of mathematizing commitments characterized by Ewald's social insurance practice. But it may still reflect the taking out of "social insurance policies" in a more extended sense as is described by Gerald Dworkin. Under the goal of justifying at least some forms of paternalistic legislation, he searches for "certain kinds of conditions which make it plausible to suppose that rational men [sic] could reach agreement to limit their liberties even when other men's interest are not primarily affected."[11] One reason for such "hypothetical consent" being given is, according to Dworkin, "a deficiency in competence ["irrational propensities, deficiencies in cognition and emotional capacities, and avoidable and unavoidable ignorance"] against which we wished to protect ourselves."[12] The other reason is more pertinent to considerations of individual protection regarding life cycle planning. Dworkin suggests that "we think of the imposition of paternalistic interferences as being a kind of insurance policy we take out against making decisions which are far-reaching, potentially dangerous and irreversible."[13]

The view of paternalistic legislation, even for the original program of social security, as social insurance to be taken out in avoidance of far-reaching and irreversible danger is doubtlessly controversial. From the standpoint of rival political philosophies to modern liberalism, the sacrifice of any present freedom for the sake of future welfare and freedom is highly contestable. Less contestable, however, are the ways in which life planning instantiates this goal of Dworkin's social insurance. Crucial to this planning are the transition periods between life stages, as Giddens explains:

> Life passages give particular cogency to the interaction of risk and opportunity spoken of earlier—especially, although by no means exclusively, when they are in substantial degree initiated by the individual whom they affect. Negotiating a significant transition in life, leaving home, getting a new job, facing up to unemployment, forming a new relationship, moving between different areas or routines, confronting illness, beginning therapy—all mean running consciously entertained risks in order to grasp the new opportunities which personal crises open up.[14]

Individuals plan with special care in regard to either the potentially dangerous or equally potentially favorable consequences of life transitions. The goal of planning with, expressed in positive terms as the anticipation and attainment of a favorable future outcome, is the responsible use of individual foresight in the preparation and sacrifice for, and the carrying out of smooth and successful transitions—the achievement of the right educational certificate, the entry into the right professional track, a timely career advancement and childbearing, and the entry into a financially secure retirement. Yet equally prominent in this planning with may well be the individual foresight undertaken for the sake of avoidance of potentially far-reaching and irreversible danger—the failing of an important examination, the temporizing of long-term unemployment, the occurrence of a painful divorce, a minimally funded retirement, or other life "crises." Perhaps only with both these forms of planning with in the present can stable and long-term occupational and relationship pathways end with "socially insured" lifetime security and the avoidance of an indigent and/or isolated old age.

In regard to the crucial transitions and their positive outcomes, not only does planning with the life trajectory but also planning upon have a prominent role to play. The modern individual is able to "plan upon" the security of state welfare assistance that is potentially administrable for the entire life cycle. This crucial factor can be conveyed in terms of being able to plan **upon** and rely **upon** social assistance in the form of educational programs, career training (and possible retraining), recovery from illness or compensation for disability, and probable receipt of at least some financial support at retirement. The "planning upon" from the individual perspective is made advantageous by the legal regulation of the work cycle and the state administration of the "welfare tracks," since both factors make a stable life course a reasonable and predictable expectancy no longer dependent totally and exclusively upon the extent of individual contribution.

Of course, earlier individuals also planned in hope of a full life of the biblical three-score and ten years, only such plans were made without the effects of social security mechanisms and other modern biopolitics. While the length and stability of the modern life cycle depends on the operations of these security mechanisms and other biopolitical measures at the level of population, it is at least equally dependent upon the activities of the subject of these mechanisms and politics.

Positive goals of achievement and negative goals of avoidance are identified in advance and strategies are mapped out for attaining favorable transition periods and preventing setbacks. Different strategies are compared and later outcomes are assessed, perhaps even by "mathematizing our commitments" as Ewald has expressed it. Even when not carried out with such formalistic rigor, life decisions are still characterized by Giddens in terms of their hypothetical reasoning as follows:

> an indefinite range of potential courses of action (with their attendant risks) is at any given moment open to individuals and collectivities. Choosing among such alternatives is always an "as if" matter, a question of selecting between "possible worlds." Living in circumstances of modernity is best understood as a matter of the routine contemplation of counterfactuals, rather than simply implying a switch from an "orientation to the past," characteristic of traditional cultures, towards an "orientation to the future."[15]

As both Ewald and Giddens indicate, the active life-planning of the individual has allowed there to be the long standardized life cycle that is actively planned and even "lived out" in advance. Hence Beck's metaphor of the "planning office" is not gratuitous, but particularly well chosen to describe the individual foresight that is demanded. The individual must, "on pain of permanent disadvantage," be one's own planning office regarding "biography, abilities, orientations, relationships," indeed one's life as a whole. Or, as Giddens has expressed the same argument in equally compelling terms:

> All individuals establish a portfolio of risk assessment, which may be more or less clearly articulated, well informed and "open"; or alternatively may be largely inertial. Thinking in terms of risk becomes more or less inevitable and most people will be conscious also of the risks of **refusing** to think in this way, even if they may choose to ignore those risks. . . . [L]iving on "automatic pilot" becomes more and more difficult to do, and it becomes less and less possible to protect any lifestyle, no matter how firmly pre-established, from the generalised risk climate.[16]

The Birth/Death of the Secure Individual

The development of the modern "planning office" and the "birth" of the "secure individual" will be dated differently dependent upon whether the "planning with" of insurance rationality or the "planning upon" of public assistance is given the greater emphasis. In accordance with the former perspective, the date could well be given with the initiation of social insurance in the 1880s and with the spread of its statistical rationality. However, in an archeological sense, the birth may even be dated earlier with an (anti-)hero of proportions equal to Quetelet in Hacking's history of statistics, Ernst Engel. Engel was the first director of the Prussian statistical bureau to face up to the challenge of coordinating geographical and anthropological data so that the combination could be administratively useful. A truly major figure in the statistical "avalanche," Engel is for Hacking the best spokesperson for "an international vision of statistics as a higher calling." His vision is expressed in his own words in 1862:

> In order to obtain an accurate representation, statistical research accompanies the individual through his entire earthly existence. It takes account of his birth, his baptism, his vaccination, his schooling, and the success thereof, his diligence, his leave of school, his subsequent education and development; and, once he becomes a man, his physique and his ability to bear arms. It also accompanies the subsequent steps of his walk through life; it takes note of his chosen occupation, where he sets up his household and his management of the same; if he saved from the abundance of his youth for his old age, if and when and at what age he marries and who he chooses as his wife—statistics looks after him when things go well for him and when they go awry. Should he suffer a shipwreck in his life, undergo material, moral or spiritual ruin, statistics takes note of the same. Statistics leaves a man only after his death—after it has ascertained the precise age of his death and noted the causes that brought about his end.[17]

Hacking's comment on Engel's vision is that it is of a new kind of man "whose essence was plotted by a thousand numbers."

From the perspective of social assistance, on the other hand, the answer could well be a very different one. Myles considers the level of assistance for retirement to be the most crucial determinant of individual security and points out that it was only very gradually that the notion of an old-age benefit system as a safety net "to prevent absolute destitution" was "displaced by the notion that it should provide the elderly with a reasonable standard of living."[18] A reasonable standard provides both "income security" allowing the individuals to maintain their earlier living standards and "income adequacy" in order to allow low-income earners to have adequate funds for their retirement living. However, the offering of such secure and adequate retirement assistance has occurred only in the thirty years after the Second World War, and standards of assistance vary from clearly adequate and secure in countries such as Norway and Sweden to scarcely adequate in the United Kingdom (the United States occupying a middle position), and even present levels of funding are, as is well known, made the subject of public debate.

As a consequence of these differing but equally plausible points of view, the date for the "birth" of the secure individual could be said to differ anywhere from the end of last century to as recent as the past generation. However, the more important consideration by far is the fact that the difference in these dates may offer much more than the occasion for a dispute as to which is the more appropriate beginning point. Rather, the dates in question may actually mark beginning and endpoints to an era of individual security that could even be judged to have already come to an end because of drastic changes in the effectiveness of life planning.

As stated earlier in the introduction, Buchmann, Beck, and Kohli have not only described and explained a process of modern standardization of life history in regard to the individual. At the same time they have pointed to more recent developments, above all in the last twenty years, which have served to make this social timetable less fixed, less standardized. Uncertainty has arisen both in regard to the stability of the family cycle and even more in regard to the Second Age of work which was to make the later ages possible. The nature and effects of what is termed the "destandardization" of work and family histories will be examined in the next section, and different interpretations of this phenomenon will be debated in the final chapters. It may now no longer be so clearly "standard" to be "secure," but the effects of this change upon the operations of security mechanisms and above all on the individual planning of the "secure individual" will have to be the subjects of careful deliberation and assessment. In particular, attention will be directed not only to the greater risks with respect to economic and familial security, but above all, to the personal "anxieties generated by risk calculations themselves"[19] in the face of these uncertainties. What must the planning office itself do in light of the new realities of economic and social impermanence?

Part II

"The New Realities":
Economic and Social Impermanence

5

The Death of Company Loyalty and the Birth of Corporate Support

A genealogy of the "secure individual" was presented in the previous section through the employment of Foucault's notions of governmentality and security mechanisms together with a broad variety of other sources on the modern state, the history of statistics, and liberal thought on social security. Within this genealogy there is obviously a close tie between the "birth" of the secure individual and the social security mechanisms of modern governmentality. However these mechanisms were not the only necessary preconditions for the "birth" of confident long-range life planning. As Guy Standing notes: "The national insurance social security system was the cornerstone of the postwar social consensus . . . It was based on two key premises: full or near-full employment, and the norm of a man in a regular full-time job with a wife and children outside the labour force."[1] The universal protection afforded by Social Security promoted individual security, but only in conjunction with the expectations of regular full-time work and permanent marriage partners.

Before the final chapter of this section takes up the impermanency of the breadwinner/homemaker marriage alluded to by Standing, this chapter and the next two chapters will deal with the fate of stable employment as a key and central linchpin for the social security mechanisms which produce or at least have produced secure individuals. The primary crisis with which most of Part Two deals—and which relates most directly to the ominous overtones of the "death" of the secure individual—is that of a potential end of the era of long-term and full time employment, "the end . . . of the age when we could all confidently expect to be employed for most of our lives if we so wanted and over 90% did so want."[2]

Full-time employment is no longer so "full-time" for millions of workers (as well as for countless others who never experienced it in the first place) as a result of foreign relocation, technological implementation, rampant business mergers, and general economic "restructuring" and corporate "reengineering" or "downsizing." Even more pertinent to the vicissitudes of our modern planning offices, long-term is no longer "long-term" for the same reasons and also due to the nature of the new occupations that are created in the restructuring process. In a book of central importance for the next three chapters, *The Age of Unreason*, Charles Handy encapsulates succinctly some of these important changes in the following anecdote:

> Thirty years ago I started work in a world-famous multinational company. By way of encouragement my employers produced an outline of my future career. This will be your life," they said, "with titles of likely jobs." The outline ended, I remember, with myself as chief executive of a particular company in a particular far-off country. I was, at the time, suitably flattered. I left them long before I reached the heights they planned for me, and by then I knew that not only did the job they had picked out no longer exist, neither did the company I would have directed nor even the country in which I was to have operated.[3]

This chapter analyzes the promise of long-term employment that this employment "pitch" so clearly expresses and contrasts this familiar framework of company loyalty to its recent replacement by corporate support programs for the enhancement of employability. The following two chapters will complete the description of the already well known insecurity of many individuals regarding long-term, full-time employment by finishing a threefold schema of negation to match Handy's conclusion to his anecdote: no longer the same company, no longer the same career track, no longer equivalent full-time employment at all.

Company Loyalty and the Good Worker

Thirty years provides the temporal framework for Handy's autobiographical anecdote and for the changes that will be considered in this chapter. He writes: "Thirty years ago I thought that life would be one long continuous line, sloping upward with luck. Today I know better."[4] The upward sloping line was something not only Handy planned with, but his company as well: "Thirty years ago that company saw the future as largely predictable, to be planned for and managed."[5] What Handy now knows "better" is "that in many areas of life we cannot guarantee more of the same, be it work or money, peace or freedom, health or happiness, and cannot even predict with confidence what will be happening in our own lives."[6]

What many workers now know "better" is to distance themselves from and even renounce any company loyalty they may have had earlier. The very title of a new handbook for management, *Rekindling Commitment*, bespeaks volumes. The purpose of the book, according to its authors, is to help "revitalize" those companies whose "employees feel betrayed and have lost faith in their organizations."[7] However, the very title of the book bespeaks that not only is corporation loyalty now being lost, but the fire is out completely and new kindling must be sought from different sources.

From the perspective of this study, the company loyalty that is now betrayed and lost will itself be considered as an economic phenomenon with its own history parallel to that of the political history of the modern social security mechanisms. Crucial to that history is, according to Richard Edwards, the attempt on the part of large companies in the middle part of this century to produce "an ideal hierarchy" of worker traits and habits in addition to "a real hierarchy" of corporate organization. The strategy for producing the "good worker," similar to liberal strategies of good citizenship, was not through the disciplinary means of "dependence on reserve-army discipline," but rather through the powerful individual incentives of "greater job security, promotion prospects, and assumption of long-term employment."[8]

Edwards describes an "organizational logic" of the modern large corporation that is characterized by "the systematic dispensation of higher pay, promotion, more responsibility, access to better or cleaner or less dangerous working conditions, better health benefits, longer vacations, assignment to work stations with more status or comfort, and the other privileges that corporations now bestow on favored employees."[9] This logic, together with other policies of "grievance procedures, seniority provisions that concentrate layoffs among workers in entry-level jobs, and the general policy of fostering low turnover," create "expectations and real experiences of long-term, perhaps lifetime, employment."[10] According to Edwards, the worker is told just as Handy was: "Stick with the corporation . . . and you can ascend up the ladder. The company promises the workers a **career**."[11]

The career promised Handy thirty years ago by a "world-famous multinational company" is characterized by length, stability, and an attractive upward slope. It is promised, of course, not for Handy's benefit but for the stability it also provides for the similarly upwardly mobile corporation. Moreover it provides "incentives for loyalty and dedication, workforce traits not relevant to efficiency but extremely profitable nonetheless."[12] The career the company promises is the reward it offers its "good" workers, and a company filled with good workers is similarly assured of its own long "career."

Handy's first company exhibits in its persuasive pitch what Edwards terms "a long-run framework for the exercise of power." Crucial to this framework is an amplitude of time—"time for workers to learn rules, procedures and expectations; time for workers to respond to the attractions of positive incentives; and time for employers to weed out troublesome, rebellious, or . . . 'mediocre' workers."[13] Yet this long-run amount of time to influence "good" workers is only possible if the company can be sure of its own "career." As Edwards writes

> **This long horizon is consistent with the core firms' ability to achieve relative immunity from the fear of short-run collapse.** Corporations have moved to guarantee their long-run futures in all aspects of their operations, from ensuring raw materials supplies to making their markets safe.[14]

Thirty years ago, companies planned and managed their futures, as Handy has indicated, with such admirably long horizons. Such planning occurred with a high degree of predictability and confidence because the huge scale and extensive market power of the large companies were assets. The story of the changes of the last thirty years is to a large degree a story of the eclipse in importance of these earlier stabilizing factors. It has been told in various terms of transformation, among them from a manufacturing society to a knowledge society or from high volume to high value. A consequence of any rendering of the tale is a deep-seated and apparently irreversible change that is visited upon the long economic horizon—an emphasis upon discontinuity for both the company and the individual who works for it.

Exporting Jobs

The first and perhaps most familiar change came from the challenge of foreign manufacturing in regard to what Robert Reich terms "high volume" production. As he explains,

> It was not just that foreign laborers were happy to work for a fraction of the soaring wages and benefits of Americans, or that foreigners had cheaper access to certain raw materials than did Americans. . . . The truly humbling discovery was that they could build and manage modern factories as effectively as could the executives of America's national champions. Thanks to emerging efficiencies in global transportation and communication—cargo ships and planes, sealed containers capable of being moved from railroad to ship to plane to truck, overseas cables, and, eventually, satellites bouncing electric signals from one continent to another—they could ship the standardized goods back for sale . . . at remarkable cost. And as commodities became smaller and lighter . . . , such costs dropped even faster.[15]

When Handy received his first job—career—offer some thirty years ago, the odds were high that it could be in manufacturing since almost "half of all workers in the industrialized countries were making or helping to make **things**."[16] What happened, according to Handy's terse formulation, is that major firms in America exported their factories instead of the goods manufactured by them.

Concerning the impact of this new export "policy," Kotre and Hall write, "Starting in the late 1970s, the United States changed in less than a decade from an economy in which blue-collar workers outnumbered professional, technical, and managerial workers by 30 percent to one in which the work force was almost evenly divided."[17] Peter Drucker states even more unequivocally: "There . . . is no parallel in history to the abrupt decline of the blue-collar worker during the past 15 years. . . . By the year 2010—less than 25 years away—they will constitute no larger a proportion of the labor force of every developed country than farmers do today—that is, a twentieth of the total."[18]

The impact of such large changes in the manufacturing sector is conveyed in a particularly strong way by the portentous change in the meaning of what was happening to blue-collar workers. According to the *New York Times* series of articles on the downsizing of America,

> the word layoff has taken a fresh meaning. In the past, it meant a sour but temporary interruption in one's job. Work was slow, so a factory shift would be laid off. But stay by the phone—the job will resume three weeks or three months from now when business picks up. Today, layoff means a permanent, irrevocable goodbye.[19]

As for impact of these layoffs upon the multitudes of blue-collar workers who experienced these irrevocable goodbyes, Steven Lazarus states in an interview for the television documentary series, *The Seasons of Life*: "A great many of them felt they had a "social contract" with their corporation. Simply stated, it was that if they performed well, their employment would continue. Suddenly, they find that contract doesn't exist, and one of the basic premises on which they built their lives turns out to be false."[20]

In regard to the importance of this basic premise for blue-collar workers, Jules Henry wrote thirty years ago that to "an industrial worker . . . to be a "success" is to have job security."[21] Hence, the consequences of the loss of security were devastating to those terminated blue-collar workers who had the unfortunate distinction of being the first to experience the end of an era of company loyalty. In an interview for the same television series on the modern life cycle, Gunhild Hagestad says of the consequences on their life planning:

> "They are men who have built strong expectations in almost a linear way. You work hard, you build security, and then you rest on your laurels and enjoy the fruits of your labor. And

suddenly, one day, all of that is gone. It could happen at any age, but it's devastating in middle age, because it's very hard to rebuild—especially for a man who has little or no formal training."[22]

The *New York Times* series speaks of "dispossessed workers" and claims that they have been and are "finding themselves on anguished journeys they never imagined, as if being forced to live the American dream of higher possibilities in reverse."[23]

Automation and the Displacement of Workers

Of course there were also companies that stayed and jobs that were not exported. However, the "hard facts of economic life" require on the part of such companies, according to Handy, three changes from the earlier principles of organization of mass production. Companies seeking to remain profitable without moving

- increasingly have to invest in smart machines if they want to be as effective as they used to be;
- increasingly want to use skilled and thinking people to use those machines in order to get the most out of them;
- need to pay those people more and therefore, if they can, to have fewer of them.[24]

The companies had to undergo a profound change from, according to Robert Reich, "high volume" to "high value." Rather than mass manufacturing with its huge economies of scale, the company that remained learned to change to what are termed economies of scope:

Not only did the list of the *Fortune* 500 top corporations . . . undergo considerable modification, their role in the economy also changed—their global employment remained stationary after 1970 (with a net loss in the United States) compared to the doubling of employment that had occurred from 1954 to 1970. On the other hand, new business formation in the United States picked up dramatically, doubling in the period between 1975 and 1981 (a deep recession year). . . . The economies of scale sought under Fordist mass production have, it seems, been countered by an increasing capacity to manufacture a variety of goods cheaply in small batches. Economies of scope have beaten out economies of scale.[25]

The high-value business both exemplifies and requires what is termed "flexible specialization" to achieve its economies of scope. Economies of scope "refer to the flexible organization of production and use of equipment so that the firm can, regardless of its size, switch production from one batch of products to another relatively costlessly and hence serve relatively small markets, regardless of their size."[26] The result is the transition, earlier alluded to in reference to Reich, from high volume to high value: "These businesses are profitable both because customers are willing to pay a premium for goods or services that exactly meet their needs and because these high-value businesses cannot easily be duplicated by high-volume competitors around the world."[27]

As indicated earlier in the quotation from Handy at the beginning of this section, high value manufacturing or service requires the introduction and integration of smart machines into the production process. As Jeremy Rifkin comments (in a section of *The End of Work* entitled "Substituting Software for Employees"), "While earlier industrial technologies replaced the physical power of human labor, substituting machines for body and brawn, the new computer-based technologies promise a replacement of the human mind itself, substituting thinking machines for human beings across the entire gamut of economic activity."[28] The implications of the introduction of automated machinery, robots, and increasingly sophisticated computers are enormous, since by Rifkin's estimates, "more than 75 percent of the labor force in most industrial nations engage in work that is little more than simple repetitive tasks."[29]

The introduction of industrial robots, for example, allows for the epoch-making introduction of "numerical control" into the production process. Quoting Rifkin,

> With numerical control, instructions on how a piece of metal should be rolled, lathed, welded, bolted, or painted are stored in a computer program. The computer program instructs the machine tool on how to produce a part, and instructs robots on the line to shape or assemble parts into a product. Numerical control has been called "probably the most significant new development in manufacturing technology since Henry Ford introduced the concept of the moving assembly line."[30]

Numerical control allows for the transfer of knowledge and skills away from experienced workers and toward the program of the computer and the operations of the robot. The process is obviously highly efficient and productive. Less obvious is the fact that it allows the production process to be controlled from a distance, by programmers and management rather than workers. This characteristic of the process reduces the need for supervision, but it also has the even more important effect of allowing detailed and significant changes in the manufacturing process to be introduced quickly through appropriate changes in the robot programming. This new flexibility helps to provide the economies of scope that characterize high value production.

The innovations of smart machinery have consequences not only for the high value companies which have stayed home, but even for the high volume companies which left. As Rifkin explains, "While cheap labor might still provide a competitive edge in some industries like textiles and electronics, the advantage of human labor over machines is fast diminishing with advances in automation."[31] The result is that companies in third world settings experience the same economic imperatives to provide high quality products and speed of delivery in the ever more competitive world market. As Rifkin concludes,

> Often, the decision to locate a plant in a developing nation is as much influenced by the desire to be close to a potential new market as by labor-cost differentials. Whether it be market performance or market location, say the editors of *Fortune*, "New technology and the continuing drive for higher productivity push companies to build in less developed countries plants and offices that require only a fraction of manpower that used to be needed in factories back home."[32]

While emphasis upon smart machinery is certainly evident in all the arenas of manufacturing, the momentum it gains touches upon all firms and corporations. As Ian Craib explains, the requirements of flexible specialization especially fit the rapidly expanding sector of services:

> The move has been away from large-scale production based on (comparatively) long-term planning towards small-scale, short-term production in which producers are not likely to find themselves stranded with large stocks of unwanted goods. In this context, the ideal product is one that only lasts until

> it is used for the first time, that is consumed as soon as it is produced: meals, hairdressing, window cleaning; in sum, the "service industries" . . . [33]

Not only are the products of the service industries ephemeral, their very existence as industries may well be ephemeral as well. The smart machinery of computer technology and tele-communications have central roles to play in coping with the ephemerality of a service business.

In the retail sector of the economy, for example, the following quick-response systems have been introduced to great effect:

> Bar coding allows retailers to keep a continuously updated record of exactly what items are being sold, and in what quantities. Point of sale (POS) data eliminates pricing and cashier errors and greatly reduces the time spent on ticketing products. Bar-code marking on shipping containers (SCM) allows the customer to log in and verify the contents of packages without having to open them for inspection. Electronic data interchange (EDI) allows companies to substitute electronic transmission of information like purchase orders, invoices, and payment for paper correspondence, reducing the need for both transportation and clerical handling.[34]

All these innovations, taken together, "allow companies to by-pass traditional channels of distribution and communication and deal instantaneously and directly with warehouses and suppliers, ensuring just-in-time inventories to meet customer needs."[35] The effect, of course, is that layers of "salespersons, account executives, truck drivers, warehouse handlers, shipping department personnel, and billing department people" are effectively eliminated.[36]

The Reengineered Inc.

The first wave of economic restructuring which so affected blue-collar manufacturing jobs was, it could be argued, offset at least in part by the simultaneous growth in the service sector and a surge in the expansion of white-collar middle management positions. More recent economic "restructuring" has affected not only the industrial worker and the service employee, but of course and perhaps above all the white-collar middle manager as well. The massive layoffs of middle managers in fields such as financial services are to be attributed by one pair of author to three factors: "corporate mergers that result in reorganization and allow for downsizing, that is, the elimination of workers who duplicate services; the rapid spread of technological innovations such as telecommunication systems; and more advanced computer networks that eliminate workers even as productivity rises."[37]

All three of these factors are very much in evidence in the example of Mutual Benefit Life which Rifkin cites in his book and which will function as the model for understanding company "reengineering" in this section:

> Mutual Benefit Life (MBL) was among the first of the nation's giant insurance companies to re-engineer its operations. Under its old system of processing applications, as many as thirty separate steps involving five departments and nineteen different people were required. Most claims took upwards of twenty-two days to process, although the actual work time expended on the application was less than seventeen minutes. The rest of the time was eaten up in the transfer of information from person to person and department to department. MBL did away with the slow, cumbersome, multilayered process and installed a single case-manager to process applications. Armed with a sophisticated PC-based workstation and programmed with an "expert system" to help answer questions, the caseworker can process an application in less than four hours. The average turnaround now at MBL is only two to five days. The savings in labor have been as dramatic as the savings in time. MBL has been able to eliminate 100 field office staff, while the new reduced workforce of caseworkers can process twice the volume of applications as before.[38]

While all three of the earlier cited factors are evident in this case, it is the first factor of corporate reorganization or reengineering which has arguably made the largest impact on the public mind. At the time of Handy's first successful interview thirty years ago, Jules Henry could argue in *Culture Against Man* with at least some plausibility that the largest challenge facing big Fortune 500 companies such as IBM and General Electric lay in keeping many of their best and brightest workers, because "when industry does get scientists it cannot hold them, because it interferes with their autonomy and growth."[39] Now, of course, the story of these same exemplars of "big business" is not that they can't keep high-salaried workers, but that they won't. Not because they don't want the workers, but because they don't want to remain "big."

If Marx could write in the nineteenth century, "Accumulate, accumulate! That is Moses and the prophets!" the contemporary business bible appears to be Re-engineer! Re-engineer! Re-engineering is now part of the standard business plan for almost any large business (and government) organization regardless of its present competitive position. When undertaken, especially when done so "consequentially" and "with resolve," it is invariably greeted with favor by shareholders and potential investors alike. In the words of the *New York Times* downsizing series, "An unforgiving Wall Street has given its signals of approval—rising stock prices—to companies that take the meataxe to their costs."[40]

There are strong historical grounds that support the approval of the investors. The 1980s were characterized by a tremendous investment by U.S. businesses in information technology of more than a trillion dollars. However, the same period was equally noted for a puzzling "productivity paradox": "Despite the large investments, productivity continued to limp along, increasing at about 1 percent a year."[41] This paradox only began to disappear in the 1990s with growth rates of 2.3 percent in 1991 and nearly 3 percent in 1992. The diagnosis of the paradox was, according to Rifkin, that "the failure to achieve productivity gains faster lay not with the new laborsaving, timesaving information technologies, but rather with outmoded organizational structures that were not able to accommodate the new technologies."[42]

For Michael Hammer and James Champy, the authors of the famous *Reengineering the Corporation*, reengineering for a company like MBL was not a luxury or even an available option but a strict economic necessity. What it had to discover was how to work smarter by rethinking its operational procedures. The same discovery was made by a very prominent example in Hammer and Champy's book, the credit division of IBM: "They found that most of it [the old management scheme] was little more than clerical: finding a credit rating in a database, plugging numbers into a standard model, pulling boilerplate clauses from a standard file. These tasks fall well within the capability of a single individual when he or she is supported by an easy-to-use computer system that provides access to all the date and tools the specialist would use."[43] A caseworker or case team approach had to be introduced in place of the clerical managerial scheme before the great efficiencies of the computer systems could be exploited. This caseworker "approach to production operates ten times faster than the older hierarchical approach to management activity, with its reliance on separate departments and vertical chains of command."[44]

Rather than vertical chains of command, the reengineered company has a flat form of organization; rather than separate departments, it creates work teams. The other features of this new form of corporate structure involve "eliminating layers of traditional management, compressing job categories, . . . training employees in multilevel skills, shortening and simplifying production and distribution processes, and streamlining administration."[45] All of these features are of course intended to take full advantage of and capitalize on the new information technologies through a leaner organizational stucture.

"I'm from the Company and I'm Here to Help You"

The impressive results of organizational reengineering together with the accompanying strong gains in productivity lead usually to major reductions in the workplace of the reengineered corporation.[46] The "argument is that some workers must be sacrificed to salvage the organization."[47] Hammer "says that reengineering typically results in the loss of more than 40 percent of the jobs in a company and can lead to as much as a 75 percent reduction in a given company's workforce."[48] Handy has his own "handy" formula to capture the dynamic: "It all puts pressure on the core, a pressure which could be summed up by the new equation of half the people, paid twice as much, working three times as effectively, an equation which, once you start believing it, has a built-in momentum."[49]

A special target for the effects of reengineering is middle management. Hammer "estimates that up to 80 percent of those engaged in middle-management tasks are susceptible to elimination."[50] Hence, one obvious consequence of corporate restructuring is that the white-collar middle manager is now experiencing the same end of an era of corporate loyalty as the earlier displaced blue-collar factory worker. Or, as Gary Loveman states the situation more bluntly, "the men and women in 'garden variety' middle management jobs" are 'getting crucified'

by corporate re-engineering and the introduction of sophisticated new information and communication technologies."[51]

Companies before reengineering, companies which promised careers in exchange for company loyalty

> used to look like a collection of ladders tied together at the
> top. A career for most people meant climbing the ladders.
> Success was rewarded by promotion to the next rung.[52]

The downsized and downsizing company with its flat organizational structure is, by contrast, "reluctant to guarantee careers
for life to everyone." More contracts are "for fixed periods of
years"; more appointments are "tied to particular roles or jobs
with no guarantee of further promotion." According to Handy,
"The help-wanted pages of the papers already reflect this trend:
the advertisements offer a job more often than they promise a
career."[53]

As for the employee of the ever-reengineering company, a
further change is also occurring correlative to the transformation from career ascendancy to job redundancy. That change is
in regard to the company loyalty that was manifested on the
basis of a lifelong career path of ascendancy. This career path
had always been premised upon the vigorous exercise of individual initiative and career planning. The change is not in the
area of individual initiative but rather in what it is now being
coupled with:

> Indeed, fewer and fewer organizations now promise to manage
> your career; instead they promise opportunities along with help
> to develop your capabilities to take up some of those opportu-
> nities. No longer is there the feeling that somewhere someone
> is thinking about your future, watching your development, plan-
> ning your next steps. . . . It is a case of "individual initiative and
> corporate support," as the Americans describe it.[54]

Corporate support is the new organizational policy of companies that "handle downsizing well" according the the authors
of *Rekindling Commitment.* As opposed to companies which see
the downsizing as an end in itself,

> Some companies understand that downsizing threatens the bond
> between organization and employee and that it is therefore
> important to concentrate on rebuilding with the people who are

left. These companies follow downsizing with programs to help those remaining increase their empowerment, learn the skills to participate in making the company successful, and work to discover new ways to achieve corporate success.[55]

Corporate support is an integral part of a new kind of work contract with the employees. The earlier type of contract, which the displaced blue-collar factory worker perceived to be violated upon his dismissal, is judged to be based on a "parental model" because it "offered to 'take care' of the employee, as long as the employee performed up to expectations."[56] Under the new contract regime, company and employee are both adults who, as self-governing units, contract with one another for their mutual benefit. Of course this dependency upon mutual benefit entails that the contract "may terminate when it is no longer workable, and as 'an adult,' the employee must understand that the company cannot be responsible for his or her welfare."[57]

The corporate support which is offered by the new work contract is couched almost exclusively in terms of offering opportunities rather than assurances.[58] And what it does assure is not employment but rather the opportunities for enhancing the **employability** of employees: "Companies that can no longer guarantee employment can at least strive to enhance their employees' 'employability.' They can offer opportunities for employees to learn new skills and to learn how to be effective learners."[59]

If the old worker contract with the long-term horizon firm offers more of a balance or indeed even a mutual reinforcement between company loyalty and personal initiative, the new contract appears overwhelmingly stacked on the side of personal initiative. The authors of *Rekindling Commitment* state unequivocally:

> Employees must build their own sense of security within themselves. This security will increasingly be based on the ability to learn, change, innovate, and adapt. . . . People have to become responsible for their own future, by maintaining their own employability.[60]

How difficult it is precisely for the employee, **any** employee—with or without corporate support—to build her or his sense of security will be the subject of the following two chapters. They will reexamine the same "hard economic facts" of this chapter, only from the specific vantage point of the employee who has to secure and maintain employability rather than rely on the corporate promise of employment. To recall the earlier Foucauldian model of governmentality as the "touching point" between techniques of domination and individual technologies of the self, we will be considering the new individual "technology of the self" that is correlative to the new economicality of flexible specialization.

6

Functional Flexibility and Job Compression

The death of company loyalty and the birth of corporate support, as momentous and striking as these developments are, represent only part of the story in regard to the economic challenges presently confronting the individual quest for predictability and security. This chapter will examine more closely the prospects of the individual achieving long-term employability in light of the new economic realities of downsizing and company reengineering. The focal point will be upon the impact of company reorganization on the security of the primary or "core" workers in the "lean" production company.

Lean production, whose familiar model is the Japanese automaking company, "differs significantly from both craft and industrial production."[1] In craft production, skilled workers make products one at a time to the precise specifications of their buyers. In mass production, "skilled professionals . . . design products made by unskilled or semi-skilled workers tending expensive, single purpose machines. These turn out standardized products in very high volume."[2] Lean production "combines the advantage of craft and mass production, while avoiding the high cost of the former and the rigidity of the latter."[3]

The lean production company avoids the costs of craft production in large part due to its exercise of what is called external flexibility. External flexibility, or **numerical** flexibility, allows the high value production company to adjust labor inputs easily to fluctuations in productive outputs. It achieves this labor input flexibility through the constellation of a "periphery" of temporary workers and subcontractors in rela-tion to the company "core" of permanent workers. As Handy explains:

> Organizations have realized that, while it may be convenient to have everyone around all the time, having all of your work force's time at your command is an extravagant way of marshalling the necessary human resources. It is cheaper to keep them outside the organization, employed by themselves or by specialist con-tractors, and to buy their services when you need them.[4]

Lean production avoids the rigidities of mass production through its development of internal flexibility. Internal flexibility, or **functional** flexibility, refers to the core itself and how this central group of workers differ from the unskilled or semi-skilled workers characteristic of mass manufacturing. Rather than be-ing merely skilled in distinction to unskilled or semi-skilled, the essential workers of the high value company must be **multiskilled** in order to perform the array of tasks required by varied small and medium batch production of goods or services.

The combination of both forms of flexibility—"fewer people inside who are better qualified, more people outside who are contracted, not employed"[5]—produces the new "lean" form of production. In cases such as automobile manufacturing, "It uses less of everything compared with mass production—half the human effort in the factory, half the manufacturing space, half the investment in tools, half the engineering hours to develop a new product in half the time."[6] As Handy provides his own encapsulation of this tremendous change, "The result is not just fewer jobs, but different organizations. . . . The demise of mass manufacturing has led to the end of the mass employ-ment organizations and a redefinition of the job."[7]

Both this chapter and the next chapter will focus on the specific aspect of job redefinition and consider it from the point of view of the flexibilities the worker must demonstrate or possess in order to keep a restructured work position. As we have already seen in the previous chapter, the long-term perspective of the career in a single company has been replaced by the present exigencies of the job and the maintenance of future employability. The nature of the job requirements varies tre-mendously depending upon whether one is located in the core and must demonstrate multiskilling or at the periphery of the restructured company organization and must have time scheduling flexibility. Both locations will be examined in detail in this chapter and the following chapter, with the attention first being directed to the core worker and the challenges of functional flexibility she or he must confront.

Continual Improvement

Core workers are distinguished from both the temporary and subcontracting periphery, as the metaphor suggests, in terms of their importance to their company. Lean companies will demand and are demanding a very great deal from their core workers in order to achieve the sought for increase in their productivity: "the organization demands of them hard work and long hours, commitment, and **flexibility**."[8] The flexibility in question is what has just been introduced as "functional flexibility" and can be elucidated preliminarily in the simple way that Handy speaks of core workers: "They are expected to go there, do this, be that, as the organization requires."[9] In the same way that the organization is required to transform from high volume, standardized production to high value, small- and medium-batch provision of goods and services, the core worker must transform from standardized labor on a single task to multitasking or multivalency capabilities. The "flexibility" of the core worker is the individual, subjective correlate to the lean and flexible structure of the high-value firm.

Put bluntly, core workers must know more on a variety of levels both than periphery employees and earlier generations of high-volume workers. Handy writes of the needs of core workers to possess technical skills, conceptual skills, and human skills. He argues that the "point about the new organization is that everyone in the core will increasingly be expected to have not only the expertise appropriate to his or her particular role but will also be required to know and understand business, to have the technical skills of analysis **and** the human skills **and** the conceptual skills, and to keep them up to date."[10]

As introduced earlier, the core worker will not be semi-skilled but a technically skilled worker, in many ways more comparable to the earlier craft worker than the mass production laborer. However, the technical skill required will not and cannot be restricted to only one area. In a metaphor quite naturally taken from computer technology, functional flexibility requires first and most directly the capability of "multitasking" or to undertake multiple and highly different roles in the production process. According to Peter Drucker in his book, *Managing for the Future*, "Machine operators getting high wages for doing unskilled, repetitive work are being replaced by knowledge-workers getting high wages for designing, controlling, and servicing process and product, or for managing information."[11] Such knowledge-workers will be characterized not only by their present skills but above all by "a high capacity to learn and to acquire additional knowledge."[12] Martin Kenney and Richard Florida find nothing amiss in comparing the multiple knowledge requirements of the core worker to the intellectual abilities of the laboratory scientist: ". . . workers actively undertake what were previously thought of as intellectual activities. In this new environment, workers are no longer covered with grease and sweat, because the factory increasingly resembles a laboratory for experimentation and technical advance."[13]

The core worker who is technically skilled and capable of performing a number of tasks in the process of high-value production is also in a much better position to have a conceptual grasp of the production process as a whole. Moreover, this new kind of "knowledge worker" also possesses the formal abilities to comprehend the company's market strategy and recognize how ultimate business success depends directly upon the increased productivity achieved by company restructuring. The demands for multiple skill development will consequently not be seen as an external and extraneous imposition, but rather as a natural requirement for the maintenance of the economic health of the company.

In a similar manner, the human skills alluded to by Handy are not extraneous but, if anything, even more essential to the economic survival of the enterprise. The multiskilled employees of the lean company work together in a "cooperative team approach": "The classical Taylor model of scientific management, which favored the separation of mental from physical labor and the retention of all decision making in the hands of management, is abandoned in favor of a cooperative team approach designed to harness the full mental capabilities and work experience of everyone involved in the process. . . ."[14]

Peter Drucker clarifies this crucial emphasis upon teamwork with a typology of three different kinds of teams. The first type of team, the baseball team with individuals working as individuals in fixed positions, characterizes the teamwork that undeniably occurs in mass production: "Traditionally, work on new products was done in a baseball-type team in which each function (design, engineering, manufacturing, marketing) did its own work, and then passed it on to the next."[15] According to him, the Japanese began around 1970 to switch to a soccer-type form of teamwork where individuals still have fixed positions but now work together **as** a team. However, the concept underlying "flexible manufacturing" which characterizes the present regime of lean production is that of the doubles tennis team where individuals both work as a team and switch positions often in doing so.

Rifkin explains the position-switching or, probably better, position fluidity involved in the new cooperative team approach again through a Japanese example involving design, engineering, manufacturing, and marketing:

> In the Japanese lean factory, design engineers, computer programmers, and factory workers interact face-to-face, sharing ideas and implementing joint decisions directly on the factory floor. . . . Workers from every department are even invited to take part in the design of new cars, a process always under the tight control of an engineering elite in the older U.S. auto companies. Concurrent engineering, as it has come to be known, is based on the principle that everyone affected by the design, scale-up, production, distribution, marketing, and sales of a new automobile should participate as early as possible in the development of a new car to ensure that each department's specific needs and requirements are taken into consideration and to help pinpoint potential trouble spots before full-scale production is set.[16]

The teamwork entailed by concurrent engineering is designed to stimulate improvements in the design process and to do so systematically rather than sporadically and infrequently. The "key to the success of Japanese production methods" is the notion of "continual improvement" or *Kaizen*. The knowledge which is gained through cooperative team settings is utilized both to pinpoint problems and to make suggestions for improvement. The "Japanese teamwork model attempts to push decision-making authority as far down the managerial ladder as possible so as to be closer to the point of production."[17] A special example of this non-hierarchical approach is the famous "quality circle" where workers meet either "before or after regular work hours to discuss improvements in the production process."[18]

Clearly one of the most important factors in the improvement of the production process lies in the improvement of the skills and knowledge of the workers themselves. Once again the goal, as explicated by one Japanese manager, is continual improvement: "One of our most important jobs is to make all of our employees willing to cooperate fully, and to make them want to continually improve themselves."[19] Consequently, the "updating" that Handy earlier referred to in regard to technical, conceptual, and human skills is not an accidental or incidental byproduct, but a basic requirement of functional flexibility on the part of the core worker in the lean production process.

Peter Drucker writes that workers "must be required to take responsibility for their own productivity and to **exercise control** over it."[20] The statement, while true, neglects to mention that workers must also exercise control over the increase in their productivity as well. The demands of multitasking do not limit themselves to the present level and range of technical skills, but extend to future functional abilities as well. Cooperative teamwork requires not only a spirit of cooperation but the abilities to cooperate across more and more divisions in the production process and to take advantage of the technological possibilities afforded by the newest telecommunications systems. Consequently, continual learning and improvement on the part of the worker are not just encouraged but actually strictly necessary. The corporate support mentioned in the previous chapter and offered in order to increase the employee's future employability is therefore in reality a condition of her or his present employment at the same time.

Half-Lives or Half-Living?

Core workers who possess the capabilities of functional flexibility and who constantly improve will be of obvious great importance to their companies. They will be paid well for their contributions, although probably a lot less well than Handy's formula in the previous chapter that mentioned income doubling. But will they be and are they now **secure** in all the ways that previous workers in the era of company loyalty were?

We have already seen how closely linked the economic health of the lean company is to its continual improvement in productivity and how closely linked in turn that improvement is linked to the continual improvement of workers. As is well known, the prototypical Japanese company itself has, during a period of "almost two decades of incessant growth in firm-size," offered lifetime security to its innermost core workers, so at least until now there appears to be no limitation within the model itself to prevent the holding of truly permanent employment. However, it is also useful to consider some of the costs of that security to the Japanese employee, before moving on to the job occupancy of other workers who have been offered the quite different promise of corporate support.

As Makoto Jumazawa and Jun Yamada explain, there is serious tension in the lean production model concerning the lifetime career formation of the worker in one firm:

> Put simply, he is expected to climb the job-ladder, or more exactly, to work his way up a grading system linked loosely with clusters of jobs, by adapting himself to frequent changes in work. In other words, he only secures his lifelong employment in competition with his fellow workers and at the cost of his ties to well-known jobs and to long-familiar work mates. . . . To stay in the inner-core section one must be ready to accept almost any job change with additional effort to acquire new skill.[21]

The Japanese worker must exercise control not only over his work and its improvement but also over his trainability for a truly wide rotation of jobs: "For example, workers in an integrated steel plan in the United States cover nearly a dozen jobs in their career but their Japanese counterparts will experience about three dozen positions."[22] Because this strong demand for job mobility is dictated by the marketing strategy of the firm, the loyalty of the employee to one firm and its promise of lifetime security to him also bring with them their own considerable cost; namely, that "the actual content of a competitively won lifelong career will not necessarily suit the individual involved."[23]

The worker who is not promised lifetime security but corporate support is of course faced with a situation with its own costs in the lean production regime. The demand for continual improvement is there, probably just as strongly as in the Japanese setting. Moreover, trainability is also clearly expected, if perhaps not to such a vast scope of multitasking. However, the offering of corporate support directs these imperatives of improvement and training not toward the promise of lifetime employment but rather to the furtherance of the worker's employability in the present company or elsewhere. Consequently, the question of great urgency is whether the continual improvement and demonstrated trainability of workers in an atmosphere of corporate support also insures their continual employability at the same time.

The maintenance of employability in an economic climate dominated by reengineering and other corporate restructuring is not only a matter of building credentials to maintain one's core employment in the same company or find core employment elsewhere. We have already seen how competition in the global economy brings about changes in the marketing strategies of companies and how these changes in turn require a general functional flexibility of workers to learn new skills and carry out different jobs in a cooperative team framework. What must be examined more closely is the threat of obsolescence in regard to the present skills, even the skills of the multiskilled worker, and the tremendous challenge it poses. In the same way that the long-term future of companies has changed dramatically and their survivability is very much in doubt, so is the long-term future of any job in the lean corporation—either of the present or the future.

Innovations in telecommunications and computer technology have not only stimulated the reengineering of corporations but actually required downsizing in order to take advantage of the benefits of increased productivity. One obvious reason that these innovations possess this great power and produce such large effects is because they make a great number of present jobs both redundant and obsolete. A particularly clear example of the capacity of these technologies to produce massive consequences in terms of obsolescence concerns "the transformation of the traditional office from a paper-handling to an electronic-processing operation."[24] In the present paper-handling office, "90 percent of all information is still stored on paper, while 5 percent is on microfiche and another 5 percent in electronic media."[25] Every business day in the United States, "600 million pages of computer printouts are produced, 76 million letters are generated, and 45 sheets of paper are filed per employee."[26] What conversion to electronic processing and storage promises, according to Paul Saffo, a directory of the Institute for the Future, is that "we are going to become paperless in the same way we became horseless . . . horses are still around, but they're just ridden by little girls and hobbyists."[27]

Many secretarial positions are now being eliminated by the assorted technological innovations of this transformation and up to 45 percent of all positions (as well as, of course, the positions of receptionists) are threatened. Moreover, the "intelligent machine is steadily moving up the office hierarchy, subsuming not only routine clerical tasks but even work traditionally performed by management."[28] The main example cited by Rifkin in *The End of Work* is The Resumix, a computerized hiring system. Employing sophisticated tools of "spatial text understanding and extraction," The Resumix "looks over each resumé, reviewing the applicant's educational history, skills and proficiencies, and past-employment record."[29] It then decides the most appropriate job category for the applicant and carries out this operation, according to field tests, more quickly than, and with at least as much skill as, human personnel directors.

The Resumix standardizes and formalizes the capabilities of the human personnel director. Its introduction, together with the inevitable promise of newer and more powerful systems, clearly undermines the attractiveness of this field and devalues its professional qualifications and skills. The research of Bernhard Buck suggests that the introduction of computer and telecommunication technologies accelerates the pace in general at which vocational and professional qualifications are devalued in general. The acceleration in the rate of obsolescence is captured in a metaphor adapted from physics: As the "cycles of innovation have become much shorter," the "half-lives" of the validity of a variety of professional qualifications are also being "reduced."[30] The consequences of the devaluation of present qualifications on the career planning of the employee are expressed technically, but clearly by Marlis Buchmann when she writes: "The rapidly decreasing half-life of the usability of acquired expertise gives rise to short-term work perpectives and induces a relatively high degree of occupational insecurity and, accordingly, a relatively low degree of calculability and predictability."[31]

But what about the new core jobs created and promoted by the introduction of the new technologies into the electronic offices and other new and sophisticated workplaces? Unfortunately the situation is not much different in regard to the usability of new expertise. As Buchmann explains, "Emerging professions, having not yet acquired social recognition, . . . are not yet linked to well-defined professional trajectories with specific rules of access, acknowledged levels of social prestige, and calculable income chances."[32] Because the half-lives of these positions are at best equal to those of which they replace, "the new professions give rise to biographical strategies with a short time perspective"[33] as well.

If the half-lives of both present traditional and new technological occupations are reducing and will reduce further as a result of the increasing functional flexibility required of the core worker, then that worker must develop an internal flexibility in seeking to preserve and enhance her or his employabililty. As Buchmann notes, "Individuals thus must renew their professional qualifications (to try to avoid their devaluation), and they must also overcome the constraints of specialization."[34] In this new context where specialization is a constraint rather than an asset, flexibility on the part of the employee entails the imperative to "acquire qualifications that open up as broad a range of employment opportunities as possible."[35]

As a consequence, the multiskilled worker appears to have to achieve the same high value goals and carry out the same imperatives of flexible specialization in regard to employability as the company for which she or he works. Moreover, this worker is planning employability in an equally uncertain environment. As Buchmann comments, "The convertibility of professional investments into occupational positions and, finally, into financial rewards is highly uncertain."[36] Individual employability strategies may be "based on anticipation of professional careers for which few chances objectively exist";[37] conversely, highly viable opportunities may be neither perceived nor utilized. The one certainty in the process is that the competition in the planning for securing individual employability and employment is at least as fierce as it is for the high-value company itself.

A final similarity between the internal flexibility of the employable, multiskilled worker and the business planning of the lean, high-value company concerns the shortening of the temporal horizon itself. If the company is no longer assured of a long horizon of secure planning, neither is the employee promised as long a time span of core employment—even with the requisite functional flexibility—as during the period of corporate loyalty. As Handy explains with great clarity and certitude:

> This compression of the job is going to happen, is already happening, not because of some miraculous rationing system but because organizations everywhere are learning how to make do with smaller bits of our time. Organizations could once wallow in our time, waste it even, when it was cheap or when everyone around them wasted it as well. A more competitive world and more expensive people demand a more careful use of time.[38]

The effects of job compression occur both at the beginning and especially at the end of the maximum core employment stay. Concerning the initial starting point, the all important first hire, the reduced numbers of the core of the lean organization entail a much greater selectivity of the company on entry.[39] Of the present prospective core employees, Handy writes, "To get one of those increasingly rare jobs in the core or the professions (less than half of all jobs by 2000 [!]), they will need to be both well qualified **and** experienced."[40]

However, the effect on the beginning point is definitely the factor of lesser importance in regard to job compression, as Handy makes abundantly clear:

> The next generation of full-time core workers, therefore, be they professionals, managers, technicians, or skilled workers, can expect to start their full-time careers later—and to leave them earlier. This is the crucial point. The core worker will have a harder but shorter job, with more people leaving full-time employment in their late forties or early fifties, partly because they no longer want the pressure that such jobs will increasingly entail, but mainly because there will be younger, more qualified, and more energetic people available for these core jobs.[41]

While the prospects of a harder job appear, at least to a non-specialist like myself, to be almost completely unavoidable, the fate of a shorter job is not quite as inevitable. There will be "glorious exceptions" among "those who control their own careers—the self-employed, the professionals, and, apparently, heads of state."[42] However, for the clear majority of core workers, the prospects are for a "shorter" but "more furious" business life: "The older men cannot always stand the pace, can get out-of-date in some technologies, or become, in general, too expensive for the value which they add."[43]

The predictable effects of job compression mean that even "those in the core will be outside for the last third of their lives."[44] How they will fare "outside" and how all the other workers are located "on the periphery" will be taken up in the next chapter, which examines the external flexibility of the reengineered company and its impact on work. Before examining these already apparently less favorably positioned work placements, it should already be evident that Handy is quite correct in writing as a consequence of job compression alone: "When society can no longer assume that we all have a paid job for most of our lives, the old recipes for dealing with the small bits at the end (pensions) and the small bits missing (unemployment benefits) become irrelevant."[45]

7

Flexibility on the Margins and the Destandardization of Work

Charles Handy employs a deceptively simple formula to illustrate the dramatic impact of job compression regarding modern work and the life cycle in general. Earlier workers who entered the work force at the age of 18 and retired at 65 worked for a period of 47 years. If they worked for 47 weeks during this time period and their work week could be calculated to average 47 hours, the sum of their work lives would be 47^3=103,823 or approximately 100,000 hours. By Handy's calculation, the core worker in a correspondingly compressed job will work about 45 hours for 45 weeks for only 25 years.[1] The total of these figures is 51,125 or approximately half as much!

The formula of 45 x 45 x 25 is not the only formula that Handy mentions, but the sum of each of his alternative formulas remains no more than half of the previous total of 100,000 hours. Workers may find themselves working part time 25 hours a week for 45 weeks a year or they might do temporary work of 45 hours a week for 25 weeks. If they work for 45 years, the sum will be the same as for the highly compressed job of the core worker.

However, it is probably going to be necessary for both the part time and temporary worker to work more than 45 years if they can. In either case "they will need to keep on working as long as they can . . . , because they will not be able to accumulate the savings through pension schemes or other mechanisms to live on."[2] This necessity is only one indication of their location on the periphery of the high-value corporation rather than within the core.

Part time and temporary workers make up only part of the periphery for the modern downsized (and downsizing) company. According to Handy's own metaphor, they constitute the flexible work force or third leaf of the "shamrock" form of modern firm organization. The first leaf, as one might expect, is the core of essential workers who work hard if not furiously. The second leaf or "contractual fringe" involves work which is understood, according to new and very strict criteria, to be nonessential to the company. This work "could be done by someone else" and is "sensibly contracted out to people who make a speciality of it and who should, in theory, be able to do it better for less cost."[3]

Both the second and third leaves of Handy's shamrock are on the periphery in relationship to the lean company's core. They form the sources of that company's external or numerical flexibility, which allows it to adjust labor inputs easily to fluctuations in production and demand. By Handy's projections, these different labor sources will comprise more than half of all work positions by the year 2000.

The effects of numerical flexibility on the positioning and the employability of these two large and important groups of workers will be examined in the first two sections of this chapter. In the third and final section, each of the shamrock leaves will no longer be viewed separately, but rather collectively. The collective effect will be to establish at least partial destandardization of the work career from the time Handy received his first company pitch until today. The chapter concludes by initiating a discussion of the possible effects of this destandardization upon the prospects of security for the life-planning secure individual. Life planning no longer is able to rely on past commitments made in the context of long standardized work histories, but rather must adapt in the present to the new employability uncertainties characteristic of destandardization.

Subcontracting Uncertainty

If downsizing is the most feared word in the contemporary quest for economic security, outsourcing is not far behind. Actually, both downsizing and outsourcing are most often invoked together. As Peter Drucker explains, "Cutting staffs to cut costs is putting the cart before the horse. The only way to bring costs down is to restructure the work."[4] The goal is, as Drucker expresses it, to work smarter, not necessarily harder, and outsourcing is certainly a major strategy for achieving this goal.

One major goal in restructuring the work is simply to eliminate what the company does not do well and does not have to do. But the other goal is to define the core of the company and to demarcate that core away from the periphery. As Drucker explains regarding the restructured company: "it itself does only work that is focused on its mission; work that is directly related to its results; work that it recognizes, values, and rewards appropriately. The rest it contracts out."[5]

Outsourcing plays a very prominent role in the model for lean production, the Japanese manufacturing company. Outsourcing allows the lean manufacturer both to drastically reduce inventories on hand and also to be "able to cut their costs fast and sharply, when they need to be shifting the burden of short-term fluctuations to the outside supplier."[6] Another of the hero companies in Hammer and Champy's *Reengineering the Corporation* is Ford Motor Company, which among other things, subcontracted its brake acquisitions to a single supplier. This change allowed Ford Motor to tell its supplier: "We like your brakes and we will continue to install them on our trucks, but until we do, they are **your** brakes, not ours. The brakes only become ours when we use them, and that's when we'll pay for them. Every time a truck comes off the line with a set of your brakes on it, we'll mail you a check."[7]

Ford's employment of outsourcing obviously allows it both to simplify greatly its purchasing and receiving procedures and to reduce its inventory levels. But, according to Hammer and Champy, the subcontracting relationship is also beneficial to the supplier:

> First, it now gets all of Ford's truck brake business instead of just some of it. Second, because the supplier is now privy to Ford's computerized manufacturing schedule, it does not have to depend on the unreliable forecasts of Ford's brake demands that it previously got from it own sales force. The brake supplier can better schedule its own production and reduce the size of its own inventory.[8]

The subcontractor might even, in light of its newly acquired reliable scheduling knowledge, subcontract out some of its parts, illustrating how these members of the second leaf of the shamrock, "although often smaller than the main organization, will have their own shamrocks, their own cores, and their own subcontractors."[9]

Outsourcing is a very popular practice in manufacturing, construction, and consumer goods. Chrysler "procures more than 70 percent of the value of its final products from outside suppliers."[10] For the Japanese automaker, the original model of lean production, the ratio is closer to 20 percent, 80 percent. Such "20/80 organizations do not always realize how large the contractual fringe has grown because it has become a way of their life."[11] This way of life is one of great numerical flexibility, and one of its consequences of this flexibility is that "Manufacturing forms are now almost totally assembly firms, while many service organizations are, in effect, brokers, connecting the customer with a supplier with some intervening service."[12]

Subcontracting is a preferred strategy for company reorganization not only due to its productivity in virtue of its numerical efficiency, but due to another equally important reason. Outsourcing profoundly decreases the risk facing the core company by shifting uncertainty to the subcontracting firm. An "outside contractor knows that he will be tossed out and replaced by a better-performing competitor unless he improves quality and cuts costs."[13] But this quite traditional uneasiness is accompanied by powerful new forms of uncertainty in the shamrock organization: "Just-in-time delivery means that the subcontractor carries the cost of any stocks. Subcontracts mean that the contractor carries the burden of any slowdown. **It is a way of exporting uncertainty**."[14]

If uncertainty is exported from the core to the periphery, from the main manufacturer or service firm to the contracting subgroups, uncertainty is also being exported—and to at least the same degree—from the workers in the core to the workers on the contractual fringe. The workers in the second leaf of the shamrock, who subcontract above all in the areas of construction, consumer goods and manufacturing, are likely to be "self-employed professionals or technicians, many of them past employees of the central organization, who ran out of roles in the core or who preferred the freedom of self-employment."[15] In running out of roles in the core, such workers have also probably run out of security as well.

The numerical flexibility afforded by subcontracting to the core company does not require of the subcontracting worker the same functional flexibility needed by the core worker. Rather than requirements of multiskilling, updating, and constant improvement, the organizational principle is simply payment for results, not time, in fees, not wages.[16]

The earlier security of company loyalty is of course out of the question, but the much lesser assistance afforded by corporate support is not a real possibility either. In the same way that the production concern of the subcontracting company lies in its immediate contract with the core company, so does its employment concern deal only with the immediate work activity of its employees. There appears to be no future employability that the worker occupying a place in the second leaf can train for, nor does the subcontracting firm have the same incentives for offering corporate support. As Handy explicates, "There is no longer a residual loyalty to be relied on, no longer any implied promise of security in return for obedient labor."[17]

Just-in-time Employment

The imperatives of numerical flexibility have also been felt strongly in the service sector, but their employment effects are often different from those in manufacturing and construction. As Handy explains, "The service industry cannot stockpile its products as a factory does."[18] What services typically do are "to expand and contract their service to match the requirements of their customers."[19] This need for flexibility is met primarily through part-time and/or temporary employees:

> Of course, the full-time core staff could be asked to work the extra hours, or enough people could be employed full time to cope with any peak and left underemployed the rest of the time. . . . It is cheaper by far, although more trouble, to bring in occasional extra labor part time, to cope with extra hours, or temporary labor, to cope with peak periods.[20]

In a previous business era, the large company may have chosen either of the core staff options which would have "made the work force more convenient, easier to manage." However, the arguments for outsourcing, explained in the previous section, now support overwhelmingly the "unbundling," to use Drucker's term, of clerical, maintenance, and support services. The subcontracting of these services will be to companies that specialize in them and may have their own cores of dedicated workers. But to achieve their own numerical flexibility in regard to "seasonal and even monthly and weekly trends in the market,"[21] these companies will also have their doubtlessly larger peripheries as well. And the brunt of the periphery will be occupied by the third leaf of the shamrock, the "flexible labor force" of temporary and part-time workers.

"The revolution in the 1990s," in an analogy made to just-in-time inventories by Nancy Hutchens, a human resources consultant, "is toward just-in-time employment . . . companies will use people only as they need them."[22] Industries where this revolution is already holding sway are industries "with large requirements for the competent but semi-skilled" such as "retailing, transport, cleaning, catering, leisure."[23] However, "the reality is that temps are being used as a substitute for permanent workers in virtually every industry and sector."[24]

Just-in-time employment has quite varied impacts on different groups in the labor pool. For a fortunate group, on the one hand, the demands of numerical flexibility for the company mirror their own needs for flexible work scheduling: "These people are not all pining for core jobs, marking time on the fringe, having to eke out an existence from part-time earnings until something better turns up."[25] For this group, the large and growing demand for a flexible work force and innovations in the fields of telecommunications and computer technology afford positive opportunities to balance a job with other important life concerns and to gain valuable, sometimes discretionary, income. For this group, the time flexibility offered by such programs as "part-time work for new parents, part-time before retirement, job-sharing, term-time jobs, four ten-hour days a week or eight-day fortnights, annual hours contracts, zero-hour contracts (being available as and when required), parental leave, career breaks, sabbaticals, time-banking (accumulating vacation time over several years), and individual hour contracts"[26] clearly outweigh the negatives of lower pay and lack of benefits.

On the other hand, for others who **are** pining for core jobs and having to eke out an existence, occupying a position in the third leaf of the shamrock is most definitely tantamount to marking time on the fringe. Laid-off workers in mass manufacturing companies find themselves working for a fraction of their former wages for subcontractors who do not provide benefits. Middle managers find themselves scrambling for part-time jobs in the service industry. Displaced clerical workers become temporary workers for temp agencies. According to Rifkin, even business professionals and scientists are being contracted out as temporary workers.[27] And of course, workers from all these groups combine two or more part-time positions and still come up short of their original position in terms of earnings and benefits.

According to Ulrich Beck, what workers in this growing part of the labor force are experiencing is a dramatic change in their work histories. Rather than the upwardly sloping to career path promised to Handy at the beginning of this part, they may expect a destandardized and unpredictable succession of jobs. The primary danger they face is no longer possible unemployment, but rather a more probable and persistent underemployment achieved after great struggle and even humiliation:

> In this game of musical jobs, people making $150,000 resurrect themselves making $50,000, sometimes as self-employed consultants or contractors. Those making $50,000 reappear earning $25,000. And these jobs are discovered often after much time, misery and personal humiliation.[28]

Or, in the more technical language of Beck, "one can say that a transition is occurring in industrial society from a uniform system of lifelong full-time work organized in a single industrial location, with the radical alternative of unemployment, to a **risk-fraught system of flexible, pluralized, decentralized underemployment, which, however, will possibly no longer raise the problem of unemployment in the sense of being completely without a paid job**."[29]

Life Planning Flexibility

Rifkin, Hutchens, and Stanley Aronowitz and William DiFazio are not nearly as sanguine as Beck concerning the passing threat of unemployment, but all concur with him concerning the strong and real economic insecurity of marking time on the fringe. Handy's most restrictive estimate for the future is that "less than one-quarter of the population will have full-time jobs inside any organization."[30] Certainly nothing that Rifkin writes in *The End of Work* or Aronowitz and DiFazio claim in *The Jobless Future* dissuades one from such an estimate of future developments. But even if the estimate is overstated, it would still appear to be true that Handy's career offer of thirty years ago is a relic of the past. Few core workers or subcontractors will work in a single, upwardly sloping career path for a single firm (or themselves) for their whole working lives. Those that do will be exceptions, perhaps in regard to energy, dynamism, and innovativeness, and it is very likely that their exceptional status will be generally perceived as such.

More but not necessarily many will be able to maintain a succession of core employment positions. These workers are those who have been able to maintain and increase their employability while working multiskilled jobs within the core. The corporate support offered them "pays off" both for the company in terms of increased functional flexibility and for the worker in terms of future employment opportunities. Although the work history will not be a single upward pathway, there are no appreciable dips of either unemployment or underemployment either, and the benefits received from the employer and supplemented to on one's own can be amassed to ensure a financially secure retirement period.

However, for virtually everyone else, the prospects appear likely of doing part-time or temporary work or even having no work during some time in their work histories. No longer is there the likelihood of lifetime employment with a single firm, no longer are qualifications acquired only once and at the beginning of the work career, no longer are the work changes expectably good or at least neutral. From a sociological point of view, "the individual's movement through the occupational system is gradually losing its highly standardized form."[31] Buchmann expresses the change brought about by this loss of standardization for the individual in the very important conclusion for this book on life planning and individual security: "The organization of one's work life as a biographical perspective no longer involves the commitment to a choice once made but, rather, the flexibility to adjust to changing circumstances."[32]

This pivotal reference to a flexibility in the present rather than a commitment to the past introduces yet another meaning for this obviously crucial term. We have examined earlier the demands for both functional and numerical flexibility on the part of firms. Correlative to these forms of institutional flexibility, we have also examined individual forms of flexibility in terms of both expanded employability and in terms of highly adaptable work scheduling. What this fifth and final form of flexibility refers to, if I understand it properly, is an intensification of the rational calculation, which we are already familiar with from Part One, in regard to individual investments and returns and the willingness to modify work positioning and qualifications. This crucial new form of life planning is no longer undertaken in conformity to secure career pathways and no longer even allows assimilation in the form of company loyalty. Rather it is carried out in reaction and in adaptation to what Buchmann terms the "partial destandardization" of the modern life cycle.

The secure individual must work much harder in regard to her or his life planning in order to remain a secure individual and bring other secure individuals into the world. Actually the goal expressed as work harder is somewhat misleading. In the same way that the modern firm must not necessarily work harder but work smarter in its organization to become more productive, the individual must plan smarter in changing circumstances of discontinuous change, uncertain future employability, and diminished organizational support. Such smart planning is required not after the reengineering occurs, but before, maybe even, as chapter 11 will suggest, when the core employment is begun (if not earlier still).

It is important to observe that in themselves both the transition from single career pathways to job pluralities and the destandardization of modern employment histories do not necessarily threaten the achievement of long-term economic security. A succession of core jobs, as we have seen, would appear to be a highly acceptable result for life planning. Moreover, many employment patterns involving the transversing of all three positions in the shamrock appear to be perfectly acceptable as well. For example, a short period of temporary work, followed quickly by increasing levels of part-time employment, a long and successful period of core employment, and a shorter, consistent period of independent subcontracting or consulting could appear to various life planners to be just as attractive, almost as attractive as, or even more attractive than the traditional single and upwardly mobile career.

The positive opportunity presented by the destandardization of work histories is the opening up toward a variety of positions which, as a group, are more appealing than the "rut" of a single job track. Handy, for example, "wonders why one career or one type of job should be the norm. Why not three careers, switching progressively from energy to wisdom as the years roll on?"[33] Why not, indeed, take advantage of the increased flexibility and fluidity of occupational pathways to design deliberately one's own employment biography and occupy the various leaves of the shamrock as one chooses? The possibility is there, as perhaps never before, for a highly individualized, if not unique, work history.

At the same time, however, the intensification of life planning also brings with it a quite negative aspect presented by the threat of the loss of employability. The same destandardization that can promise a highly individualized and fulfilling occupational resumé also carries with it a pressing uncertainty as to whether a present secure position will last and whether the future job (or joblessness) will be in any way as good. From the perspective of the first shamrock leaf, the positions of the other leaves are marked by the element of contingency, if not even greater anxiety: "Most Americans feel trapped by the new lean-production practices and sophisticated new automation technologies, not knowing if or when the reengineering drive will reach into their own office or workstation, plucking them from what they once thought was a secure job and casting them into the reserve army of contingent workers, or, worse yet, the employment line."[34] Unemployment or, perhaps more likely, underemployment, and not necessarily for a short period of time, is a real danger and, it is unclear how this threat to one's employability can be defused through even the best flexible planning done in the most anticipatory way.

The following paragraph from *The Seasons of Life* captures well both the potential promise and the great threat that appear to be necessarily bundled together in the destandardized work history:

> The U.S. economy is changing so rapidly—and we're living so long—that it's difficult to find lifetime security, much less lifetime satisfaction, in any single job. Perhaps in our work, as in our lives, we have to think in terms of seasons. Not one career for one life, but several careers, each in its own time, each

with its own sense of purpose. From this point of view, nothing can be more damaging than ending one career of employment with no way of beginning the next.[35]

The third section of this book will discuss in detail both the positive panorama and the looming threat expressed so poignantly in the above quotation. On the positive side, we will take up Handy's powerful claim that "for the first time in the human experience, we have a chance to shape our work to suit the way we live instead of our lives to fit our work."[36] But we will also ask: How important is actual employment now in relationship to the preservation of employability? More importantly, how much is it the case that employability is actually achievable in virtue of smart, i.e. flexible, life planning? Having in the first section provided a genealogy for the birth of the secure individual, we will look in the third section at the tremendous threats—above all regarding employability—to her or his survival.

Before beginning this most crucial task of the book, we must look at other sources of the destandardization of life history in the present. An earlier work history of lifetime employment and the expression of company loyalty to a single company was often, if not normally, accompanied by a lifelong spousal commitment in a framework of family loyalty. The at least partial destandardization of temporal frameworks regarding relationships and family life will be examined in the final chapter of this section.

8

Intimacy, Independence, and Insecurity

The first group to feel the full effects of economic restructuring were the blue-collar workers who were laid off in masses from their factory jobs. Part of the intensity of the pain they felt came, as noted in the previous chapters of this section, from a sense of betrayal of their company loyalty and the long number of years they had worked within a career ladder pathway for the same factory. But an even greater part of their pain came from being no longer the main means of financial support for their families. Their earnings had provided their families with both the necessities of life and the wherewithal for a good standard of living. No longer "breadwinners," they had the new identity of "breadloser" to cope with and very minimal chances to recuperate their lost family function.

If the status of being the family breadwinner carried great pressures with it, it also had a positive side as well. Correlative to the identity of family breadwinner was the identity of the homemaker, "a woman full time in and around the home, on permanent assignment to clean it up, care for the children, prepare the meals, see to everyone's comfort."[1] Probably the greatest plus of being the family breadwinner was the lack of primary responsibility for the nurturing of children and the drudgery of housework.

The most important underpinning of the breadwinner identity was the real and likely possibility of earning a one paycheck male "family wage."[2] But another underpinning for the role of family homemaker was even more critical for the family system as a whole. The expectation of a permanent and stable marriage supported the domesticity of the stay-at-home housewife by making, as Kathleen Gerson has pointed out in her well-named volume, *Hard Choices*, the status of economic dependency and the task of full-time mothering options that were even possible to entertain.[3] As Barbara Bergmann adds: "The marriage ceremony was supposed to obligate her and her husband to stay together until one of them died. There was a strong taboo against having children out of wedlock. These arrangements made life comfortable and secure for many people. . . . "[4]

The breadwinner/homemaker family, never a universal matter of fact, is no longer the prototype or cultural norm; rather, it now occupies the status of one alternative among many. The presence of many alternatives to the "traditional marriage" opens the issue of marital restructuring and a destandardization of family histories similar to the destandardization of work histories described in the previous chapter. This chapter will certainly not take up all the issues involved in such destandardization and in particular will not address the most important issues of social justice regarding either the traditional cultural norm or present governmental programs of family support.[5] Rather, the focus is on the effects of destandardization upon the security earlier afforded by the underpinning of permanent and stable marriage. Above all, we will have to deal probatively with the judgment of Bergmann that the "assumption that a marriage was for life created feelings of security that now have been lost"[6] both in regard to the social changes which have produced this loss and with respect to the effects that a loss of that security may have on the economic life planning of the individual "standing by herself."

Marital Layoffs

The loss of security and the crushing of a cherished assumption of permanence and stability in marriage were probably most intensely felt by housewives in their late forties and fifties who had to confront the realities of unanticipated divorce at approximately the same time as the effects of factory layoffs were starting to be felt by middle age workers. The depths of their pain and the feeling of their betrayal were at least the match of their blue-collar age cohorts.

In Bergmann's words, "The treatment of the 'displaced homemaker'—a person who has been a housewife for a long time but whose 'job' has ended through separation or divorce—is a national scandal."[7] Of such displaced middle age home-makers, she elucidates: "When the divorce comes late in life, usually it is very late for the woman to start a serious career of her own, even if she has the resources, will, and self-confidence. She finds that many of the married people she considered good friends are not willing to continue as friends. Lonely, neglected, robbed of their previous status and of almost everything that made life worth living, many divorced house-wives eke out a miserable existence in a marginal job."[8]

Newly divorced or separated housewives had expectations of permanence and stability at least as firmly established as the long-term factory workers who worked for "good compa-nies." They

> were encouraged by their parents to search for spouses who would be "good earners." Having found and captured the affec-tions of a man willing to marry her, a woman was taught by the prevailing culture that any effort to sell her own labor in a hostile marketplace would be unnecessary and undesirable. A wife was not, of course, infallibly secure. She might be impov-erished by her husband's failure as worker or business man or farmer. He might sink into alcoholism, go to prison, or die an early death, leaving her with no source of income. . . . The one calamity from which she was supposed to be safe was her husband's desire to terminate the marriage, provided that she remained faithful to her marriage vows.[9]

When the unexpected calamity did indeed occur after all, the loyal homemaker made the unfortunate realizations that her assumed lifetime vocation was in reality a job subject to "foreign competition," her relationship with her "employer" had been on surprisingly shaky grounds, and her unanticipated "layoff" was for all intents and purposes permanent. The divorced home-maker faced a precipitous drop in income. She experienced a sharp feeling of isolation from both her husband and her circle of married friends. She also felt an intense feeling of betrayal.

Doris Reiney, a divorcee in the early 1960's, articulates all these feelings in a most compelling way:

My mother's generation really had the security of being supported. They knew that that was their husband's obligation and that they were supposed to be taken care of. They accepted a lot of crap in exchange for it, but the deal was there. My generation came along and everybody said that the wedding ring was the end of the rainbow, that if you behaved yourself, learned to play a good game of bridge, and stayed attractive, if you did that . . . a man would take care of you forever.

And then partway through the game, they changed the rules and men were running off with their secretaries because they wanted to be fulfilled. You were old hat and old-fashioned. So your husband left you for some lady at the office who was doing really important stuff rather than staying home, raising children, and becoming old hat. My generation is full of displaced homemakers. People who played by the rules and got screwed. So I think my mother at least had society on her side. Every time I turned around, it was a new set of rules.[10]

Isabel Sawhill offers a possible analysis of the change of rules spoken of so painfully by Reiney. According to the earlier rules,

Marriage is a partnership with a lifelong commmitment to another individual and a complete sharing of economic costs and rewards. Implicit in the lifelong-partnership view is the idea that the risk of divorce is small and that alimony provides a kind of insurance against this risk. . . . A second view of marriage is that it is a limited partnership in which husbands share their incomes with their wives, but only for as long as their marriage is intact. . . . The real problem arises when women agree to marry and be homemakers under the terms of the lifelong-partnership model and later discover that the limited partnership model is in effect.[11]

Sawhill's framework of differing kinds of contracts for comprehending the crushing nature of Reiney's discovery is quite similar to the differences between the implicit contract that the loyal factory workers felt they had with their company and the present realities of short term corporate support. These women had worked hard in **their** homes and were on the way to building up security that was going to last for a lifetime, only to have their limited partnership be dissolved unilaterally. Like the middle-aged factory workers, they now faced an uncertain future only without mate, without friends, without immediate prospects of employment, and likely without the home as well.

Till Disadvantage Do Us Part

Sawhill makes a strong legal argument from the principles of lifetime contract that the ex-housewife should be compensated through alimony for the loss of her earning power from the beginning of the marriage up to the present time. However, such compensation, even if it were awarded as a matter of actual legal practice, only compensates partially for the totality of the injuries she had suffered. Not only was the homemaker **discharged** from her economic position like the blue-collar factory worker, but at the same time she felt the intense pain of being **discarded** from her marital position and her social position with her friends. Conversely if she and her spouse were to decide to remain together after all, then it may no longer be because of the foundation of lifelong commitment but rather due to the power of the motivation of a new kind of fear: "What threatens or is feared beyond marriage and the family is perhaps the most stable foundation of marriage, despite all the crises and conflicts: loneliness."[12]

These sobering reflections concerning the twofold "displacement" of the homemaker suggest that the short term perspectives of limited partnership have even more ramifications regarding the security of personal relationships than they do in the sphere of employment. The final form of economic flexibility analyzed in the previous chapter requires on the part of the present-day individual no longer a commitment to a past decision but rather a concentrated adaptability to the present economic situation. Such flexibility demands above all the preservation of one's employability not simply in the present but throughout one's job history. Flexibility in a marriage based on the principles of limited partnership would appear to involve an even more daunting challenge. The fear of separation, divorce, or desertion would appear to require that, given legal realities concerning both the awarding and the receiving of alimony, one should preserve one's employability and, additionally, that one foster, maintain, and enhance one's "marriageability"[13] beyond the present marriage as well. The potential loss from the discard as well as the damage from the discharge must both be overcome.

"If marriage is then finally conducted 'subject to recall'— 'suitable for divorce', so to speak (as the marriage counseling books flooding the market demand through contractual agreements covering everything from splitting property to extramarital sexuality)," Beck argues that the "split which was to be avoided is simply anticipated, and the unequal consequences of all the decisions and regulations emerge more and more openly."[14] If he is correct that the split is simply anticipated— or even if a separation simply **might** be anticipated—then strategies are required **in the present** to avoid the implications of possible future loneliness and of financial setback from the unequal consequences of divorce. Some of these strategies must be undertaken with one's present economic situation and future employment prospects in mind. However, other strategic considerations will concern present familial responsibilities and future relational possibilities as well.

Given what Bergmann entitles *The Economic Emergence of Women* and the new improvement in employability and economic independence it has brought for many women, not all of the effects of the loss of orientation to a past decision of commitment are of course necessarily negative. Enhanced prospects for reciprocity and equality in marriage occur when the "husband of a woman capable of financial independence at a fair standard of living must, if he wants to keep her, earn by his behavior her desire to continue in the relationship, just as she must earn his." It is even "entirely possible that there are more happy marriages today, rather than fewer."[15]

Moreover, as Marlis Buchmann argues, the economic independence of women allows them both to dissolve marriages which are injurious to their interests or the interests of the children and to entertain and experiment with new family models and family forms. Among the "pluralization of family forms" that Beck mentions are: "childless marriage, temporary and unofficial marriage, parenthood late or delayed, . . . professional parenthood, that is parenthood limited to a small number of families. . . . family communes, senior communes and family units of single unmarried adult and one or more children. . . . A new type of 'extended family,' in which children have multiple parents."[16]

Such pluralization of family forms offers both opportunities and pitfalls, very much analogous to the destandardization of work histories. For individuals with secure employability, the presence of a new variety of options allows them to escape the "rut" of conventionality of a standardized family cycle and seek a variety of relationships at different times in their lives. More importantly, the constrictions associated with a narrowly conventional view of marriageability can be broadened, if not transgressed, by the entering into of quite different types of partnerships and unions. Primary relationships may concentrate on either a moderate or a radical alternative to traditional marriage or be formed between parent and child; they may fluctuate between the nuclear family and other ways of life or simply between alternative lifestyles themselves; or they may multiply, so that "each individual family member is a member of many families" in a new form of extended kinship. Any of these alternatives can be chosen consciously and a whole highly individualized pattern of relationships can be planned in advance and even carried out according to plan. There are the opportunities for a multitude of many individual recipes for sharing parenting, pooling economic resources, and achieving happiness.

However, especially for many (and there are of course many) who lack present economic resources and future employability, an unanticipated change in their standardized family cycle may have only threatening or chaotic consequences. The presence of children functions in their cases not only as a source of personal realization, but also as an economic obstacle to both their employment advancement and the finding of a new marriage partner. For those who are in poverty or have become single again in later life, the expectation may be not of a new stable and permanent marriage but rather of no new marriage at all. For those in less disadvantageous circumstances, new partners may be found, but only for short terms of duration in a succession that may appear chaotic as much as, if not more than, planned. Even those who possess a secure economic future may face a new situation under the fear of making a rather strong compromise in earlier plans for a family and ideals of intimacy. In all of these cases, the destandardization of marriage life may mean not so much an opportunity for self-discovery, but rather the looming threat of non-marriageability or at least under-marriageability for the future.

Finally and more subtly, Beck proposes a potential conflict between the very framework of the individual life planner and the relational demands of the other in general. The argument is couched in terms of marriage and family relationships but appears to be obviously true in regard to unconventional alternatives as well:

to the extent this individualized mode of existence succeeds, the danger grows that it might become an insurmountable obstacle to the kind of relationship (marriage, family) which still is basically desired. In the single life, the longing for the other grows just as much as the impossibility of integrating that person into the architecture of a life that now really is "one's own." That life was fulfilled with the non-presence of the other. Now, there is no space left for him or her. Everything breathes the resistance to loneliness: the variety of relationships, the rights one grants them, living habits, control of one's schedule, the ways of retreating to cope with the agonizing pains behind the façade. The delicate and carefully adjusted balance of all this is endangered by the desired partnership. The designs of independence become the prison bars of loneliness. The circle of individualization closes.[17]

The "Till disadvantage do us part" of limited partnership is superseded by the "Till disadvantage do us join" of unlimited individualism.

Having It All, Doing It All, Planning It All

For those who seek to avoid the short term perspectives of either limited partnership or unlimited individualism and to pursue the framework of lifetime commitment, the consequences of the real chances of separation and divorce and of the real effects of the limited partnership model are still not easily escaped. Ruth Sidel establishes the reason for the title of her study of the life planning of late adolescent and young adult women, *On Her Own*, as follows: "What is new about the dreams of many young women today is not only that they are the central characters in their plans for the future but that they believe they must prepare themselves to go it alone. Young women of all classes talk about the need to be independent."[18]

Women "have come to realize that whether because of divorce, ... childbearing outside of marriage, the inability of many men to earn an adequate 'family wage,' or their remaining single—either through design or through circumstance—they must be prepared to support themselves and anyone else for whom they feel responsible."[19] This perspective of individual responsibility is true, as Sidel reports, just as much for the "Neotraditionalist" young woman who plans with a primary focus on being a partner in a permanent and stable marriage as it is for anyone else.

However, this attitude of independence is even truer of a larger group of Sidel's interviewees whom she dubs the "New American Dreamers." The New American Dreamer

> has heard the message that women today should be the heroines of their own lives. She looks toward the future, seeing herself as the central character, planning her career, her apartment, her own success story. These young women do not see themselves as playing supporting roles in someone else's life script; it is their own journeys they are planning. They see their lives in terms of **their** aspirations, **their** hopes, **their** dreams. . . . They will work at jobs men work at, earn the money men earn; but many of them also plan at the same time to play all the roles women have traditionally played.[20]

The "emphasis among the New American Dreamers is on doing, on career, on material rewards."[21] Each is under pressure "to work out a way for oneself to live the good life." This good life is achievable if it is properly planned for: "Above all, she is convinced that if she plans carefully, works hard, and makes the right decisions, she will be a success in her chosen field; have the material goods she desires; in time, marry if she wishes; and, in all probability, have children."[22] The New American Dreamer "plans, as the expression goes, to 'have it all.'"[23]

How possible is it to plan "having it all" in advance"? More seriously, how can having it all be achieved without, as Judith Sprankle poses, "having to do it all" at the same time?[24] The planning of the New American Dreamer—probably of either gender—depicts a dual income marriage with each partner allotting high priority to career success. There remains, of course, the responsibilities of child care and the burdens of housework that fell to the traditional homemaker to perform.

The previous privileges of the breadwinner in the breadwinner/homemaker household must be negotiated. But Bergmann points out two very different frameworks according to which negotiations can occur. According to the first model, all contributions to the family are valued in money terms. If one partner brings in more of the family income, perhaps far more than half, then the other partner should do more than half of the housework. In addition, the housework itself is to be valued in terms of the low market-set wages. Under this model, the "husband who is not allowed to buy his freedom—who contributes lots of money and half the housework, too—is exploited."[25]

According to the alternative "sharing ethic," each "spouse's contribution might be valued as proportional to the total time the person devoted to the family's economic well-being—time devoted to a paid job (including commuting) and time devoted to housework."[26] Moreover, each "hour would be valued inversely to the pleasure the activity gave" so that the drudgery of housework chores would receive a diametrically opposite value to the competing market model. The goal would be to share both the benefits and the burdens of the marriage responsibilities equally.

Any disparities in income due to the effects of the earlier family wage system work to the benefit of the husband in the marketing ethic alternative. Moreover considerations of a limited partnership nature may also be used to the benefit of the larger wage earner: "The way the disparity in economic power works to keep the housework fastened on the woman is that repeated requests for a change in the sharing of housework may bring in return a threat on the part of the husband to leave."[27] According to Bergmann, the "disparity in raw economic power between men and women is one basis for the adoption by about a quarter of working couples in the United States" of what she terms "the drudge-wife family style"[28] or what Arlie Hochschild has famously called the "second shift."[29]

Of course, more couples are now negotiating and new American dreamers are definitely planning in accordance with the sharing model. But even in this instance, Bergmann's judgment that "the disparities in economic power between men and women are being reduced faster than the housework burden is shifting"[30] remains true. Progress has definitely been made in regard to the sharing of child care, and models of the "new" father typically convey a high commitment to involvement and the nurturing of children. But the gap between the amount of time devoted to the chores of housework remains and the second shift persists, even regarding spouses with egalitarian attitudes, and its diminishment may have less to do with any increase in husband involvement than with a decrease in the time available for the wife to clean and cook.

Moreover, even in those cases where an equality of time is given to the carrying out of household chores, there is likely to remain a disparity in the responsibility of planning the housework. This disparity is particularly evident in the case of upper middle class and upper class dual-earner families where the majority of all the domestic tasks regarding children, education, medical care, upkeep of primary and secondary homes, and entertainment are carried out by people other the spouses themselves. Aasta Lubin terms this support system the "sustaining crowd" of the family and uses the principles of modern organizational theory to analyze the workings of the "high-echelon" dual-earner family.

According to Lubin's analysis in *Managing Success*, which parallels the analysis above of the success of modern corporations, women in such families have the responsibility to organize and plan and their role is best understood as that of a general manager:

> The women are the hub, general managers and members of the board who develop strategies to run the family in a way that frees sufficient time for them to devote to their careers. Thus the career is the core department around which the family department has to adjust. Sometimes strategies are developed in conjunction with another member of the board (husband), who frequently functions also as administrative assistant. However, the daily running of the household is almost exclusively in the women's hands.[31]

The wives in the families of Lubin's study exhibited great skill in managing, above all through their assembling of "support systems" for the family "department." According to the principles of external flexibility elucidated above, "cleaning people, caterers, restaurants, stores, hairdressers" and the like could be contracted for the family department as the need arose. More important, of course, were the responsibilities to find the right private schools and medical professional help that could be viewed as second shamrock subcontractors. Also necessary—above all in emergencies—were the possibilities of the husband or an understanding secretary to take control of the unexpected situation when the wife's own responsibilities precluded action.

However, the major organizational requirement of the complex structure in upper echelon dual-earning families is the obtaining and keeping of a good housekeeper: "The housekeeper emerges as the women's number one practical and concrete support in regard to the children. The husbands come next; they support both practically and emotionally. They complete the circle, making everything right in their world if they are supportive. . . . But the housekeeper is the main factor in making possible the career women's success."[32] The housekeeper is frequently a "green card lady" from the West Indies, Mexico, or Central America, or the Orient according to geographical area. The "basic requirement for the career woman's housekeeper is that she take care of the child and be available whenever needed. The standards set for the rest, such as housekeeping, meal-cooking, laundry, etc., are much less vital. Most career women have additional cleaning help anyway."[33]

According to Lubin, "there is a greater interdependence in the relationship between the career women and the housekeeper than in the usual employer-employee relationship. The career women will go to great lengths to ensure that the housekeeper is content and will therefore in turn function well in her job as her major support system."[34] The greater interdependence in the relationship is a reflection of the tremendous work demands of the wife's career. However, the "housekeeper is, figuratively speaking, often as much of a slave to her employer's work as the career women themselves are."[35] As Lubin and other researchers have pointed out, "she functions to some extent like a wife in the traditional family.[36]

While wives in these higher-echelon families have the responsibility to organize the complex family system, what appears to stand out is not so much the inequality of the burden but rather the accomplishment and excellence with which the planning is carried out. Among "the strategies they use to keep their social system working are to plan, to delegate tasks and responsibilities, to instruct in regard to these, to surround themselves with competent people whom they can trust and use to do the work they cannot or do not want to do themselves, to lower standards in some areas . . . , to compartmentalize in order to keep one role from interfering with another, and finally to see to it that the reward systems are adequate for the people involved, including themselves."[37] Yet what makes all of this impressive planning possible is the ironic preservation of the role of the traditional homemaker—only now "displaced" into a home which is not even her own. As one of the women in Lubin's study comments, "It's like she's the wife staying home to look after the children and I'm the breadwinner who goes to work and has an interesting time."[38] Consequently, the only solution that successfully appears to avert the "second shift" of family housework is achieved not through equal sharing of work and planning between spouses, but through a remarkably interdependent, yet subcontractual preservation of the long first shift of the traditional homemaker.

Stand by Yourself

At the conclusion of her book, Sidel poses a series of critical questions that strike at the heart of the title of "on her own":

> But what about the notion of going it alone? Is that belief on the part of young women an expression of hope or of despair? Is it a reflection of strength that stems from the recognition now emerging—at long last, some might say—that women must be complete human beings with their own identity, income, and independence, or is this an image of aloneness, of isolation that stems, rather, from the recognition that there are few supports remaining in American society and that one had better be able to survive alone?[39]

Sidel's own answer to these and other equally striking questions is that the responses of her interviewees combine both of these factors together with the "individualism that 'lies at the very core of American culture' and at the very core of the American Dream."[40] Given the doubtless correctness of this answer, it says a great deal not only about the life planning of Sidel's young women but of the challenges facing any would be secure individual today.

The New American Dreamers, and not they alone but all the women in Sidel's study, do not rely on the assurance of spousal support throughout their career and family life. According to Barbara Ehrenreich in *The Hearts of Men*, this is a totally appropriate stance to take, since "the collapse of the breadwinner ethic, and with it, the notion of long-term emotional responsibility toward women, affects not only the homemaker who could be cut loose into poverty, but the financially self-sufficient working woman, not to mention the children of either."[41] She continues:

> For better or for worse, most of us grew up expecting that our lives would be shared with those of the men in our generation; that we would be married, or as we later put it in the modern

vernacular, that we would have "long-term committed rela-tionships." Only within those relationships could we imagine having children (and not only because of the financial conse-quences of motherhood) or finding the emotional support to do what we increasingly identified as **our** own things. Yet we—and the "we" here includes many more than feminists, profes-sional women and others that conservatives might dismiss as marginal groups—face the prospect of briefer "relationships," punctuated by emotional dislocations and seldom offering the kind of loyalty that might extend into middle age.[42]

To recall the distinction from Part One between "planning with" and "planning upon," the young women from Sidel's study, but older women and any other would be secure individuals as well, appear not to plan upon or rely upon the promise of permanent spousal support or the extension of sufficient social support from the extended family, the community, or the gov-ernment. How, then, can they still be at all independent and optimistic life planners of their future, when they start out so strongly "on their own"? The answer to this question lies in what they—or perhaps we—still plan with or calculate upon achieving in regard to their—or our—work futures.

According to Sidel,

> Perhaps the most startling aspect of my interviews with young women was their vision of their future work lives. The young women had basically four scenarios for the future: they would enter high-status, high-income professions, such as law, medi-cine, and business; they would enter more traditional women's occupations such as art, design, modeling, or the health pro-fessions; they would be home with children for the first few years and then find part-time work that was compatible with a primary commitment to child rearing and homemaking; or they could not imagine the future at all. But with the excep-tion of the last group, the theme that transcends the vast majority of the responses is the desire—indeed the intention to be affluent. . . . However they plan to achieve it, the image of "the good life," the affluent life, is the common thread in nearly all the interviews.[43]

Crucial to the affirmative stance of the interviewees to-ward being "on one's own"—as a stance of independence and not only isolation—is the confident planning by the individual of success at work and the successful subsequent attainment of a high level of stable economic earning. Indeed such confidence in success is crucial to the attainment of a sense of independence and individualism that characterizes the activism and the optimism of the planning of the secure individual in general. However, Sidel's study demonstrates that the viability of such planning with is not required today solely for its own value and the economic benefits it might bring. Rather the planning and achievement of success appear to be equally necessary as compensation and insurance for the lack of ability to plan upon significant enough social support from a spouse, a neighborhood, or a government.

With respect to the actual prospects of economic success, Sidel finds that her interviewees are unaware of the consequences of job discrimination against women and the difficulties in landing jobs sufficient in income to support their family plans. As Ehrenreich writes, "there is only one thing left of the family wage system: the fact that women, on the average, are paid less than a family (at current urban rents, less that a very **small** family) requires for a moderate standard of living."[44] She adds: "For women as a group, the future holds terrifying insecurity: We are increasingly dependent on our own resources, but in a society and an economy that never intended to admit us as independent persons, much less as breadwinners for others."[45]

Sidel's greatest concern is that her interviewees, and other adolescent women as well, have no real comprehension of the "terrifying insecurity" they face. Indeed, Ehrenreich shows that the concern is valid on an even more general basis: "It will not help to break out of women's occupational ghetto if there are fewer and fewer well-paying jobs outside of it, and it is hard to insist on higher pay from employers who are already busily disinvesting, fleeing overseas or replacing human labor with robots and microcomputers."[46] Not only the young women of Sidel's study but every would-be secure individual must plan for economic success in the face of the contemporary business demands for functional and external flexibility in their workforces. The successful negotiation of these demands is essential for everyone, apparently not only in view of the need for secure earnings, but also as a result of the lack of other reliable and adequate social support upon which to rely.

The third and final section will deal only indirectly with the destandardization of family life as it relates to the challenges of the planning of economic success. This planning now appears both to bear the brunt of the load in the attainment of security and even to have to compensate for the lack of social support that was earlier there. But exactly how securely can the economic future be planned in the present business environment and will the economic resources of such employment be sufficient to compensate for the lack of sufficient social supports to "plan upon" regarding children, marriageabilty in late middle age, and "Third Age" resources for living? The optimistic and pessimistic answers to these questions will be introduced, considered, and compared.

Part III

The Struggle for Employability and
The Fear of Inadequacy

9

The Planning Office as Opportunity and as Self-Expression

Probably the most central theme of the last part concerned the different meanings and requirements of flexibility in regard to work. Companies need functional flexibility in regard to their core employees; core workers must become multiskilled and technologically up to date so that they can work in effective teams with similarly multiskilled workers. Companies need numerical flexibility regarding their peripheral workers and the varying demands of their customers; subcontractors and part-time or temporary workers must adapt to highly variable work scheduling in accordance with such fluctuations. Finally and perhaps most importantly, any present or would-be employee appears to have to be able to plan flexibly in order to preserve employability in the present and enhance it in the face of an uncertain work future.

Particularly the latter meaning of flexibility, which is echoed in the discussion of marriageability in the previous chapter, signals a change in the temporal organization of life history. As has been quoted above from Marlis Buchmann, life planning "no longer involves the commitment to a choice once made but, rather, the flexibility to adjust to changing circumstances." Moreover, the uncertainty of these circumstances—the challenges of having to adapt in the present to new global conditions and to the new rules of production—also makes it appear that life planning is now becoming more intense and consequently more difficult. Planning flexibly in the present would appear to require having to plan—and having to work—harder in the present and future as well.

Discussions of individual strategy typical of the managerial literature admit the difficulties posed by the new developments in lean production and the telecommunications industry and the threats posed by the outdating of qualifications and the outsourcing to external vendors and producers. However, they also contend that the assumption of a frankly entrepreneurial attitude on the part of the employee will disclose the sizable opportunities stimulated by the information technology revolution as well. It may even be possible through planning smarter—not necessarily harder—to survive and, according to some of the literature, even thrive.

According to outplacement executive William Morin, "You have to see yourself as a business."[1] Consequently, the picture of the planning office, which has accompanied all the discussions of life planning so far, no longer functions here as merely **a** metaphor but rather as **the** recipe for how the individual should function in "the enterprise culture." Planning smarter entails acquiring the acumen of "the enterprising self" appropriate for "the enterprise culture."

The qualities of the enterprising self are "self-reliance, goal orientation, activism and reward expectation."[2] Reward expectation, probably the most interesting quality, is not a misleading or unreasonable stance, because opportunities are out there, or so the argument goes, for those willing to engage themselves actively in the pursuit of their self betterment. The present and future employment uncertainties need not be feared, and the flexibility that is required can be viewed optimistically as a real opportunity rather than a threat.

This chapter will present the case for the worker as enterprising self, before the next chapter gives a quite different picture of the obstacles, limitations, and challenges of job planning. However, the authors whose ideas will be examined in this chapter are not selected for proclivities to promise a proverbial pot of gold at the end of the reengineered rainbow, but rather for realistic strategies for easing the effects of work and life discontinuity. In the first section, William Bridges' advice that the worker "start thinking like an external vendor" will be explained in regard to both its justification and implications. Above all, one of the most important implications, the assemblage and living out of the "composite career" will be highlighted through a metaphorical comparison between chains and cables. In the next section the composite career will be further elucidated through Charles Handy's richly suggestive notion of the worker "portfolio." The chapter closes with an argument for the need to combine the perspectives of both authors in order to achieve, on the one hand, the material returns and, on the other, the richness of the work experience sought by each respectively.

You and Co.

The pivotal advice that Bridges offers for his readers of *Jobshift* is that "workers need to develop a mindset, an approach to their work, and a way of managing their own careers that is more like that of an external vendor than that of a traditional employee."[3] The old mindset of the secure career pathway was more than understandable; it was almost natural—"It isn't your fault that you were brought up on a diet of Get-a-Good-Job-and-You're-All-Set. Of course you bought into it. Everyone did."[4] However, it now is no longer workable and in fact is positively disadvantageous: "the good job, which was once the definition of responsibility, is now a very risky business. And the old kind of freelance activity that was once risky is now in tune with the future and is becoming the choice of many people who want to act responsibly."[5]

The required change of attitude follows from the change that workers ought to make regarding the way they approach their work. The company has changed in the way it approaches its employees, and employees need to change as well. Above all the company has changed in the way it uses external vendors:

> Today, as more and more organizations decide to focus their resources on exploiting their own distinctive "core competencies" and "unbundle" their other component elements, the old boundary between the self-contained organization and its market "environment" becomes not only irrelevant but dangerously misleading. As organizations increasingly replace many of their support functions (and even parts of their central operations) with services provided by external vendors, they invite market forces into their interior workings. Employees find themselves being evaluated in comparison to (and even bidding against) external suppliers.[6]

Consequently the company's own workers "must either learn to view the organization as a marketplace or else lose the organization's business to someone else who does."[7] They must approach their work in the same way that an external vendor to the company does, as the title of one of Bridges' chapters, "Run 'You & Co.' As a Business," well indicates.

The external vendor is of course outside the company, but Bridges' advice is that the core employee, although inside the company, must act as though she or he is outside at the same time. The crucial insight is that "you must see yourself as a self-contained economic entity, not as a component part looking for a whole within which you can function."[8] As a component part, the company has found ways to identify and promote your individual multiple skills. It's now up to you "to identify and find new ways to exploit your individual 'core competencies,' just the way your organization is."[9] According to Bridges,

> It's a case of joining 'em when it's too hard to beat 'em. . . . In an earlier day this idea of "being in business for yourself" while still drawing a paycheck would have been viewed as the height of disloyalty. Today it provides the organization with useful and highly motivated assistance, which is what the organization needs today far more than it needs the kind of old-fashioned loyalty that is really the dependency that grows from an inability to be self-sufficient.[10]

The training required for becoming a self-sufficient You & Co. is in no way simple. It is

> training in "reading" a market, in spotting change-generated needs, and in defining one's product in terms that make sense to people that have those needs. It is training in personal benchmarking, so that you know how well other service vendors do what you propose to do—and how they get those results. It is training in being your own sales department, in being your own R&D group, in continuously improving the quality of what you do.[11]

However, there is also a noteworthy strategic benefit that comes from all this effort. If you run your business self so that you are able to exploit your core competencies for yourself as well as your employer, you are going to be doing more than one thing both inside and outside the company as well. In other words, you will have a **composite career** not only over time but in the immediate present as well. Such a composite career may appear to force you to "split your time between different roles, locations, clients, teams, schedules—whole different work worlds."[12] But the composite career also pays off in the acquisition of security because of its diversification and multiple work worlds.

According to Michael J. Piore, a development which rivals the change away from the single-dominant-wage-earner family in importance is "the increasing porousness . . . of the boundaries of business enterprises."[13] His prognostication is that "employment will be associated less and less with a single firm and more and more with a community of firms consisting of suppliers, customers, clients, and even erstwhile competitors of what used to be a stand-alone enterprise."[14] Such networks of firms should, in his estimation, "be able to provide the portfolio of employment opportunities that would create the employment security that single business units, even relatively large corporations, no longer seem able to provide."[15]

According to the metaphorics of Bridges, the earlier career pathway was like a chain, with each successive transition in the pathway serving as a link, a single identifiable and definable step along the way. The composite career, on the other hand, is: "more like a woven cable, made up of multiple twisted strands of wire. The strands are assignments and projects, often for different organizations and sometimes involving wholly different personal products."[16]

With the contrast between these two metaphors in mind, the case for the composite career is an easy one to make:

> The job-chain career provided strength, but it was only as strong as each individual link. These days, the job links break far too easily. The strands of the composite career, however, begin and end at various points and weave a more flexible kind of strength out of their multiplicity. Any one strand can break without destroying the career cable.[17]

The external-vendor minded employee will be able to benefit through her or his development of such a flexibly strong cable. She or he will be able to survive the breakage of a strand because of the multiple connections with other firms in the broader, porous network. This is because she or he or you or I have learned to manage a work career in the same way that an external supplier has learned to survive and perhaps prosper in such competitive circumstances. We will have learned to run You & Co. as a technology of the self correlative to the way business is run under today's conditions.

You and Your Portfolio

When Piore refers to a portfolio of employment opportunities, it is with the picture of the investment portfolio in mind. Bridges has something very similar in mind in putting forward the cable analogy. In fact the other analogy he uses to argue for the composite career is that of diversified investing. The "vocational investment in the composite career's multiple activities and sources of income is like a financial investment (e.g., a mutual fund or a portfolio of stocks, bonds, cash, and real estate) that spreads the risk around."[18]

However, the term "portfolio" of course can have a quite different meaning deriving from art and the compilation of an ensemble of works representing one's talents and abilities at self-expression. Charles Handy combines both of these meanings in proposing and extolling the advantages of the "worker portfolio." Such a worker portfolio diversifies and minimalizes risk in the manner of the diversified financial portfolio. However and more interestingly, the worker portfolio also expands and greatly revises the very notion of work of which it is a compilation. According to Handy, "'What do you do?' no longer means 'What is your job?' but 'How do you occupy your time?'"[19] And you or I will occupy our time with the job demands of our organization, but also with "work rediscovered, work redefined to mean more than selling your time to someone else, work that is more in tune with the rest of life, work that is more personal, more creative, more fun than most jobs can ever be."[20]

Handy distinguishes among five different kinds of work, all of which are able and ought, in his opinion, to fit in a worker portfolio. Wage work and fee work are kinds of work done for money either for the time given or the results delivered. But there is also homework and gift work and study work which are not done primarily for money. The variety presented by all these kinds of "free" work has been missing in the career pathways in the earlier era of the strictly defined corporate ladder. But a compilation of all of these kinds of free work can be the defining characteristic of the portfolios of workers who are now outside the restrictions of such rigid expectations.

The opening up of the worker portfolio to an expanded and revised notion of work couples the earnings of different forms of money work with the meaningfulness of free work. Crucial to its success and attractiveness is yet again a further application of the now most familiar core/periphery distinction. As Handy explains in his own instance,

> I looked for a job that would provide me with interesting and exciting work, work, too, that I would be proud of doing. I also wanted enough money and the chance to make more of it if I needed to, good companions and a pleasing location with the chance of travel. Needless to say, I never found the perfect job. There was, however, a . . . solution. If I adopted a "portfolio" approach to life, meaning that I saw my life as a collection of different groups and activities, I could get different things from different bits, done for different people. A part of that portfolio would be "core," providing the essential wherewithal for life, but it would be balanced by work done purely for interest or for a cause, or because it would stretch me personally, or simply because it was fascinating or fun.[21]

The application of the core/periphery distinction to the worker portfolio reacts back on Bridges' metaphor of the cable to suggest that some strands of the now expanded cable will be more important than others. Indeed, Handy admits that for most of the core employees in the new working organization, "the job will fill the whole portfolio to bursting point with just one item."[22] However at another time, not all that far in the distant future, as we "become used to the idea that the full-time executive or skilled worker fades in his or her late forties, in most occupations,"[23] the "core" of the portfolio will not be so singularly determined and the portfolio will not be so monotone: "Like it or not, the ex-core employee will be forced into a portfolio life, and life without some work, as any of the long-term unemployed will confirm, is life without meaning."[24]

Portfolio thinking can open up a quite different perspective to the import of this transition and the way it is understood. "Early retirement" used to be a formula "spoken in a hush." Now for many people it is a situation to be managed and arranged, a situation "signifying release or a key to new possibilities."[25] According to Handy,

> Ask those people what they will do next, and they do not talk of wage work but of ways of keeping their hand in (some small free work), of time for old enthusiasms, or new causes and hobbies (gift work), of helping out more with household chores or parenting (homework), or of taking up a new interest (study

work). They don't call it work, but they should. They are
building up a new portfolio and in so doing redefining their
lives and themselves.[26]

Portfolio thinking is intended not only as a coping device for
the difficult transitions that simply have to be undergone, but
much more as a stimulus for undertaking sequencing on one's
own. A variety of sequencing patterns is possible, and each can
allow for individualization and for some form of free work to
complement the money work core. Among the possibilities that
Handy mentions: "Some will want to interleave their careers with
periods of study. . . . Others, particularly but not only women,
will want to interleave the career with periods of raising a
family. . . . Some will want intense and early careers allowing
them the possibility of a second kind of life before they get too
old to do it well. Some will use the organization as a training
ground and, then, in their thirties, become more independent."[27]

The portfolio orientation may even be employed to promote
the mutual negotiation of sequencing in personal relationships.
Handy develops an entire typology of relationships involving
combinations of "involved," "thrusters," "carers," and "loners"
primarily to argue for "a portfolio of possibilities," the flexibility
"to move from one pattern to another when the need demands."
If the relationship starts involved-involved, it may change to
thruster-carer, but only temporarily before moving back to
involved-involved or changing to the pressures of the high-level,
dual earning thruster-thruster. Handy even argues for the "possibility in a dual portfolio life of mixing the patterns monthly,
or weekly, or even daily."[28] There could be thruster-carer days,
involved-involved weekends, loner-loner holidays, and carer-
thruster repartees. In any case, a "portfolio marriage" may well
be the most appropriate way of joining two portfolio lives.

Handy admits that the bits and pieces of a diverse and
maybe even fragmented worker portfolio may "sound a poor
second best to a proper job and a proper career."[29] However,
he also argues: "We overdo the core. In our personal lives we
often exaggerate the necessities. Few need as much as they
think that they do, or as much security as they hanker after."[30] What the portfolio metaphor is meant to convey is the
value that lies in the whole, in the balance achieved between
money and free work and in the complete assemblage of all
the bits and pieces.

The sequencing involved in the worker portfolio envisaged and lived by Handy is intended to be quite different from the fixed career pathway on the corporate ladder of an earlier era of work. While perhaps less certain than that secure pathway, it can at the same time be a sequencing "of our choice, in our time and under our control."[31] According to Handy, "for the first time in the human experience, we have a chance to shape our work to suit the way we live instead of our lives to fit our work."[32] With this major opportunity for self organization and self expression in mind, we "would be mad to miss the chance."[33]

Portfolio Cables

Both Bridges and Handy emphasize self-initiative in life planning but in quite different ways. For Bridges the initiative is that of the worker who adapts the perspective of the external vendor. Such a worker takes the initiative to work hard both inside and outside the company and also to train smartly in the promotion of self-advancement. For Handy the initiative is one of self-expressiveness characterized by the artistic component in the worker portfolio. The individuality of the worker is evidenced in the portfolio by the particular mix between money and free work and above all by the sequencing of the different bits and pieces that make up the whole portfolio.

Both of these senses of initiative—or, once again, flexibility—are not only useful but arguably even necessary for the individual planning of the contemporary worker. The tough-mindedness of Bridges' external vendor appears essential for securing the core of Handy's portfolio, since it offers the means by which the resources of the necessary financial wherewithal are reliably obtained. On the other hand, the tender-mindedness of Handy's worker-artist is necessary to prevent the planning office from becoming not simply an appropriate strategy but rather an exhaustive description of the worker's present and future.

Bridges' directives regarding training are necessary for beginning the cable or getting the core of the portfolio beginning at all. "Fewer people mean better people,"[34] so there is obviously greater selectivity on entry. Since the requirements for obtaining a multiple-skilled and knowledge-based core position are greater and the competition is stiffer, getting that first important strand in the multiple cable going is likely to prove to be a difficult challenge.

Vendor mindedness is also obviously important in securing the other strands of the cable as well. To have a thicker cable, it will be necessary to establish connections and working relationships with other enterprises in the porous network of related firms. It may even be necessary to switch primary core employment among firms in the network and perhaps quite often. The larger the network and more established the connections, the thicker the cable and the more secure the present and future employability.

Tough-mindedness is also required when Handy's original calculation for the career demands of core employment—45 hours x 45 weeks x 25 years—proves severely undercalculated in regard to its hourly work demands. As Handy admits in his later work, seventy hours is quite often the more appropriate figure and quite often over more than forty-five weeks. The core worker may indeed amass the 100,000 hours of the traditional careerist, only over the span of a much shorter work experience of thirty years or less and under considerably more pressured conditions.

Finally, the discipline of Bridges' detached perspective is required to save financially and to prepare for the transition from core employment that is coming far earlier than at the traditional retirement age. In the previous period of the secure career ladder, the loyal employee could not only count on having a job with the company up to the retirement age, but also on earning high pay during the later years in virtue of the length of the seniority that had been accumulated. Indeed the period between the age of fifty and retirement was characteristically the period of maximal savings because the family was also grown. Now it appears, by contrast, that this period could well signal a time of dramatic decline in earning. Consequently, the savings have all to be accumulated **before** fifty in order to have the financial means to "manage" early retirement after being pressured out of or at least no longer measuring up to the challenges of core employment.

However, Handy's "tender-mindedness" is also needed precisely for this same "Third Age" transition from an emphasis upon money work to free work. The definition of work dominated by the presuppositions of long careers and secure fees will no longer suffice for the entire time period of the traditional career. Consequently, gift work and homework and study work are not simply poor substitutes for high-earning money work, but essential components that are needed to complement a too monetaristic understanding of work and its rewards. While such work may be situated at the periphery of the portfolio at some periods of the development of the worker portfolio, it is in no sense damaging but rather salutary that they occupy core positions at other times.

Moreover, not only is there no perfect job which combines high monetary rewards and personally meaningful service, but the contemporary pressures of functional flexibility are making jobs less and less perfect all the time. Because there are such great difficulties in either achieving the meaningfulness of gift work or doing the necessities of housework within such jobs, the artistic dimension to the portfolio is just as important as the financial one. Without it the standpoint of the external vendor is simply that of the modern planning office without any exception or remainder.

The composite career must be only a part of a composite life. At the same time that composite life will need the strength of the flexible cable of the composite career in order to accomplish its balance and completeness. Bridges' cable career modifies but also, I would argue, re-expresses through its emphasis upon continuous strands the Neo-Stoic attitude of constancy articulated by Lipsius for the military commander and the dedicated bureaucrat in a literal time of chains. While it needs Handy's portfolio for completion, the synthesis provides strategies for fighting and not fleeing under conditions of heightened competition and compressed job histories. The multidimensional planning office may succeed through intensified constancy where more restricted planning will almost certainly fail.

But even by the appropriately modified criteria of security as explained by Piore above, is the employability afforded by the composite career able to supply a sense of security at all analogous to that provided by the earlier career ladder? In the next chapter, the technology of the self begun by Lipsius for military life and reinterpreted by Bridges in terms of You and Co. will be compared to a quite different interpretation of what the present-day struggle for employability entails and when it begins. Crucial to the comparison will be a very different attitude of planned abandonment and an equally different metaphorics involving videotape.

10

Work as Chapter and as Episode

Throughout these last two sections of the book, Foucault's notion of governmentality has been applied outside of its original purview as a means of interpreting the latest changes in the business strategy of corporations and other economic organizations. The changes have not been examined so much for their own sake, but for their implications for individual technologies of the self which have been adopted in correlation to these changes. The final changes entailed by the worker's adaptation of the viewpoint of the external vendor have even been justified as a matter of "joining 'em when it's too hard to beat 'em."

This chapter will, at the risk of testing the patience of the reader, take one final look at the strategies involved in the business practices of reengineering and their upshot regarding the longest stage of the modern life cycle devoted to work. The central emphasis in the presentation so far has been upon the need on the part of the company for continual improvement. This need was met on the side of the worker with the requirements to be more and more multiply skilled and technologically sophisticated.

This chapter will examine the contention of Peter Drucker that the imperatives of continual improvement are only one part of a threefold program of corporate improvement and innovation. In this more comprehensive and ambitious program, the new part of greatest importance is the need for the company to plan rigorously and vigorously for the abandonment of the production of its present products or the offering of its present services. It is this suggestive but complicated notion of "planned abandonment" which will be examined again not primarily for its own sake, but rather for its implications for the individual planning of employment.

A further examination of the preservation of employability and its relationship to present employment will be offered through the aid of Zygmunt Bauman's even more global analysis of modern identity. For Bauman, there has been a new and significant transition from identity formation in lasting frames that control the future to a fixation, if one will, on not being fixed at all or on not mortgaging the future. The repercussions of this attitude of "leaving 'em before it is too late" will be explicated through a quite different metaphorics than in the previous chapter; namely, through Bauman's comparison between photography and videotape.

Planned Abandonment as a Production Goal

Peter Drucker is one of the most persuasive business analysts on the need for the application of the Japanese technique of continual improvement. At the same time, however, he is the most compelling writer on the inadequacy of continual improvement alone. The Japanese have developed a more comprehensive approach to corporate innovation for which continual improvement is only one of the crucial steps. Drucker believes that companies which overlook this comprehensive approach will do so only to their own competitive disadvantage.

According to Drucker, the Japanese lean production firms are "systematically starting out with a deadline for **abandoning** today's new product set on the very day on which this product is first sold."[1] Conventional economic wisdom would appear to dictate "that a product becomes more profitable the longer its product life."[2] But the conviction of the Japanese companies is "that the only alternative to themselves shortening the life cycle of the product is for a competitor to do so—and then the competitor will not only have the profits but the market as well."[3]

The Japanese strategy involves "reorganizing research and development so that it simultaneously produces **three** new products with the effort traditionally needed to produce one."[4] The first of these new products is to come from the already familiar process of *Kaizen* or organized, continuous self-improvement. This process has "specific goals and deadlines—

e.g., a 10 percent reduction in cost within 15 months and/or a 10 percent improvement in reliability within the same time, and/or a 15 percent increase in performance characteristics."[5] Given the cumulative effect of these changes over time, the "aim of *Kaizen* is to improve each product or service so that it becomes a truly different product or service in two or three years' time."[6]

The second product will be achieved by learning how to exploit, "that is, to develop new applications"[7] from the product's successes. This middle product will be a "leap" from the original one.

The third and most important product genuinely will be new in comparison to the others. It will be the product of a systematic research and development effort devoted to supplant the previous product. The purpose is not to undermine the profitability of that product, but to create a different pathway to profitability through the development of a different and more desirable product. This product is brought about not only through its own research and development, but also through the "planned abandonment" of the original product.

The organization that learns how to plan abandonment has learned, in Drucker's very important analysis, how

> to ask every few years of every process, every product, every procedure, every policy: "If we did not do this already, would we go into it now, knowing what we now know?" And if the answer is no, the organization has to ask: "And what do we do now?" It has to **do** something, not just make another study. Increasingly, organizations will have to **plan** abandonment rather than to prolong the life of a successful policy, practice, or product...[8]

The successful business enterprise must be "organized for systematic abandonment of the established, the customary, the familiar, the comfortable—whether products, services, and processes, human and social relationships, skills, or organizations themselves."[9] Otherwise, it "soon will lose performance capacity, and with it the ability to attract and to hold the knowledge specialists on whom it depends."[10]

The Discipline of the Second Curve

If the company stands the risk of losing its performance capacity by prolonging the same product line for too long, the employee also stands the risk of losing employability "capacity" by hanging on to the same job for too long. The issue is whether the employee must pose the same sort of blunt question—"If I did not do this already, would I go into it now, knowing what I now know?"—and then have to **do** something if the answer is negative. Is there an individual strategy of planned abandonment which is not only possible but even actually required by the present employment climate and, if so, what implications might the adoption of such a strategy carry with it?

A very common model for illustrating the developmental strategies of companies is the life cycle itself, and this fact can be exploited (in a non-leaping fashion) for the establishment of a strategy that does not exemplify planned abandonment. Charles Handy, for example, in his second book on the latest business changes, *The Age of Paradox*, introduces the sigmoid curve in discussing both organizational and individual adaptations to the continual change in business:

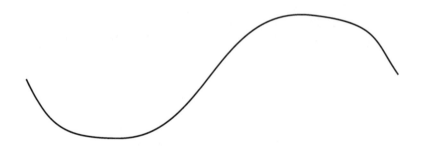

This curve "sums up the story of life itself."[11] We "start slowly, experimentally, and falteringly; we wax and then we wane."[12]

The authors of *Rekindling Commitment* give a much less poetic rendering of the same life cycle for the business firm:

> First, there is a period of inner development, slow growth as the system develops a new idea. . . . After its founding, an organization can experience fast growth and development, as it exploits the results of its innovative product or service. But after the period of fast growth every living system, from people to organizations, reaches a period of maturing, in which growth slows. Organizations at this developmental stage predictably become set in their ways and lose the ability to innovate and respond to the marketplace. . . . The product can no longer be

refined or fixed enough in order to compete; or the way a group works is no longer efficient enough to beat the competition, or everyone feels they are getting stale and exhausted without any really new ideas or innovations. . . . The only possible ending for a system that does not have a major change is decline, or even death.[13]

Handy and the authors of *Rekindling Commitment* and others who use this developmental picture employ it for the purpose of arguing for the need for the organization to make a decisive change before it is too late to avert the looming decline in the s-curve. For Handy the lesson is to initiate the change at point A in the curve rather than point B:

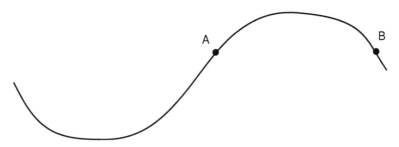

What makes it difficult to initiate change at point A is that "all the messages coming through to the individual or the institution are that everything is fine, that it would be folly to change when the current recipes are working so well."[14] Nevertheless, point B is obviously too late when the pink slip has already been received or the market already lost. Consequently, "Wise are they who start the second curve at point A because that is the . . . way to build a new future while maintaining the present."[15]

Those who have the wisdom that Handy counsels will possess the "discipline of the second curve." To the inevitable question of how far one is along the first curve, they are willing to entertain the answer of farther along than has been heretofore admitted. The "discipline of the second curve requires that you always assume that you are near the peak of the first curve, at point A, and should therefore be starting to prepare for the second."[16] The assumption may turn out wrong and the first curve may be prolongable, but nothing will be lost by exploring the need for the second curve. The "discipline of the second curve keeps one sceptical, curious, and inventive—attitudes essential in a time of change . . . "[17]

Organizations "should assume that their present strategies will need to be replaced within two or three years and that their product life cycles are shorter than they were."[18] However: "What is true of organizations is true of individuals and their relationships. A good life is probably a succession of second curves, started before the risk curve fades."[19] Consequently, individuals "should also work on the assumption that a new direction will be needed in two or three years."[20]

Abandonment and the Threat of Lost Employability

The discipline of Handy's second curve counsels "that the past may not be the best guide to the future, that there can be another way, and that some 'myths of the future' . . . will help."[21] However, he also counsels that we must "be wary that we do not abandon the first curve too early," since the "second curve needs the resources and time that only the first curve can provide."[22] The picture is, once again, similar to the earlier discussion of the worker portfolio, one of balance, only this time struck between the continuity with the past and the innovations of the future.

Drucker's picture of the same process, at least on the organizational level, is, by contrast, one of much greater discontinuity. If "society, community, family are all conserving institutions," the "organization of the post-capitalist society of organizations is a **destabilizer**."[23] The innovation required by such organization can only be produced, according to Drucker, by what Joseph Schumpeter has termed "creative destruction."[24]

The difference in Drucker's accentuation on constant upset, disorganization, and destabilization is accounted for by the great emphasis he places on planned abandonment rather than the *Kaizen* of continual improvement that both he and Handy share. The difference is felt most in the time point that both place as neccesary for the initiation of the dramatic change. For Handy the point is at the near **endpoint** of an upswell of impressive first curve growth. For Drucker, by contrast, it is at the very **beginning point** when the product is first introduced, the policy enacted, the practice initiated. Planned abandonment in this sense is for him clearly the most important goal in a threefold process of innovation that also includes continual improvement.

Drucker makes a strong case that his timetable of planned abandonment and innovation represents the better business strategy for maintaining corporate performance capacity in the face of strong competition from other lean firms. The crucial issue for the correlative individual technology of the self—indeed perhaps the most crucial issue in this book—is whether the flexible planning of employability has to adhere to the same timetable for preserving and enhancing employability rather than the more gradual sigmoid curve of Handy. In other words, is the most prudent strategy of the worker to plan the "abandonment" of the job position even when she or he is first starting the job?

If an intense competitiveness also exists for the employee in regard to employment that extends not only to the present position but any future job promotion, demotion, or loss, then Drucker's counsel to plan at once for being a maker of the genuinely new product or a provider of the truly innovative service appears to be as compelling for the individual as it is for the company. Indeed the contemporary economic technology of the self appears to dictate the assumption of this attitude of planned job abandonment for fear of the loss of competitive employability for the future.

The implications of the assumption of this kind of worker strategy are, in my estimation, enormous. To plan to leave an employment position as soon as it is begun entails that the employee view her or his work in just as non-permanent terms as the company does. It is a job to be kept as long as one has to. However, it can't be kept too long or the job will be "abandoned" by the company or maybe its career "half-life" will even expire altogether.

The present job cannot be a fixation; future options cannot be neglected or, worse yet, closed off; employability can, must, and will have to be maintained. The worker who is judiciously concerned about the future does not plan on staying on the job for too long. She or he will not get too committed to the organization or the fellow workers, but will be a Bridgean "external vendor." But above all the present position will not be thought of solely as an asset; it could quickly become—and may even already be—a liability. It might be impeding the development of new skills or at least the right skills which will be crucial in the obtaining of the next round of employment.

The present job offers employment "until further notice." That notice can either come from the company or oneself. Notice coming from the company is bad, but notice from oneself need not be catastrophic. Rather it can offer an opportunity to latch onto a new product line or be the provider of a new service.

The real fear is that of inadequacy when the notice comes. The paradox is that at the very moment when present adequacy is demonstrated by the beginning of the job stint, the fear of future inadequacy has already commenced. The internal distance required by Bridge's external-vendor attitude is intensified and extended. There is the real fear of being unable to secure the future employment position one needs, wants, and/or aspires to. And beyond the fear of never reaching the peak, there is the fear of being unable to stay on it, should one make it.

As Zygmunt Bauman expresses it, the "fear of uncertainty has been reforged into the fear of personal self-forming ineptitude."[25] There is the fear of growing rusty or stale at the job. The worry of being stuck in a dead-end or at least non-progressing post. The peculiarly contemporary anxiety of becoming overspecialized for the market. The deep-seated dread of becoming perhaps irreparably out of date or falling behind the technological juggernaut.[26]

Neither employment nor skills can be accumulated and saved. Jobs, "formerly seen as being 'for life,' are more often than not merely temporary, and may even disappear virtually without notice, together with the factories or offices of bank branches that offered them."[27] "Trades and professions . . . have acquired the confusing habit of appearing from nowhere and vanishing without notice," while "the demand for the skills needed to practice such professions seldom lasts as long as the time needed to acquire them."[28] Perhaps most crucially, "what is vaunted and recommended and hammered home today is treated with disdain tomorrow—that is if still remembered."[29] The resumé cannot be predicted reliably in advance or even beyond the present employ.

The result of all this uncertainty and fear of inadequacy is a further addition to, and intensification of, Buchmann's transition from past commitment to the adaptation to present circumstances. In addition to this transition, there is the transition from commitment to present employment to the preservation of present employability. Crucial to the maintenance of this all important capability is a vigilance toward not putting one's employability at risk. As Bauman analyzes this transition in even more general terms,

> In such a world it is wise and prudent not to make long-term plans or invest in the distant future (one can never guess what the attractiveness of the presently seductive goals or the value of today's assets will then be); not to get tied down too firmly to any particular place, group of people, cause, even an image of oneself, lest one find oneself not just unanchored and drifting but without an anchor altogether; to be guided in today's choices not by the wish to **control** the future but by the reluctance to **mortgage** it. . . . To be free to move when opportunity knocks. To be free to leave when it stops knocking.[30]

According to this strategy of life planning, it "is just the ability not to stand still that counts."[31] That ability comes from having present employ**ability** which becomes strongly prioritized in importance over what the present employ**ment** actually is. Indeed the present job no longer appears to function as either a link in a solid chain or as a strand in a flexible cable. Rather the job history now looks more like a collection of happenings or, in Bauman's terminology, of "episodes." Such episodes are characterized thusly: "each with a beginning and an end but with neither pre-history or future; that there is little or no logical connection between the episodes, even their succession looking suspiciously although purely coincidental, contingent and random; and that much as they come from nowhere, episodes go by and away without leaving lasting consequences."[32]

Photographic Album and Videotape Cassette

The interpretation just put forward regarding individual employment planning is quite different in both tone and content from what Drucker has in mind in proposing the strategy of planned abandonment for companies. For Drucker the ability of the company to stimulate and even indeed to plan innovation will allow it to survive and perhaps even thrive in the future. Planned abandonment is indeed an effective means of planning for the organization which will allow it to control its future in ways that other companies will not be able to.

Bauman's claim concerning the life planning of the individual, by contrast, is that being "prudent and provident, thinking of the future, become ever more difficult."[33] The basis for the claim and this difficulty is "the overall tendency to dismantle, deregulate, dissipate the once solid and relatively lasting frames in which life-concerns and efforts of most individuals were inscribed."[34] For Bauman the focus is not on planned abandonment, but rather on what the individual has been forced to abandon, a "lasting frame" of past commitment and future control. Thus the abandonment of a potentially dead end position, **even if planned**, signals the weakening of individual planning that occurs under the new circumstances: "'to be provident' means now more often than not to **avoid commitment**" for the sake of keeping the future open.[35]

Bauman relies on Paul Valéry in claiming that the modern individual is "intoxicated by energy," "besotted by haste":

> It does not matter so much what is being done and what targets are chased; what does matter is that whatever is being done be done quickly, and that the chased targets escape capture, move and keep moving. To be "intoxicated with energy" means to be intoxicated with the **ability** to move and act, not with any particular work to be done or particular destination to be reached.[36]

The concentration on the ability to move and keep moving carries with it an ambivalence which is already familiar from the discussions of destandardized work histories and relationships in Part Two. Bauman designates this ambivalence in terms of horror and allurement: "The horror of the new situation is that all diligent work of construction may prove to be in vain; its allurement is the fact of not being bound by past trials, being never irrevocably defeated, always 'keeping the options open.'"[37] The horror aspect, as applied to the struggle for employability, carries with it a distancing from and a relegation of the present work position which may of course not "work out" or be the "right move." The allurement comes from not being defeated by these possibilities or even confined by their limitations, as one stays "on pace" or even still "on the fast track."

The weakening of the life planning comes both from a game-like attitude which is assumed toward the events and a splitting up of the game into smaller episodes: "a sensibly played game of life calls for the splitting of one big all-embracing game with huge stakes into a series of brief and narrow games with small ones."[38] The key advice is "to take care that the consequences of the game do not outlive the game itself, and to renounce responsibility for such consequences as do."[39] The past is no longer to bear on the present, indeed the previous lasting frame is to be cut off from both ends, which had earlier served to "fix" the present. As stated earlier, "there is no more 'forward' and 'backward'; it is just the ability not to stand still that counts."[40]

According to Bauman's metaphorics, the medium of the lasting frame was that of photographic paper which can be used only once and with no second chance. The major vehicle for expressing the lastingness of that frame was the family album: "Think of the family album, filled with yellowing portraits of grand- and great-grandfathers and mothers, innumerable aunts and uncles, all with a name attached, **all counting and to be reckoned with**, all adding their stones to the castle of the slowly accumulating family tradition, in which no part can be taken away or eradicated, in which everything is for better or worse—forever."[41] The new medium of the highly mobile present is videotape, "eminently erasable and reusable, calculated not to hold anything forever, admitting today's events solely on condition of effacing yesterday's ones, oozing the message of universal 'until-further-noticeness' of everything worthy of recording."[42]

The medium of the album conveys the lasting frame of the secure individual among other secure individuals, each with their standardized histories. They "count and are to be reckoned with," because they have also been able to plan with long perspectives and reckon with the assistance of the insurance state. The financial stability of the framework allows for if not the building of a castle then the affording of a family home. And the album both goes back for generations and yet reads forward as a narrative of increasing material success and progressive financial and planning security.

The medium of the videotape, by contrast, has a quite different story to tell. That story is one of novelty commensurate to the new technology it introduces, but also, according to Bauman, a novelty permeated by "until-further-noticeness." What the technology allows for is, as the advertisement (for photography, actually!) says, "to capture the moments of our lives." But the immediacy and the spontaneity of the moments can wane, and then new moments can be recorded over them. Rather than accumulating, they are erased over; or, if accumulated, they do not fit easily into any larger constellation analogous to the family album.

Families can and do have both cameras and videorecorders. But if not the moments but the family fortunes wane, probably the first item to go in the garage sale or to repossession will be the videorecorder. The last item to be parted with, in any case, will be the family album. But if anything has to be sold at all, a new frame of reference will enter into the viewing of that family album. The garage sale will in no way represent an anticipated shift from comparative plenty to want as experienced by the hard-working family depicted in the Rowntree quotations at the beginning of the century. Moreover, the sense of "until further notice" will preclude any anticipation of a re- reversal of the shift toward plenty anytime soon. As argued by Bauman, the secure framework of the standardized past no longer will remain. The sense of personal control will be lost in the struggle not to mortgage the family album and family dreams. A videotape "gap" will intrude into the past chain or cable of family employment history.

11

The New Insecurity

In Part Three a multitude of metaphors—chains and cables, portfolios, photography and videotape—have all been introduced in order to encapsulate different individual strategies for dealing with the impermanence of employment and uncertainty about the future. The first group of these metaphors, elaborated on in the first chapter of this section, were presented as modifications of standard career strategies in line with the new demands of composite and portfolio careers. By contrast, the thesis of an at least partial destandardization of modern lives, first introduced in Part Two, was illustrated in a dramatic way through Zygmunt Bauman's metaphorics of videotape. According to it, the intensified individual initiative now demanded in work and relationships is shot through with the sense of "until further notice." This sense pervades the struggle to preserve employability in the present without the past guarantees of secure employment. Moreover, a different kind of fear, more personal in nature, was also introduced in the immediately preceding chapter. That fear of self-forming ineptitude was meant to capture the individual feelings of inadequacy that are likely to arise while planning under such uncertain and highly competitive conditions.

In this chapter the struggle for employability and the fear of inadequacy are brought together in a more comprehensive argument about their effects on life planning. The argument claims that there is a "new insecurity" in individual life planning and that this analysis of adaptability to the present should succeed earlier social criticism of present adaptability in terms of conformity and assimilation. The new insecurity may take any or all of three powerful forms which are explained in the first three sections of this chapter. First, there is the fear for the preservation of employability in a time where having employability is more important than being employed. Second, there is the more personally felt fear of inadequacy, or incompetence, in being able to be the highly skilled planning office that appears to be more necessary now than ever. Finally, there is even the anxiety about the futility of life planning at all in light of past lack of success and frustration produced so far.

The fourth and final section of this chapter relates each of the three forms of insecurity to Bridges' and Handy's strategies for preserving security in a period of discontinuous change. While pointing out the significant merits that composite work cables and multifaceted portfolios possess, the concluding section indicates occasions where concern for employability and the fear of inadequacy show up in spite of these strategies. The conclusion of the section—and of the larger argument of the chapter as a whole—is that any one of the challenges alone or any combination together is sufficient evidence that a quite different kind of insecurity is manifest in the life planning of individuals today and characterizes their adaptation to destandardized circumstances.

The Firm Commander of the Past and the Flexible Worker of the Present

Part One began the genealogy of the secure individual and all the deliberations on economic strategies that followed with descriptions of the disciplined body of Foucault's *militaire* and of the constant mind of Oestreich's steadfast commander. According to Bauman, this beginning point was quite appropriate given that under "modern conditions human individuals were constructed mainly as **producers/soldiers**; that is, the roles of producers and soldiers, which all or most were meant to perform and for which they were groomed, supplied between themselves the main patterns and the criteria of evaluation serving the formation of individuals."[1] The genealogy of the secure individual was a historical narrative of the liberal initiation of social insurance and assistance programs with which and upon which such producers/soldiers could plan. Later on, the blue-collar workers and white-collar middle managers whose fates were presented and discussed were the descendants of Oestreich's standing army of soldiers and sitting army of bureaucrats.

For the factory worker or manager, the job history of the bygone era of company loyalty described in Part Two may have been a brief "I was an A" or "I worked for A, Inc." In Part Three the job planning suggestions of Bridges' cable and Handy's altered sigmoid curve amend the narrative significantly to read "I was an A then a B then a C" in a work with many, but not too many, highly interrelated chapters of varying, but not too varying, lengths. The job history of the successful "job abandoner" described in the immediately previous chapter does not necessarily have any more segments; however, this history differs from all the others insofar as employability is preserved by getting out of A and then B and then C **at the right time**.

The maneuverability of present employability is something to be sought after and preserved at all costs in the work history of Bauman's "videotape" era. The flexibility of erasability afforded by the videotape conveys a quite different goal from the unequivocal decision to fight in the religious wars which was made by Lipsius's Neostoic commander in Part One.[2] Fight, don't flee was the counsel given then; flee, don't stay—or at least don't stay too long—the advice given now.

The technology of the self of the resolute military commander was based on the attainment of constancy, a firmness of mind and a concentration of energy focused on staying the course and not deviating from it. The figurative "mother" of constancy was an attitude of patience and quietness of mind in the face of public evils like war, pestilence, famine, tyranny, and massacres. Such patience and constancy were both the virtues and the requirements of the military life of the *miles perpetuus*, a term Lipsius coined for the lifetime soldier.

Of course such self-discipline was not the particular province of the soldier alone. As seen above, the state bureaucrat should also be constant. The lifetime worker as well. Work, don't be idle was the correlative technology of self-discipline and frugality of the hard worker to match that of the steadfast soldier.

Now, however, the military is downsizing even as business is, and the mass movements of large armies are replaced by the

precise interventions of single weapon systems and the technological development of "smart" weapons. And at least the retirement pensions of the lifetime military are argued to be a drag
on the efforts to balance the national budget.

In a period when the employability of the soldier is no
more permanent than that of the industrial worker, constancy
could be the wrong strategy, a bad move in a game of employment preservation that is being played with constantly changing rules and with characteristically incomplete information.
Rather than constancy, the strategy of "until further notice"
extends itself to the depth of the social relationships made at
work, the temporal commitment devoted to the present job,
and to the personal assessment of the job's value. The present
job is not permanent or at least cannot be responsibly viewed
as permanent, and the next job cannot be reliably predicted or
even necessarily expected. Consequently, it is more important
not to compromise or foreshorten employability for when change,
either self-initiated or otherwise, almost inevitably will come.

Unlike the period of producers/soldiers, fitness now stands,
in Bauman's estimation, "for the individual's bodily and spiritual
capacity to absorb, and creatively respond to, a growing volume
of new experience, ability to withstand a fast pace of change,
and ability to 'keep on course' through self-monitoring and cor-
recting the inadequacies of performance."[3] However, in this instance, staying the course refers primarily to the challenges of
private life and the private "evils" of unemployment and divorce
or, even more dire, unemployability and unmarriageability. If the
technology of the self of the firm commander of the past confronted the public evils of the time, the new technology of the self
exhibited by the flexible worker of the present seeks to avoid the
private evil at all costs. The new virtue of necessity for this
technology of the self is the tenacity to move and keep moving,
to escape the "capture" of unemployability. "I am a downsizing
survivor" or, as the English put it, "I have avoided redundancy."

The employment content in the work history no longer
counts for so much when the premium is placed so strongly on
not mortgaging the future. For the downsizing survivor, A, B,
C, et al. no longer function as "chapters" of a life stage. Rather
they are "episodes" which attest to the "until-further-noticeness"
of employment. The fact of employment is superseded in importance by the ability to move and the struggle for the more
necessary employability.

The priority of employability over employment creates the insecurity of shortened temporal horizons for the new life planner. It is difficult both to ask the question—"If I did not do this already, would I go into it now, knowing what I now know?"— and then to do something if the answer turns out negative. However, even more insecurity is caused by the intensified uncertainty as to the right strategy for preserving employability in the present. Past employment wisdom has lost its currency and no new formula has taken its place. The flexible worker may choose to stay, but can't stay for too long. Job training will probably help, but may not pay off at all. The struggle grows more difficult as one grows older and less capable of change. In all these ways, the struggle for employability functions as perhaps the largest source of individual insecurity in a destandardized world.

The Era of Company Loyalty as a Time of Secure Planning

"Do not build on the good old days, but on the bad new ones" is a quote attributed to Bertold Brecht by Walter Benjamin. For an earlier generation of social theorists and critics, the era of company loyalty was a bad new day and justifiably so. In a new time with its new uncertainties and pressures, the era starts to look different and to be quite open to reassessment. However this alteration in the focus of social criticism is once again because of the need to criticize new bad days far more than the inclination to celebrate past good ones.

For an earlier generation of social criticism, the employment of the loyal employee joined with roles in the family, politics, and consumption to form the world of "total administration" characteristic of "one-dimensional" society. Politics of the era were criticized above all because of the non-resistance to fascism by the "totalitarian personality" or the "mass individual" or the "outer-directed personality." Consumption was dominated by the effects of "hidden persuaders" upon *homo advertisus* and by the viewing habits of large audiences stimulated by the "mass entertainment industry." If advertising and entertainment produced "euphoria in unhappiness," a similarly uneasy sense of comfort was also said to pervade the routinization of marriage between the breadwinning "organization man" and the homemaking wife-consumer of hi-tech kitchen gadgetry. Thus the exhibition of uncritical company loyalty took its place as only part of the larger phenomenon of mass conformity and individual assimilation.

However, a new generation of social criticism now faces new "bad days" which also have the effect of putting the past era of loyalty and security in an entirely new light. Thirty years ago, the life planning entailed by Handy's first job offer, which acted as a stimulus for all the reflections in Part Two, was primarily a matter of fitting in the clearly demarcated career pathway and being loyal to the company by being a good employee. Now, however, this era has been replaced by a new regime of individual initiative and corporate support. In this period of new economic realities, the emphasis falls primarily upon individual initiative and the efforts of the employee to preserve employability within the company and elsewhere. Hence, adaptability to present circumstances no longer means conforming and being assimilated, but rather having to plan the future without guarantees in highly uncertain and even more highly competitive circumstances. There is *The Fear of Falling* (Ehrenreich) out of the middle class or the prospects of *Falling from Grace* (Newman) of sizable, stable earnings.

The previous generation now appears not so much as a quagmire of conformity but rather as a period of life planning security. According to Katherine Newman in another of her books, *Declining Fortunes*, life planning for that generation of Americans could be encapsulated in the following precepts: "Hard work leads to success; living close to the margins is a recipe for disaster; caution is better than taking risks."[4] For new generations of life planners, however, these precepts and the conservative strategies they exemplify no longer guarantee success:

> Our economy has grown increasingly more fragile, buffeted by forces we barely understand and cannot seem to control. With every day that goes by, these unseen hands seem to interfere more and more in our most intimate decisions: when to marry, when to have children, where to live, how easily we can remain close to our extended families, whether we will be able to enjoy our sunset years or will have to fret over every dime. . . . Decisions that were once left to the vagaries of emotion are now calculated down to the last nickel; risks that could once be taken in education or career are now out of the question. . . . in truth, being careful and making all the right choices is no guarantee that the future will work out well.[5]

Being cautious and simply fitting in do not always pan out today, for the reasons that were explained in the remainder of Part Two on company and employee flexibility. If companies must improve continually, so must their core employees. However, the new accumulation of multiple skills does not necessarily guarantee employment beyond the application of these skills in the present work position. The effects of job compression are at work in regard to both the outdating of work qualifications and even the usefulness of past work history and employment training. The period of potentially high employment earnings constricts for core employees to approximately the time they turn fifty. Even worse off are the situations of subcontractors and part-time or temporary workers who occupy the positions of the other two leaves in Handy's shamrock and may not experience any high earnings at all.

Under these new circumstances of job insecurity and intensified life planning, the earlier era of company loyalty will not be lamented for the uncritical assimilation that undoubtedly took place. Rather the long-term temporal frameworks of the career ladders which were offered many will be envied by those caught up in the struggle for preserving their employability. Adaptability to the present now means for them the continual coming to terms with uncertainty in their lives. The fears they experience while planning for the future in the face of the "new realities" are the "bad new days" which cause them to see the old days so differently.

The fear of inadequacy is familiar from the discussion of the fear of not mortgaging the future in the previous chapter. This fear begins with the threat of the ultimate loss of employability, and that kind of fear probably remains its most prevalent form. This is the fear that has also already been documented and described by Ehrenreich and Newman as the fear of "falling" or falling from "grace." It is the individual fear of *The End of Work* which is the subjective correlate to the larger structural changes that Rifkin describes. It is finally the fear of which Tracy Chapman sings even more dramatically and compellingly in terms of a "cold blue light" shining down in the sleep of the subcity resident.

However, the fear of inadequacy may also take an even more personally directed form. The experience of being downsized or being reengineered out of the company or being outdated or simply being unnecessary may also lead to Bauman's "fear of self-forming ineptitude." Such fear is that of not measuring up to the new competitive conditions. The perception is one of being insufficiently able to be the individual planner which the contemporary technology of the self obliges one to be.[6] Perhaps most damagingly, it produces the sense of individual failure which so often follows upon unwanted economic news.

The individual planning office can no longer plan its work history with the confidence it once had when promises of career employment were more readily made. However, the planning office is very likely to hold itself just as responsible for its self-perceived failures and shortcomings when the company breaks off its ties. The bad news is taken as proof for the ineptitude that is perceived simply to have to have been there. If only I would have planned better, if only I **could** plan better— so begin the personal recriminations in the "bad new days" of insecurity which now look so different from the "good old days" of company loyalty.[7]

The Planning Office in Question

The third challenge is much more indirectly expressed, if indeed it is expressed at all. It is motivated by an anxiety not only about being employed or keeping employability, but about planning itself and its ultimate usefulness. There is a possible fear that not only is my planning inadequate but planning itself is no longer helpful. There is doubt that the life planning that has been so important and useful in the era of the secure individual will "deliver the goods" in the way that it once did in a period of permanent employment.

The planning office we must be, as quoted from Beck in the introduction, is required "on pain of permanent disadvantage." "Living on automatic pilot," to return to Giddens' phrase, simply produces an unacceptably high amount of contingency and unpredictability. The "highly structured occupational trajectories" of Buchmann, on the other hand, are supposed to produce "well-defined timetables" and highly sequenced, lifelong trajectories. If, however, the highly structured trajectory has gaps in it of work or non-work episodes that are unplanned and may even be interpreted in terms of personal failure, then the difference between structure and nonstructure in destandardized work lives is no longer so clear. It is perhaps even uncertain that the highly planned and the decidedly unplanned work histories will be all that different; instead they may be similarly—depressingly—chaotic.

The erasability of the videotape work episode bespeaks its "until-further-noticeness," its potentially limitless revisability. This "episodic" character contrasts strongly with the "chapters" of employment in earlier work histories, and not only in regard to the prioritizing of employability over employment. There is also the further matter of the game-like character of the episodes, as described by Bauman in the previous chapter.

Bauman contrasts a strategy of "floating" with that of "fixing." As he remarks in regard to floating, "In this strategy, insecurity is escaped rather than fought, in the hope that security may be found, at a lesser cost and with less onerous an effort, elsewhere."[8] The strategy is one "of 'cutting one's losses,' of 'not throwing good money after bad,' of giving up trying and looking elsewhere for another try once the gains seem to have fallen below the level of expenses needed to secure them."[9] In regard to employability and the putting together of a work history, the strategy involves the assuming of a game-like posture and the splitting up of the big "all-embracing" game into "brief and narrow" games with smaller stakes.

To turn employment into a game and then break the game into smaller ones is a way to keep moving and avoid being caught—avoid being "fixed"—in a dead end situation. The attraction of the floating strategy is the way it keeps the options open and avoids the very threatening feeling of foreclosure. However, many of the smaller games offer real possibilities of non-work or underemployment. Moreover it is by no means clear how small these game episodes will actually turn out to be. Consequently the "allurement" of open options may be clearly outweighed by the "horror" of the destandardized situation; namely that "all the diligent work of construction" has indeed proven to be "in vain."

To experience work in a game-like way may thus be an invitation to undergo in an even more tangible way the frustration of not having what earlier generations had. Future games lose their appeal, when the immediately preceding ones turn out so badly. Disappointment, if not failure threatens, and the individual advantage of the life planning of the modern planning office appears to be no longer guaranteed as it once was. What good, then, after all is the diligent work of planning in the first place?

Life Planning Shift

The third form of uncertainty is, in my estimation, probably unlikely given the dangers of not planning at all, but
certainly the anxieties of the first level concerning loss of employability and perhaps the self-recriminations of the second
concerning one's planning capabilities are not. The individual
who is fearful for the fate of one's employability, or indeed
fearful of one's adequacy as a modern planning office at all, or
even fearful of the worth of planning itself, is not in a position
to feel that she or he controls the future that is being planned.
Consequently each of these three fears—the fear for preserving
employability, the fear of one's inadequacy as a life planner,
and the fear of the futility of life planning itself—is so powerful
that, either alone or in tandem with the others, it is a strong
basis for maintaining that the previously secure individual is
no longer secure in the planning of one's life.

Nevertheless, the composite career from Bridges and the
worker portfolio of Handy do deserve to be taken seriously as
interesting and complementary technologies of the self for coping with the perplexing difficulties in life planning today. Both
offer strategies, and very good strategies at that, for maintaining continuity in individual planning and living during a period
when being cautious and fitting in do not always pan out.
However, either strategy alone or the two in combination are
still, in my view, insufficient to overcome all the sources of
insecurity that have come about in the encounter of individual
planning with the challenges of the new economic realities.

Bridges' promotion of the stance of the external vendor
counsels the worker to adopt an attitude of being outside of
and independent from the company. Yet in doing independent
work for other firms in what Piore described as a "porous"
business network, the employee is not actually so much **outside** the company as occupying multiple positions **inside** the
larger and more significant network of firms. Consequently, the
multiple strands of the composite career offer the promise of
security for those fortunate to be so positioned, or multipositioned, inside growing or at least stable multifirm networks.

Handy's worker portfolio is also a savvy strategy of adaptation for dealing with the compression of jobs and the loss of
permanent employment. Even a composite career faces the
problem posed by the peripheral position of leaves two and

three in Handy's shamrock. Portfolio thinking allows for the integration of periods of part-time work, subcontracting, and study during the primary period of employment and for the meaningfulness of volunteer work when the effects of job compression kick in.

Both strategies work at the level of employment to make it, although of course in no way permanent, still continue to have many of the same features of security that the earlier permanent job possessed. Consequently both strategies, while sound, are vulnerable when and if considerations of employability enter and threaten to gain the ascendancy in priority over employment itself. If Bridges' cable gets its ultimate strength from the larger outside network of firms within which the employee is multiply positioned, those who are not so positioned will be far more concerned about their employability than secure in their present employment. If Handy's portfolio offers the "chance to shape our work to suit the way we want to live instead of always living to fit in with our work," the fear of the real loss of employability is that there will not actually be the high value work either to shape or even to fit in with.

Where the strategies of Bridges and Handy can be easily and successfully implemented, the "LifePlanningShift," to modify the title of Bridges' book, may appear to be less threatening and consequential. Otherwise, however, the concern for one's employability finds expression in the fear of inadequacy and, more particularly, the fear of personal self-forming ineptitude described in the previous chapter. There is the worry that there will be, to return to the mixed metaphor at the end of the last chapter, an unanticipated videotape "gap" of indeterminate length in the network cable. Indeed, given the fears of intense job competition, of being laid off due to downsizing, and of becoming outdated in one's qualifications, there is the worry that there will be not just one gap but several, or one exceedingly long and painful gap that threatens to outlengthen the cable itself. Even present composite employment or multifaceted portfolio involvement loses priority to the struggle to keep or even simply to have options that preserve employability.

In addition, there is the even deeper-seated anxiety that there will be strong personal self-forming ineptitude in the worker portfolio. The role of life planning should be to eliminate the gaps in the history and promote individual and family progress, but if these are exceedingly difficult goals to accomplish, then the fear of ineptitude may spread to the life planning itself. The fear is one, as Bauman expresses it, not of deviance from the norm, but of disfunctionality or incapability in a situation without the earlier promises of company loyalty and clear career pathways.[10] Such disfunctionality or incapability does not come about because of lack of docility or determination, but rather because of the lack of a qualification or ability which really could not be anticipated or planned. Nevertheless, the individual is responsible—or holds herself or himself responsible—for the inability either to maintain employment or to anticipate the need for another job transition that produces the unwanted gap in the planned strategy.

The presence of many gaps or even just one painfully long one may even challenge the very worth of life planning itself. Especially for the laid off worker toward the end of her or his work history, the frustration multiplies from having to start over again. Even as a game, the need to make another change both grows old and wears thin. It is not the way things were supposed to work out or the way things worked in the past. It is certainly not the way it was planned.

The struggle for employability is not simply a transient phenomenon that appears likely to disappear soon. For the individuals who must work in the destandardized context of the new economic realities, the real prospect of prolonged periods of under- or unemployment and retraining is the most personal, the most daunting, and the most powerful implication of the "LifePlanningShift" they face. Nor is the fear of inadequacy simply an individual phenomenon attributable to the lack of nerve or the absence of personal responsibility. No wonder workers of today no longer feel secure when they compare their situations to earlier forms of lifetime career promises and envy the expectability of success of earlier generations they know. The looming prospects of "the end of work" have both larger social significance in terms of accelerated change and instability and definite personal impact in terms of insecurity as well. The destandardization of work is in no way the peculiar fate of any individual, but more and more characteristic of the population as a whole.

12

The Prospects of the Secure Individual

According to the argument of the last chapter, social criticism is beginning and should continue to look at the employment of individuals differently than in the past. Adaptability to present conditions no longer means the comfort of career conformity but the insecurity of having no larger enterprise to be loyal to or to be assimilated by. There is the struggle for employability because continued employment is no longer promised. Personal planning ineptitude is to be feared, because factories leave, jobs become outdated, and firms become leaner and meaner. Even the value of planning is put into question as large gaps of unemployment or underemployment in the past threaten to make a mockery of the planning in the present.

This final chapter relates this description of "the new insecurity" to the liberal social security mechanisms described in Part One. According to that section, these social security mechanisms were instrumental in the producing of secure individuals who could plan with the rationality of social insurance and plan upon the reliability of governmental assistance. However, according to the description of the new insecurity, the secure individual produced by these social security mechanisms may well be no longer secure due to the struggle for employability, the fear of personal ineptitude, and the frustrations of life planning. What, then, are the present prospects for individual security—and for the social security mechanisms which originally helped to produce it?

The examination of these questions in this chapter begins with an "end" of community loyalty on the part of companies similar to the earlier "end" of company loyalty in Part Two. The purpose once again is not to pursue the theme for its own sake, but for its correlation to an individual form of conduct, in this case the ascendancy of the taxpayer role in contemporary political discussion. A dynamic of taxpayer opposition will be described, both as it is particularly aimed at what are perceived to be "spongers" and as it spills over with general ramifications for all forms of public funding.

The next section presents what is probably—at least initially—a most implausible connection between the taxpayer in ascendancy and the interviewees of Ruth Sidel's study whom she termed New American dreamers. Both undeniably adhere to strong beliefs concerning the importance of independence and the value of individualism. But the argument put forward in this section is that the taxpayer in opposition to taxes is also similar to the adolescent dreamer in a third way; namely, in the strong belief in standing by oneself because one has to. This sense of isolation should be incorporated, it is argued, into a threefold political perspective which includes a fear of insecurity in addition to the perspectives of individualism and independence. This fear is not understood in terms of personal failing or weakness, but rather in terms of widespread uncertainties resulting from the destandardization in employment and marriage described in Part Two.

The recognition of a broad-based fear of insecurity rooted in no longer standard jobs and families could open a quite different perspective toward the mechanisms of social security than the dynamics of taxpayer opposition. Theda Skocpol argues for the wisdom of this perspective in proposing modifications in and additions to the traditional programs of social insurance. In reaction to problems of family security, she proposes a "family buffering program." This program will be examined for its own merits in the third and final section of the chapter, but even more as a springboard for the exploration of another kind of program designed to help offset the destandardization of employment. A major problem caused by this destandardization has been described (in mixed metaphors, assuredly) as the presence of one or more videotape gaps in the employment cable history. The general idea of income assistance will be introduced as a way of alleviating the impact of these gaps and thus avoiding financial instability and turbulence.

The End of Community Loyalty and the Birth of Taxpayer Opposition

One final parallel between the new economic realities of larger business and the strategies of individual life planning allows for and even encourages a more political dimension to enter into the discussion of the possibly no longer secure individual. Not only the old social contract between the large company and the loyal employee has been put in doubt by unannounced and unanticipated mass layoffs. Community loyalty has been put in doubt as well, as factories and major offices make surprise closings of their facilities in communities they have long-standing ties with and then reopen in new areas.

Not by choice but under the pressure of global competition and the potential loss of market position, "business is on the lookout for any means of cutting expenses, including business taxes."[1] Communities who are "hungry for economic stability have traded corporate tax breaks for jobs"[2] in their courting of new factories and offices to locate in their areas. Many companies have taken advantage of such competition to bargain hard for valuable tax concessions and relocate in such hungry communities. The old communities, which relied heavily on these tax revenues in the past, lose out through the closings in terms of both jobs and lost revenues. The communities that win, on the other hand, also realize that the victories are not likely to be as long-term as in the past and that they may be subject to new concessions at later times. Thus the new social contract between company and community, similar to the new contract with the employee, very much appears to be no longer a matter of past commitment but rather till disadvantage do us part.

Individual taxpayers for their part are not rushing to offset the losses in revenue incurred by the tax concessions. Rather they are seeking with the same determination—and arguably the same sense of necessity—to lessen their own tax burdens. As incomes do not increase and even decline and as jobs are lost by economic restructuring and corporate reengineering, the value of the amount of taxes paid increases and the imperative to reduce the tax burden grows urgent. There is the danger, according to Bauman, that "we confront the community, common needs and common causes solely in the capacity of taxpayers,"[3] that we recast communal action "from the pledge of the individual's security it used to be, into the individual's burden and bane; an extra load to carry, adding little to one's personal weal, yet something one cannot, regrettably, easily shake off though one would dearly like to."[4]

There comes into play in this dynamic a kind of political core-periphery distinction which is different from the economic distinction which has been spoken of so much. The political distinction is roughly similar to the one referred to passingly in the discussion of Lubove's critical questions on the future of social security in Part One; namely, between the socially insured employed and the unemployable outside it. According to Bauman, the contemporary form taken by this distinction is between the taxpayer and the "sponger" who does not work but still "takes advantage of" unemployment assistance, health care, food stamps, and/or family assistance. The "political realities" in this instance are quite different from the economic ones, since the numbers are in no way on the side of the periphery: "as the numbers of those who give money overtake the numbers of those deprived of value, the fate of the 'spongers' is sealed. Their claims and grievances have every chance of being voted off the agenda . . ."[5] The "political realities" of taxpayer opposition can and do succeed against the perceived laxities of spongers.

The dynamics of taxpayer opposition not only affect the issues of welfare assistance but all aspects of public funding. As Bauman explains with primary reference to his English context:

> It is only natural that the taxpayer wants to pay less taxes. (Just as a beast of burden wants the burden to be smaller.) The outcome is, of course, that the quality of services collectively provided slides down a steep slope. . . . If we can, we buy ourselves individually out of the underprovided, shabby schools, the overcrowded, undernourished hospitals, the miserly state old-age pensions—as we have already bought ourselves, with consequences which most of us belatedly bewail, out of the shrinking and wilting public transport. The more we do so, the more reasons we have for doing it, as the schools grow shabbier, the hospital queues longer, and old-age provisions more miserly still; and the fewer reasons we see to make sacrifices for the sake of those who failed to follow our suit.[6]

The Adult Taxpayer and the Young Adolescent Dreamer

The explanation Bauman provides for the ascendancy of the taxpayer role fueling the opposition to sponging and to general public funding allots a prominent role to the loss of individual security: "The weaker and less reliable are the guarantees of individual security communally offered, the less justified and more burdensome seem the communal claims for joint effort and sacrifice."[7] The natural rallying cry is "no new taxes." No new program, whatever its merits, should be funded now and whatever program now being funded should be funded in the future at lower levels. Old programs have allegedly "failed" and new programs offer no better chances for being successful.

But have the programs of collective insurance and social assistance failed? Or has the nature of the risks and emergencies changed? Did the rationality of social insurance and the protection of social assistance not work to reduce insecurity when the secure individual (which is of course quite different from saying all individuals) had the prospects of permanent employment and marriage was more so? Is it not in fact the change in the expectation of these stabilities which has brought the dissatisfaction with the political programs which were based on them?

The ascendancy of the taxpayer role in political debates and elections stands in a curious similarity to the planning of the New American Dreamer described by Ruth Sidel in Part Two. Both adhere to the desire for independence and both subscribe to a strong belief in individualism. But both also count on either getting or keeping economic success to such a degree that it not only provides economic security but even compensates for the loss of expectations for the job and family future and for the lack of social support available to the individual. The adult taxpayer, like the adolescent dreamer of Sidel's study, in part stands by oneself because one has to: "the new spirit is sceptical about the possible uses and benefits of acting together, joining forces, holding hands; and resigned to the idea that whatever you want to achieve, you had better look to your own cunning and ingenuity as the principal resources."[8] A sense of isolation joins the desire for autonomy and the affirmation of individualism in motivating the ascendancy of taxpayer concern.

How capable is the framework of taxpayer opposition by itself of coping with and alleviating such fear of isolation? From the taxpayer framework of the political contract, "it is no more a question of our shared responsibility for, and collective insurance against, everyone's mishap and misfortune—but a question of how much it will cost me to provide for those who cannot provide for themselves."[9] But the question then inevitably arises how certain am I that I will be able to provide for myself alone without the past communal and political bases of collective security to rely on?

The brute fact of the matter is that my guarantee that I can provide for myself is no stronger that the assurances I have of employability. However, there is no core-periphery distinction between taxpayer and sponger concerning the loss of permanence of jobs, and no distinction concerning the unexpectability of permanent marriage either. Rather these developments are sources of real fear of inadequacy as has been described in the previous two chapters. The fears of losing employability and lacking marriageability are in no way confined to the periphery alone—either economically or politically. Rather they extend to a whole population having to adjust with flexibility to the "new economic realities" of destandardized work and family lives.

The sense of isolation and fear of inadequacy cannot be overcome or compensated for by the other elements of individualism and independence. In spite of the great value of both of these latter elements, the one time secure individual stands on the brink of being no longer secure in regard to life planning. The difficult political challenge is to admit this fact and make it the basis for a threefold political perspective including the fear of insecurity rather than a twofold formula of individualism and independence alone.

The inclusion of a fear of inadequacy in a threefold perspective need not be dismissed as a sign of either lack of independence or individual failure. Rather it can be interpreted as an appropriate reaction to the destandardized work history with its real prospects for prolonged periods of under- or unemployment and retraining. Such destandardization, it has been argued, is not peculiar to the individual, but more and more characteristic of the population as a whole. A recognition of that fact can open up a different vantage point toward the collective endeavor to provide social insurance and social protection described in Part One than that of the taxpayer's concern for costs and burdens alone.

The roots of taxpayer opposition are admittedly real, indeed so real that they probably affect most of us. They reflect true burdens "attributable to higher bites from payroll taxes, the effects of inflation and bracket creep on federal income taxes, and increases in state and local taxes."[10] Indeed there has been since the 1970s a definite "pincers effect on blue-collar and middle-income white-collar workers and their families" which is explainable in terms of flat or "declining real income combined with a rising tax burden that appeared to yield no tangible benefits."[11]

Nevertheless, the individual security afforded by the rationality of social insurance and the protection of social assistance has also been valuable to the individual. In fact, according to Theda Skocpol, while the concern for tax burdens is undoubtedly real, it is equally true that "Americans are happy enough to take benefits from the government when they are widely distributed and mesh well with private interests."[12] The meshing has allowed those fortunate enough to be secure individuals to plan their future with confidence and without the fear that some unforeseen emergency would cause irreparable damage. Moreover social security has also been helping the poor by not targeting them as a welfare group, but benefitting them at levels above their contributions in regard to retirement, Medicare, disability, unemployment, and survivor's insurance.[13]

Now individuals are fearful for the permanence of their jobs and the real value of their employability. The loss of job permanence has impeded the planning with of the secure individual who planned with job security and social insurance in order to be able to withstand the difficulties of an admittedly uncertain but still overall stable work future. The loss of expectation of permanent marriage has similarly compromised the social supports of family, neighborhood, and community the secure individual could plan upon in looking toward the future. The recognition of these new insecurities could result in a wider public openness not simply to defend social insurance programs against taxpayer opposition, but to change them in accordance with the most pressing individual concerns we now have.

Family Buffering and Income Assistance

The lastingness of the collective endeavor to provide security ought to be reaffirmed on moral grounds of past commitment, on community grounds of social relationship, and on grounds of egalitarian social justice. But collective endeavor is also needed because of individual concern as well, in particular the life planning need of the individual to preserve the collective insurance against her or his own mishap and misfortune. Insofar as destandardization is becoming, almost paradoxically, more and more "standard" with respect to job and family, the insecurity that is experienced in life planning becomes more and more similar in its scope to the earlier fears of physical disability, premature death of spouse, and old age indigency which prompted the social insurance programs described in Part One.

Skocpol proposes a "family security program" which modifies the present programs of social insurance and assistance in ways that pertain directly to the pressing individual insecurities involved in the planning of work and family. The first individual concern she identifies is that of "making employment sustainable along with parenthood."[14] As she states, "both dual-parent and single-parent families . . . need help with the growing challenges of balancing parenting and work outside the home."[15] Paid parental leave and tax credits for child care are proposed as appropriate means to "buffer families from the extra stresses of childbirth or adoption or to help them find and finance adequate child care while both parents work."[16]

For single custodial parents the most crucial part of the program would be a policy of "child support assurance." This assurance would require all absent parents to pay proportions of their wages as child support through an automatic program of wage withholding. Support would come from the government and "would nearly equal the amounts collected from absent parents, except when the monies were not collected or fell below a minimum benefit needed to raise children, in which case the custodial parent would get the minimum payment from public funds."[17] The minimum payment "would not disappear as soon as the mother went to work."[18]

The second concern identified by Skocpol is even more relevant to the emphasis on economic insecurity in this book.

That concern, as she expresses it, is "help for all adults who are looking for jobs." The help she envisions takes the form of a "federally run labor market system." Such a market would "identify jobs and areas of the country where new workers are needed," "provide transitional unemployment benefits and perhaps housing subsidies," and, quite importantly, "train or retrain people to help match their skills to available jobs."[19]

Skocpol successfully identifies the two concerns which are brought into prominence by the conditions of destandardization and consequently puts forward a comprehensive program for restoring individual family and work security. However, there is still an issue whether the concern for economic security is sufficiently addressed by a program of transitional unemployment benefits and job retraining. Earlier forms of social insurance, similar to Skocpol's proposal, were geared, quite naturally so, to the expectation of full-time and permanent employment. Now, however, full-time employment, especially on the periphery, may no longer be so crucial and, in almost all cases, lacks in the permanency it once had. If such permanency of employment is no longer likely, then the preservation of individual employability may have to take its place—not just as the "second best" goal but as the most appropriate strategy to adopt in light of the new economic "realities."

What individuals who are engaged in the economic competition for today's jobs need is assistance in the struggle to preserve employability. They fear for their ability to control the future because they fear a real and imminent danger of losing their present income and suffering a precipitous and perhaps irreversible loss of funds. Those who find themselves located on the periphery (or worse, not located at all) fear that control of the future has already been lost. All fear the videotape gap of unemployment or at least underemployment in the desired for cable of continuous employment history.

Programs of job training and retraining are needed to prevent the one or more gaps of un- or underemployment from becoming even longer. But some direct form of universal income assistance may be needed as well to deal with the new kind of transition from plenty to comparative want which the contemporary successors to Rowntree's laborer family are experiencing. Programs proposing either (1) a guaranteed basic income, or (2) a participation income, or (3) a social insurance program of income buffering could offset, in varying degrees, the strong fluctuations in earnings that today's job histories are prone to. Moreover, they would not substitute for individual choice in life planning, but on the contrary would maintain its active possibility by lessening the impact of radical job transitions.

The different nuances of the three alternatives for income assistance, their positive consequences for alleviating income fluctuation and turbulence, and their various responses to the taxpayer concern for free-riding and sponging will all be examined in the following Appendix. However, should there already be an openness and a willingness to consider them as well as Skocpol's proposed policies for family buffering? The history of collective insurance is that it has worked in the past for those who, from today's point of view, must appear blessed to have had permanent jobs and stable marriages. However, if these programs do not change, the individual will stand by herself and himself not only in regard to job and family responsibilities, but also in regard to possibly wild fluctuations in income from un- and underemployment gaps in the employment cable.

The admission of a sense of isolation and a fear of inadequacy need not paralyze the other components of individual autonomy and individualism which come more to the fore in the taxpayer stance of concern. But without the appropriately sober, non-hysterical recognition of the new fears of insecurity we face regarding job and family and the accompanying alteration of the present programs of collective security to accommodate them, we will no longer be able to plan either our economic or social futures with confidence. Programs of income assistance and family buffering may well offer the best possibility of protecting ourselves against the worst consequences of these new insecurities. It is up to us to take them seriously.

Appendix: Three Proposals for Income Assistance

The final chapter of this book argues that conditions which lead to the new insecurity of destandardized employment could at the same time lead to a new willingness to examine programs of income assistance. In particular, the lack of standard job expectations of permanency makes urgent the problem of videotape gaps in the employment history cable. The individual facing the new economic realities of unemployment must fear strong fluctuations in income and even the possibility of a long-standing gap or, as in this chapter, a near permanent "pothole." Consequently, there should be a public openness to the idea of a mechanism to buffer income and prevent the wild fluctuations in earnings that are likely in the new employment histories and struggles for employability.

This appendix introduces and compares three different kinds of income assistance programs. However, the comparisons are undertaken with a quite limited set of objectives. My objectives are: 1) to introduce the three different programs of a guaranteed basic income, a participation income, and a social insurance program of income buffering; 2) to explain their respective merits with regard to addressing the problems of no longer standard job and family lives; and 3) to explore how each proposal is able to respond to the powerful objection described in the previous chapter in terms of the taxpayer opposition to spongers.

The carrying out of these objectives, even if successful, in no way constitutes a full-blown discussion of the public policy of income assistance or even the establishment of a firm policy recommendation. Nevertheless, what has not yet been contributed fully to the discussion of this public policy is precisely the value that programs of income assistance could have in coping with the sorts of life planning insecurity and income instability which more and more of us are having to face. Nor have answers to taxpayers' concerns about free-riding and sponging always been forthcoming in sufficient detail. In these regards, this appendix is useful if it can plug some important gaps and fill a few deep potholes, even if it is not the whole answer itself.

The Firm Floor of a Basic Income

The meaning of the title of a central book in Part Two, *The End of Work*, is explained by Jeremy Rifkin when he states that, after "centuries of defining human worth in strictly 'productive' terms," the "high-tech global economy is moving beyond the mass worker" and leaving her or him "without self-definition or societal function."[1] He puts forward these claims in order to argue for a fundamentally quite different "end of work" than the simple threat of the loss of employment. Rather, he argues for the end of work as the sole determinant of income and for its replacement/displacement by "some kind of government guaranteed income" for those who have been permanently displaced by automation and by the reengineering of their previous companies and organizations.

A government guaranteed income is a nearly complete solution to both the struggle for employability and the fear of personal planning inadequacy which characterize the new insecurity. At the same time, however, the guarantee of a basic income entails truly fundamental changes in the very bases of economic functioning, individual planning, and even human worth.

According to Philippe Van Parijs, a "basic income is an income unconditionally paid to all on an individual basis, without means test or work requirement."[2] It is paid "irrespective of any income from other sources" and, much more controversially, "without requiring any present or past work performance, or the willingness to accept a job if offered."[3] In Van Parijs' words, it involves "the replacement of the safety net, in which the weakest and the unlucky get trapped, by a firm unconditional floor, on which they can securely stand . . ."[4]

The individual recipient of a basic income stands securely on a firm floor because of the "decommodification" brought about regarding her or his work. According to Gøsta Esping-Andersen,

> To understand the concept, decommodification should not be confused with the complete eradication of labor as a commodity; it is not an issue of all or nothing. Rather, the concept refers to the degree to which individuals, or families, can uphold a socially acceptable standard of living independently of market participation.[5]

What matters is the introduction of schemes that permit individuals "to be paid while pursuing activities other than working, be they child-bearing, family responsibilities, re-education, organizational activities, or even leisure."[6]

With the decommodification provided by the guarantee of a basic income, "individuals could go through repeated and protracted periods in which their activities earned them less than a subsistence wage—for example, as they retrained between two jobs, as they learnt new skills on the job, as they kept old skills alive in a period of reduced professional activity, as they launched new businesses, and so on."[7] According to Guy Standing, people would have "real choices between high-income/high-work and lower-income/lower-work options."[8] A basic income would "encourage self-employment" and "reduce the stigma of unemployment, while dispensing with the situation whereby, for many, benefits are paid **only** if they remain idle (unemployed)."[9] It would also "avoid the inflexible institution of 'retirement' and arbitrary notions of retirement age, while enabling the elderly to avoid the unfairness of 'earning rules' that determine receipt of state pensions."[10] According to Beck and Beck-Gernsheim, it would even: "slow down the roundabout forcing people to decide in favour of their jobs and against their families. At least there would be a place to try out living together."[11]

For all these reasons, discontinuity in employment and change in job and family status would no longer be as feared as they are now. According to Claus Offe, "the option of discontinuous participation in employment would cease to be considered second best . . . and would instead be seen as the most-preferred alternative—even under conditions where full employment was thought to be feasible."[12] The burden of full-time and lifelong employment would be loosened in favor of "a significantly reduced share of lifetime in employed work for the average person."[13] The recipient of the government guaranteed basic income would want to live the portfolio life as described by Handy but without the need for Bridge's employment cable. Therefore, it is easy to see how the idea of a firm unconditional floor of an adequate and secure income is highly appealing to the life planner involved in a struggle to maintain employability and fearful of personal inadequacy.

An Income for Participation?

The great heat generated by controversies concerning the economic impact and political feasibility of a guaranteed basic income has overshadowed the even more intriguing issues concerning its impact on human worth. If the individual is freed from dependence upon the pressures of the market through such a program, she or he is also loosened from identification with paid work in terms of her or his personal identity. In a society which begins its process of socialization with the question "What are you going to be when you grow up?" and the expectation of an occupation as the answer, the response of "recipient of a basic income" is at least initially neither particularly socially or personally informative.

Offe recognizes the great change that the implementation of a basic income would entail in the definition of human worth when he argues for a displacement of the measurement of that worth from employment in paid occupations to participation in "useful activities." He argues that "Extensive co-operative and other institutional forms of non-wage labour outside formal employment must be experimentally developed in order to expose the near-monopoly that the institutional arrangement of formal employment holds over the universe of useful human activities in competition with alternative modes of 'getting things done.'"[14] Important human skills and untapped personal potential could be exploited in "useful activities, alone and in co-operation with others, that are normally underutilized in employment in general and in unemployment in particular."[15] The distinction drawn by Handy in his own portfolio life between a core of employment responsibilities and a periphery of useful activities could thereby be deconstructed according to

Offe. Regarding the formation of personal identity, homework, gift work, and study work could hold equal pride of place to wage and fee work in a life no longer dominated by the struggle to achieve financial subsistence.

Offe's proposal for the revaluation of "useful activities" vis-á-vis the social recognition given paid labor has two important applications. Not only does it clarify the largest, most challenging, and most intriguing ramifications which would be brought about by the introduction of a basic income, but it also opens the perspective for discussion of another alternative, but related, form of income assistance. By far the most controversial aspect of the basic wage proposal is the unconditionality of the benefit. What if the benefit were not unconditional, but it was also not premised on paid labor employment either? What if instead the benefit were made conditional upon involvement in useful activities as they have been broadly defined by Offe, or by participation in any of the core **and** peripheral forms of work enumerated by Handy?

In an interesting address on the Beveridge Plan fifty years after, A.B. Atkinson proposes the idea of a "participation income." Such an income would be offered to any individual not unconditionally, but dependent upon her or his participation on grounds of: "work as an employee or self-employed, reaching pension age, inability to work on grounds of disability, unemployment but available for work, engaging in approved forms of education or training, caring for young, elderly or disabled dependants, undertaking approved forms of voluntary work, etc."[16]

The proposal of a participation income is not presented as an alternative to present programs of social insurance, but as a complement to them. In addition, the "participation income" proposed by Atkinson would not overturn popular support for the conditionality of public assistance. However, it displaces the conditionality from participation understood in terms of paid economic employment to a larger definition of making a useful social contribition. Anyone who contributes in this larger sense of doing useful work would also be protected in view of their contribution. The level of protection could vary, dependent of course on whether only small or major changes are made in the taxation schema, from a safety net level (£18.25 per week) to something quite approximative of Van Parijs' firm floor (between £37 and £39 a week).[17] At the latter level of support, the participation income would provide most of the same benefits to the newly insecure life planner as those of the guaranteed basic income explained above.

Income Buffering

Less developed than either the proposal for a guaranteed basic income or even Atkinson's proposal for a participation income are the basic ideas for a social insurance program of income buffering. Nevertheless, William Bridges does write in *Jobshift* of the need for "some kind of income buffering" which "is going to be necessary, especially during the difficult period during which jobs are being replaced by kinds of work that are much more like self-employment."[18]

Income buffering addresses the problem of the videotape gaps (or in Bridges' language, "income potholes") in the work cable. At a more modest level of assistance, it would lessen the effects of wild swings in income. At the more ambitious level as Bridges envisions, it consists "of a variable payout that would keep relatively constant the level of disposable income under circumstances where earnings fluctuate."[19] He argues in regard to the need for this concept: "We need to detach such support from the idea that it is a 'jobless benefit.' Most people are going to be jobless. This benefit is, rather, an income supplement to buffer the drops in income that the self-employed are prone to."[20]

The mechanism by which the funding for such buffering would be accumulated is not described in great detail. One part includes at least partial self-funding for most individuals. It could take the form of "an 'account' into which deposits are put during good times and from which they are withdrawn during hard times" or alternatively the "deposited money" might be "better spent purchasing 'income subsidy insurance' from a private carrier."[21] The rest of the funding would come in the form of a governmental income subsidy to provide for "temporary support when income levels fall, as they must in the dejobbed world."[22]

Such subsidies would go in effect at higher income levels only "during those rare times when all earning stopped." In middle income ranges, the subsidies would fill the videotape gaps/income "potholes" and help ameliorate the otherwise strong fluctuations in earnings. At lower income levels, they "would constitute a constant supplement to (but never replacement for) what was being earned"[23] in the part-time and temporary work characteristic of Handy's third leaf in the shamrock. According to Bridges, "the real need is for a system that would both subsidize those at the bottom of the income ladder and encourage them to keep working and earning."[24] That of course, is the same goal of social protection that the liberal proponents of social insurance and social protection also had in mind in designing the first programs of social insurance and later extending the benefits at proportionately higher levels to the lowest groups of contributors.

What is striking about the proposal for income buffering is not its difference but rather its similarity to Bridges' earlier proposals concerning the composite career and the situating of the employee within a multiple and porous network of firms. The promise of security issues in this instance from being not singly positioned but multipositioned in the network of work. The proposal of income subsidy coupled with employee self-funding expands the network further to include the government and allows for one more opportunity for multipositioning, only this time with a buffering function. For those without such porous networks to begin with or those navigating their way between positions, it could prove to be the most important position of all by helping them both to achieve the re-employment that they strive for and to protect their families from economic turbulence and emergency.

Responding to Taxpayer Fear and Suspicion

My only aim in discussing opposition to programs of income assistance will be to discuss the one crucial objection they all share in various forms. As explained in the final chapter, the taxpayer who feels more and more forced to "stand by oneself" has a difficult time with those who are perceived to fail to do so. Programs of income assistance have no choice but to deal with the charge of helping undeserving free-riders or spongers.

The charge of sponging is raised most strongly and passionately against the basic income proposal, even if the charge reappears in reformulated terms against the other proposals as well. Relating directly to the dynamics of taxpayer opposition and the appellation of "spongers," the objection attacks the unconditionality of the benefit of a sizable basic income. In an atmosphere of debate in the 1960s and early 1970s on the proposal of a guaranteed income in which, according to Senator Daniel Moynihan, "it was not likely that as many as a dozen U.S. Senators understood the subject,"[25] Senator Russell Long was understood when he said that the "objection is paying people not to work." Similar to the present polemic against welfare, there was a "rising objection to people who lay about all day making love and producing illegitimate babies."[26]

Both the present polemic on welfare and the earlier political discussion on guaranteed income reflect the bifurcation beween welfare and social security analyzed by Theda Skocpol and referred to earlier at the end of Part One of this book. Essential to that bifurcation and to these debates is a strong distinction between contributors—those who work and pay into social programs—and non-contributors. If support is felt at all for the latter, then it is certainly extended only to those who truly are unable to contribute. Anyone else is and, according to the argument, deserves to be called a "sponger."

The unconditionality of the guarantee of a basic income represents a full frontal assault against the dynamics of taxpayer opposition and the bifurcation between welfare and social security. It attacks the distinction between contributors and non-contributors both in regard to participation (or non-participation) in the labor force and in regards to payment (or non-payment) into programs of social insurance. Consequently, the most passionate objection against the introduction of a basic income is "that it would amount to an institutionalization of free-riding, to the exploitation of hard workers by those able-bodied people who would choose to live on their basic incomes."[27]

Atkinson's proposal of a participation income avoids the stigma of the original "sponger" label which is so readily given by the burdened taxpayer to the unconditional recipient of a guaranteed income who is not disabled. By moving the main consideration from distinguishing between contributors and non-contributors to the differentiation between participation and non-participation, the idea of a participation income thus defuses some of the most passionate and vociferous opposition to the idea of income assistance. However, the proposal is still open, unfortunately, to objection on grounds recognizably similar to the original "sponger" charge.

Crucial to Atkinson's (and Offe's) core idea is a larger notion of social contribution than one measured in terms of paid work. Gift work, homework, and study work, to use Handy's terms, are rightly seen as important activities, and to participate in such work is to make an important social contribution worthy of financial assistance. But the sponger-related argument counters that community service and beautification, child and elderly care and house cleaning, and job retraining and vocational re-education, even if socially useful, are not "real work" and that their forms of participation are not "real jobs." Only the participant in a "real job" who does "real work"—paid labor—is, so according to the new extension of the argument, not in fact a "sponger."

The fecundity (if not the virulence) of the sponger argument is a clear indication of the strength of resistance there is to the implementation of any form of income assistance. Indeed the social insurance system of income buffering is also not immune from its attack. The form the attack takes in this instance is a perhaps more attenuated one, but real nevertheless. The argument is probably best interpreted cross-generationally, in terms which pit the relatively secure past against the unpredictable present. The cross-generational comparison begins with generations who have reliably worked and contributed to their social insurance programs. These "hard-working" generations have the opportunity to contrast themselves with the alleged lack of direction, confusion, indecisiveness, if not immaturity of the present-day members of "Generation X." Any new form of income buffering which might help members of this generation cope with the new, discontinuous economic realities they face must stand therefore under yet another form of suspicion of coddling the non-contributor. The contemporary "slacker" is, then, yet another reincarnation of the sponger according to the truly omnipresent anti-sponger suspicion.

However, if the argument of the previous chapters is correct, the new insecurity and its attendant fear of personal inadequacy are in no way confined in their effects to the members of Generation X. More importantly, the so-called indecision and lack of direction of the "slacker" may represent instead very real and necessary re-adjustments in life planning brought about by new challenges in the struggle for employability. The fluctuations of keeping moving may not be acts of personal irresponsibility, but rather express the adoption of the right strategy of not mortgaging the future and keeping the options open. Indeed the main cross-generational comparison may and ought not to be between the hard-working past and the irresponsible present, but rather between the long-range and clearly defined career trajectories of an era of the photographic album and the episodic contrasts in an era of videotape in which the struggle for employability has replaced and displaced the earlier certainty of employment.

Consequently, the proposal of a social insurance program has resources within itself for responding cogently to its form of the sponger attack. Because of its nature as a social insurance program, it also avoids the most forcible form of the same argument which is advanced stridently against the idea of an unconditional and guaranteed basic income. If the objection of free-riding was raised against a guaranteed income earlier in times of relative economic security when the idea of a basic income was first debated, it is certain to be urged now with greater tenacity and even ferocity when there appears to be such an overwhelming need to have to stand alone. In an atmosphere in which welfare programs involving means testing are being transformed into workfare programs, the proposal of a guaranteed basic income, whatever its merits, has much less a chance for success than the reversal of this trend or tide.

As for the relationship of the social insurance proposal to the proposal for a participation income, that may be a more complicated story about potentially complementary responses to taxpayer worry and work insecurity. A social insurance program of income buffering also avoids the form of sponger argument based on "real jobs" and "real employment" which may be employed against the income participation scheme. But the focus on paid employment may not be appropriate for the nature of the new economic realities we face, as both Handy and Offe realize for their own very different reasons. A "significantly reduced share of lifetime in employed work" may be the fate that the average person living the "portfolio" life is going to have to face now and will continue to have to confront in the future. If this diagnosis of the present and future is accurate, then the broadening of economic valuation to include socially useful activities is desirable and the privileging of "real jobs" is best understood as a bias from a more secure past.

The social insurance program of income buffering ought not to be conceived primarily as an alternative to a participation income scheme. Rather it is a possible steppingstone to the implementation of such a larger program of economic assistance based upon participation in socially useful activities. The social insurance program offers the first line of defense against both the fear and the suspicion of free-riding and sponging. The participation income proposal represents the further program of income assistance which is the most appropriate for the new economic realities and may be the most worthy of the social insurance line of defense.

Notes

Preface

1. Since 1995 real family income may be increasing. For the argument that slower economic growth is not simply cyclical but structural and permanent, see *The End of Affluence* by Jeffrey Madrick (Random House: New York, 1995), above all chapter 3, "What We Lost."

2. Many of the sentences of this paragraph are taken almost directly from an article titled "Running Scared" by Robert Schmuhl, *Notre Dame Magazine* (Autumn 1995, p. 42).

3. Of course Americans are also afraid for their personal safety, the lives of their loved ones, and the security of their property. This quite different but equally important sense of insecurity is not addressed directly in this book.

4. "Marriageability" is to be understood with a very broad meaning beyond the limits of legal definition (in the same way that "employability" refers to being employed beyond the strict sense of market employment). What is struggled for is participation in a long-term personal and intimate relationship. It is also important to add what Ulrich Beck and Elisabeth Beck-Gernsheim point out in their book, *The Normal Chaos of Love* (Polity: Cambridge, 1994): "Using uniform terms such as family, marriage, parenthood, mother, father and so on disguises the growing diversity of the lives concealed behind them" (p. 15).

5. For a description of the structure of the insurance state in most industrial-era welfare states, see Nancy Fraser, "After the Family Wage: Gender Equity and the Welfare State," *Political Theory*, Vol. 22, No. 4, November 1994, pp. 591–2.

6. For a clarification of the different rationales for the implementation and for an explanation of the different accentuations in assistance each provides, see Part I, "The Three Welfare-State Regimes," from Gøsta Esping-Andersen, *The Three Worlds of Welfare Capitalism* (Princeton University Press: Princeton, 1990).

7. Paul Tough, Ronald Blackwell, Albert Dunlap, George Gilder, Edward Luttwak, Robert Reich, "Does America Still Work? On the turbulent energies of the new capitalism," *Harper's Magazine* (May 1996), p. 44.

8. Peter Drucker, *Post-Capitalist Society* (HarperBusiness: New York, 1993), p. 215.

Introduction

1. I will use the first person plural both in the context of this chapter on the standardization of life history and in later discussions on the secure individual. Concerning especially the latter context, Ian Craib has written an explanation of his use of the first person plural which is much better than I could do and very relevant to my purposes at the same time. This explanation appears in his *The importance of disappointment* (Routledge: London, 1994) and can be modified to fit my purposes completely simply by substituting "insecurity" for "disappointment":

> Who is this "we" I am talking about? Much of the time I am describing a normal human difficulty, so the "we" is everybody. However, perhaps these difficulties are more pronounced for some than others. By "we" I mean primarily people like myself. The social changes I am concerned with affect most strongly those who might once have been called "middle class": . . . those of us who have a comparatively uncertain future, reasonable levels of education, who range from the comfortably off to the comparatively poor, but who are not entirely trapped. There are many who do not fall into this category: there are those who have been consistently disappointed [insecure], whose life does not often rise much above a matter of day-to-day survival and who have little material out of which to form choices for the future. Such people might be in the majority—their existence, I suspect, acts as a permanent threat to those of us who try to avoid disappointment [insecurity]. (pp. 2–3)

2. Ulrich Beck, *Risk Society: Towards a New Modernity* (Sage Publications: London, 1992), p. 135.

3. Charles Handy, *The Age of Unreason* (Harvard Business School Press: Boston, 1990), p. 43.

4. Marlis Buchmann, *The Script of Life in Modern Society: Entry into Adulthood in a Changing World* (The University of Chicago Press: Chicago, 1989), p. 25.

5. Martin Kohli, "The World We Forgot: A Historical Review of the Life Course," *Later Life: The Social Psychology of Aging*, ed. Victor W. Marshall (Sage: Beverly Hills), p. 277.

6. John Kotre and Elizabeth Hall, *Seasons of Life: Our Dramatic Journey from Birth to Death* (Little, Brown and Company: Boston), p. 9.

7. Kohli, p. 278. Kohli explains that this change can be graphed interpreted statistically as a process of "rectangularization."

8. Ibid.

9. Ibid., p. 279.

10. All quotes are from "The State and the Structure of the Life Course," *Human Development and the Life Course: Multidisciplinary Perspectives*, eds. Aage Sorensen, L. Sherrod, and F. Weinert (Erlbaum: Hillsdale, N.J., 1986), pp. 232, 233.

11. See chapter Two, "The Social Clock," from Kotre and Hall and the references there to the research of Bernice Neugarten.

12. Beck, p. 131.

13. Ibid., pp. 130–31.

14. Buchmann, p. 18.

15. Beck, p. 130.

16. Ibid., p. 131.

17. Buchmann, p. 40.

18. Ibid., p. 31.

19. Ibid., p. 40.

20. Ibid.

21. Ibid.

22. Ibid.

23. Ibid., p. 41.

24. Beck, p. 135.

25. Ibid., p. 136.

26. Ulrich Beck, Anthony Giddens, and Scott Lash, *Reflexive Modernization: Politics, Tradition and Aesthetics in the Modern Social Order* (Stanford University Press: Stanford, 1994), p. 14.

27. Beck, 135.

28. Ibid., p. 90.

29. Ibid., p. 136.

30. Ibid., p. 131.

31. There is of course work of the greatest social theoretical significance and greatest practical urgency which gives priority not to individualized risk but to global or "manufactured" risks. Ulrich Beck's books, *Risk Society* and *Ecological Enlightenment*, are used in this study for their passages on individualization, employment, and family structure, but the primary theses of these books are about the importance of the risks of nuclear fission, radioactive and other forms of scientific waste, and other forms of environmental pollution and ecological neglect, and these theses simply must be considered in any larger account of modern risk. In a similar manner, Anthony Giddens has developed the leading social theoretical account of trust in modernity and related such trust to the risk of "manufactured" uncertainties in *The Consequences of Modernity*, *Modernity and Self-Identity*, and *Beyond Left and Right*. I emphasize that no priority is claimed for the sorts of privatized risks which this work takes up.

32. B.S. Rowntree, *Poverty: A Study of Town Life* (Macmillan and Co.: London, 1902), p. 137. Rowntree also notes that "the women are in poverty during the greater part of the period that they are bearing children" and provides this larger overview of the life cycle of the laborer:

> The life of a labourer is marked by five alternating periods of want and comparative plenty. During early childhood, unless his father is a skilled worker, he will probably be in poverty; this will last until he, or some of his brothers or sisters begin to earn money. . . . If he has saved enough to pay for furnishing a cottage, this period of prosperity may continue after marriage until he has two or three children when poverty will overtake him. This period of poverty will last perhaps for ten years, i.e. until the first child is fourteen years old and begins to earn wages. . . . The man enjoys another period of prosperity only to sink back again into poverty when his children have married and left him and he himself is too old to work, for his income has never permitted his saving enough for him and his wife to live upon for more than a very short time. (p. 136)

33. W.H. Beveridge, *The Pillars of Security* (Allen and Unwin: London, 1943), p. 60. Quoted in *The Dynamic of Welfare: The Welfare State and the Life Cycle*, ed. Jane Falkingham and John Hills (Prentice Hall/Harvester Wheatsheaf: Hertfordshire, 1995), p. 13.

34. "The Life Cycle: Public or Private Concern?" in *The Dynamic of Welfare*, p. 17.

35. Michel Foucault, *Michel Foucault: Politics, Philosophy, Culture: Interviews and Other Writings*, tr. Alan Sheridan and others, ed. Lawrence D. Kritzman (Routledge: New York, 1988), p. 160. For a discussion of the welfare state inspired by this aspect of Foucault's thought, see Nancy Fraser's description of a "Juridical-administrative-therapeutic state apparatus" in *Unruly Practices* (University of Minnesota Press: Minneapolis, 1989), pp. 154ff.

36. Ibid., p. 161.

37. The significance of "*The Foucault Effect*" can be readily seen in the appearance of a new volume of important essays written in its same spirit, *Foucault and Political Reason: Liberalism, Neo-liberalism and Rationalities of Government*, edited by Andrew Barry, Thomas Osborne, and Nikolas Rose (University of Chicago Press: Chicago, 1996). Especially important to the genealogy of the secure individual which is attempted here are the analyses of advanced liberalism by Nikolas Rose and Pat O'Malley. O'Malley observes a shift in the conception of risk from pathology or danger to opportunity within neo-liberalism, and both he and Rose describe the technique of neoliberal prudentialism—the privatization of risk management—which corresponds to this shift. While publication deadlines did not permit me the opportunity to incorporate these ideas in Part One of this book, I would wish to argue (1) that the collectivized form of risk management is not simply blamable for welfare dependency but rather equally responsible for much of the individual autonomy so emphasized by neo-liberalism and (2) that the "new economic realities" carry with them risks that are not solely opportunities but also threats and that these threats are inadequately addressed by prudentialism.

38. Colin Gordon, "Governmental rationality: an Introduction," *The Foucault Effect*, eds. Graham Burchell, Colin Gordon, and Peter Miller (The University of Chicago Press: Chicago, 1991), p. 20.

Chapter 1

1. "Is it really important to think? an interview with michel foucault," tr. Thomas Keenan, *Philosophy and Social Criticism* IX, 1 (spring 1982), p. 38. Quotation is not from the interview itself but

from an unpublished lecture, "Subjectivity and Truth," delivered at Dartmouth College, November 17, 1980.

2. Gerhard Oestreich, *Neostoicism and the Early Modern State*, eds. Brigitta Oestreich and H.G. Koenigsberger, tr. David McLintock (Cambridge University Press: Cambridge, 1982), p. 50.

3. Ibid. In a footnote to this sentence, Oestreich claims that a "discussion of modern militarism is fruitless without an account of the history of the relevant ideology."

4. Ibid., p. 75.

5. Ibid., p. 18.

6. Michel Foucault, *Technologies of the Self*, ed. Luther H. Martin, Huck Gutman, and Patrick H. Hutton (The University of Massachusetts Press: Amherst, 1988), p. 19.

7. Michel Foucault, *Discipline and Punish*, Alan Sheridan, trans. (Pantheon:New York, 1979), p. 168.

8. Ibid., p. 210.

9. Ibid., p. 152. Compare the discussion of rhythm with William H. McNeill's discussion of dance and drill in human history, *Keeping Together in Time* (Harvard University Press: Cambridge, 1995). In chapter 5, "Politics and War," McNeill compares Maurice of Orange's use of drill with the close-order drills of Ch'i Chi-kuang in China.

10. Ibid., p. 153.

11. Ibid., p. 158.

12. Ibid., p. 161.

13. Ibid., pp. 158–59.

14. Hubert Dreyfus and Paul Rabinow, *Michel Foucault: Beyond Structuralism and Hermeneutics*, Second Edition (University of Chicago Press: Chicago, 1983), p. 155.

15. *Discipline and Punish*, p. 146.

16. Ibid., p. 163.

17. Ibid., p. 164.

18. Ibid., p. 162.

19. Compare the following quotation from p. 166 of *Discipline and Punish*:

All the activity of the disciplined individual must be punctuated and sustained by injunctions whose efficacity rests on brevity and clarity; the order does not need to be explained or formulated; it must trigger off the required behavior and that is enough. From the master of discipline to him who is subjected to it the relation is one of signalization: it is a question not of understanding the injunction but of perceiving the signal and reacting to it immediately, according to a more or less artificial, prearranged code. Place the bodies in a little world of signals to each of which is attached a single, obligatory response: it is a technique of training, of *dressage*, that "despotically excludes in everything the least representation, and the smallest murmur"; the disciplined soldier "begins to obey whatever he is ordered to do; his obedience is prompt and blind; an appearance of indocility, the least delay would be a crime."

20. Ibid., p. 138.

21. Oestreich, p. 83.

22. Ibid., p. 78.

23. Ibid., p. 79.

24. Ibid.

25. McNeill points out the importance of the requirement of digging trenches as a way of banishing idleness for Maurice of Orange on p. 129.

26. Ibid., pp. 52–53.

27. Ibid., p. 54.

28. Ibid., p. 19.

29. Ibid., p. 23.

30. Ibid.

31. Ibid., p. 29.

32. Ibid.

33. Ibid., p. 55.

34. Ibid., p. 18.

35. All quotations are from ibid., p. 160.

36. Ibid., p. 30.

37. Ibid., pl 270.

38. Ibid., p. 68.

Chapter 2

1. Michel Foucault, *Politics, Philosophy, Culture: Interviews and Other Writings 1977–84*, ed. Lawrence D. Kritizman (Routledge: New York, 1988), p. 63.

2. Ibid., p. 69.

3. Ibid., p. 70.

4. "Foucault at the Collége de France II: A Course Summary," tr. James Bernauer, *Philosophy and Social Criticism* VIII, 3 (fall 1981), 356.

5. *Discipline and Punish*, p. 82.

6. Gordon, pp. 2–3.

7. *Philosophy, Politics, Culture*, p. 76.

8. Michel Foucault, *Power/Knowledge: Selected Interviews and Other Writings 1972–77*, ed. Colin Gordon, trs. Colin Gordon, Leo Marshall, John Mepham, Kate Soper (Pantheon Books: New York, 1980), p. 170.

9. Michel Foucault, "Governmentality," Burchell, Gordon, and Miller, p. 91.

10. Ibid., p. 92.

11. Ibid., p. 94.

12. Ibid., p. 92.

13. *Philosophy, Politics, Culture*, p. 79.

14. Gordon, p. 10.

15. Ibid., p. 12.

16. *Foucault: A Critical Introduction* (Continuum: New York, 1994), p. 121.

17. Ibid.

18. Gordon, p. 20.

19. Ibid., p. 25.

20. Oestreich, p. 156.

21. Ibid.

22. Ibid., p. 153.

23. Ibid., p. 157.

24. Ibid., p. 158.

25. Ibid., p. 157.

26. Ibid., p. 265.

27. Ibid., p. 265.

28. Ibid.

29. Ibid.

30. Both quotations are from "Governmentality," p. 99 and p. 100.

31. Ian Hacking, *The Taming of Chance* (Cambridge University Press: Cambridge, 1990), p. 7.

32. Ibid., p. 29.

33. Gerd Gigerenzer, Zeno Swijtink, Theodore Porter, Lorraine Daston, John Beatty, Lorenz Krüger, *The Empire of Chance* (Cambridge University Press: Cambridge, 1989), p. 62.

34. Hacking, p. 40.

35. Ibid., p. 107–8.

36. Ibid., p. 107.

37. Ibid., p. 118.

38. Ibid., p. 137.

39. Ibid., p. 160.

40. Ibid.

41. Ibid., p. 2.

42. Ibid., p. 1.

43. Ibid., p. 168.

44. Ibid., p. 178.

45. Ibid.

46. Ibid., p. 16n.

47. Compare also what the authors of *The Empire of Chance* have to say about the enumeration of statistical data and the implications this has on political assumptions:

> Statistics, as a numerical science of society, was from the beginning a part of nineteenth-century liberalism. . . . To count each individual for one had hardly been possible in

old-regime societies of estates and orders. But centralizing monarchs, assisted by bureaucracies, pursued precisely this flattening of the social landscape that straightforward enumeration implied, even if they were inclined to view the information obtained as a state secret. (EC, 68)

48. "Governmentality," p. 101.

49. Ibid., p. 100.

50. "Foucault at the Collége de France," p. 356.

51. Ibid.

52. Gordon, p. 15.

53. Ibid., p. 17.

54. Albert O. Hirschman, *The Passions and the Interests: Political Arguments for Capitalism before its Triumph* (Princeton University Press: Princeton, 1977) pp. 86–7. Quoted in Colin Gordon, "Afterword," *Power/Knowledge*, p. 249.

55. Gordon, p. 17.

56. Michel Foucault, "Space, Knowledge and Power," *The Foucault Reader*, ed. Paul Rabinow (Pantheon: New York, 1984), p. 242.

57. Ibid.

58. Ibid.

59. "Governmentality," p. 100.

60. Ibid.

61. Quoted in Gordon, p. 17, from a lecture delivered to the Collége de France, April 5, 1978.

62. Quoted in ibid.

63. Quoted in ibid., p. 19.

64. Ibid., p. 20.

65. Ibid.

66. "Foucault at the Collège de France I: A Course Summary," tr. James Bernauer, *Philosophy and Social Criticism* VIII, 2 (summer 1981), p. 241.

67. Ibid.

68. Gordon, p. 24.

69. Ibid., p. 20.

70. Ibid., p. 24.

71. Ibid., p. 20.

Chapter 3

1. Gordon, p. 355.

2. Ibid., p. 28.

3. Ibid., p. 35.

4. "Preface," *Readings in Social Security,* eds. William Haber and Wilbur J. Cohen (Prentice-Hall, Inc.: New York, 1948), p. v.

5. Daniel Defert, "'Popular life' and insurance technology," *The Foucault Effect,* p. 232.

6. Haber and Cohen, ibid.

7. François Ewald, "Insurance and Risk," *The Foucault Effect,* p. 199.

8. Ibid.

9. Ibid., p. 200.

10. Ewald, p. 202.

11. Ibid.

12. Ibid., p. 203.

13. Defert, p. 219.

14. Ibid.

15. Ewald, p. 204.

16. Quoted in Ewald, pp. 204–5.

17. Ibid., p. 209.

18. Ibid.

19. Defert, p. 211.

20. Ibid., p. 215.

21. Ewald, p. 207.

22. Ewald, p. 207.

23. I.M. Rubinow, *Social Insurance* (Henry Holt and Company: New York, 1916), p. 482.

24. John Myles, *Old Age in the Welfare State: The Political Economy of Public Pensions* (University Press of Kansas: Lawrence, 1989), p. 15.

25. Ibid.

26. Ibid.

27. Maurice Stack, "The Meaning of Social Security," *Readings in Social Security*, p. 46.

28. Gerhard A. Ritter, *Social Welfare in Germany and Britain: Origins and Development*, tr. Kim Traynor (Berg: Leamington Spa, 1986), p. 4.

29. Ibid., pp. 4, 47.

30. Ibid., p. 131.

31. Kohli, p. 288.

32. Ritter, p. 131.

33. Michael Freeden, *The New Liberalism: An Ideology of Social Reform* (Clarendon Press: Oxford, 1978), p. 206. According to Esping-Andersen, Barnett's type of distinction is characteristic of liberal welfare states in general, which tend to demand means testing in the offering of unemployment relief. Note also the discussion later in this chapter of the bifurcation in American social assistance between social insurance programs of Social Security and welfare programs involving means testing.

34. Ibid., p. 233.

35. Ibid., pp. 233–34.

36. Quoted in Freeden, p. 204.

37. Ibid., p. 236.

38. Ibid.

39. Quoted in Freeden, pp. 227–28.

40. Ibid., p. 228.

41. Quoted in Freeden, p. 236.

42. Gordon, p. 34.

43. Ibid.

44. François Ewald, *L'Etat providence* (Editions Bernard Grasset: Paris, 1986), pp. 407–15. I am indebted to Kevin Olson for this reference.

45. Ibid., p. 67.

46. Ewald, *L'Etat providence*, pp. 528–9. Again I am indebted to Kevin Olson for the reference.

47. Haber and Cohen, p. 72.

48. Stack, p. 53.

49. Ibid., p. 54.

50. Ibid.

51. Ibid.

52. Ibid., pp. 54–5.

53. Ibid., p. 55.

54. Ibid., p. 56.

55. Ibid., p. 57.

56. Ibid.

57. Ibid.

58. Quoted in Freeden, p. 237.

59. S. Fleming, quoted in Anne Hélène Gauthier, *The State and the Family: A Comparative Analysis of Family Policies in Industrialized Countries* (Clarendon Press: Oxford, 1996), p. 60. Gauthier's book as a whole is an excellent study of the historical phases of the development of family assistance and other forms of social security.

60. Theda Skocpol with Edwin Amenta, "Redefining the New Deal: World War II and the Development of Social Provision in the United States," *Social Policy in the United States* (Princeton University Press: Princeton, 1995), p. 168.

61. Skocpol, p. 31.

62. Roy Lubove, *The Struggle for Social Security* (Harvard University Press: Cambridge, 1968), p. 180.

63. For an excellent critique of the notion of welfare dependency, see "A Genealogy of 'Dependency': Tracing a Keyword of the U.S. Welfare State" by Linda Gordon and Nancy Fraser in Fraser's *Justice Interruptus* (Routledge: New York, 1997), pp. 121–49.

64. Skocpol's strategy is distinctive in the American context, but very standard in the more social democratic welfare regimes. See the discussions on "Stratification in Socialist Social Policy" and "The Social Democratization of Capitalism" in Esping-Andersen's *The Three Worlds of Welfare Capitalism*, pp. 65–69 and pp. 108–11 respectively.

65. Skocpol, p. 265.

66. Ibid., p. 264.

67. Ibid.

68. Ibid., p. 265.

Chapter 4

1. Gordon, p. 39.

2. Burchell, pp. 145.

3. Ibid., pp. 144–45.

4. Ewald, p. 207.

5. Anthony Giddens, *Modernity and Self-Identity: Self and Society in the Late Modern Age* (Stanford University Press: Stanford, 1991), p. 28.

6. Freeden, p. 236.

7. Ibid.

8. Giddens, p. 75. Giddens' claim can be compared with the emphasis which Thomas Ziehe places on "makeability"—"a demand and a capability to regard more and more things—like one's own or one's children's selves—as possible to shape and produce according to a project or a plan rather than as an outcome of natural developments or given traditions" (Quoted in *Cultural Theory & Late Modernity* by Johan Fornäs (Sage Publications: London, 1995), p. 45.

9. Ibid., pp. 75–6.

10. Ibid., p. 85.

11. Gerald Dworkin, "Paternalism," *Morality and the Law*, ed. Richard A. Wasserstrom (Wadsworth: Belmont, 1971), p. 120.

12. Ibid.

13. Ibid., pp. 122–23.

14. Giddens, p. 78.

15. Ibid., pp. 28–9.

16. Ibid., pp. 125–26.

17. Hacking, p. 34.

18. Myles, p. 45.

19. Giddens, p. 182.

Chapter 5

1. Guy Standing, "The Need for a New Social Consensus," *Arguing for Basic Income—Ethical Foundations for a Radical Reform*, ed. Philippe Van Parijs (Verso: London, 1992), pp. 54–55.

2. Charles Handy, *The Age of Paradox* (Harvard Business School Press: Boston, 1994), p. 286.

3. Charles Handy, *The Age of Unreason*, p. 6.

4. Ibid.

5. Ibid.

6. Ibid.

7. Dennis T. Jaffe, Cynthia D. Scott, Glenn R. Tobe, *Rekindling Commitment* (Jossey-Bass Publishers: San Francisco, 1994), xii.

8. Richard Edwards, *Contested Terrain: The Transformation of the Workplace in the Twentieth Century* (Basic Books: 1979), p. 181.

9. Ibid., pp. 142–43.

10. Ibid., p. 153.

11. Ibid., p. 21.

12. Ibid., p. 152.

13. Ibid., p. 151.

14. Ibid.; emphasis added.

15. Robert B. Reich, *The Work of Nations: Preparing Ourselves for 21st-Century Capitalism* (Alfred A. Knopf: New York, 1991), pp. 69–70.

16. Handy, p. 50.

17. Kotre and Hall, p. 289.

18. Peter Drucker, *Managing the Future: The 1990s and Beyond* (Truman Talley Books/Plume: New York, 1993), p. 132.

19. *New York Times*, Sunday, March 3, 1996, p. 14.

20. Kotre and Hall, p. 288.

21. Jules Henry, *Culture Against Man* (Vintage Books: New York, 1965), p. 30.

22. Kotre and Hall, p. 289.

23. *New York Times*, ibid.

24. Handy, p. 149.

25. David Harvey, *The Condition of Postmodernity: An Enquiry into the Origins of Cultural Change* (Basil Blackwell: Oxford, 1989), p. 155.

26. Stephen Wood, "The Transformation of Work," *The Transformation of Work*, ed. Stephen Wood (Unwyn Hyman: Boston, 1989), p. 13.

27. Reich, p. 83.

28. Jeremy Rifkin, *The End of Work: The Decline of the Global Labor Force and the Dawn of the Post-Market Era* (G.P. Putnam's Sons: New York, 1995), p. 5.

29. *Ibid.* The *New York Times* series makes the point more colorfully: "Behind every A.T.M. flutter the ghosts of three human tellers" (p. 16).

30. Ibid., p. 67.

31. Ibid., p. 204.

32. Ibid.

33. Ian Craib, *The importance of disappointment* (Routledge, London, 1994), p. 106.

34. Rifkin, pp. 103–4.

35. Ibid., p. 104.

36. Ibid., p. 105.

37. Stanley Aronowitz and William DiFazio, *The Jobless Future: Sci-Tech and the Dogma of Work* (University of Minnesota Press: Minneapolis, 1994), p. 4.

38. Rifkin, p. 145.

39. Henry, p. 37.

40. *New York Times*, ibid.

41. Rifkin, p. 91.

42. Ibid., p. 92.

43 Michael Hammer & James Champy, *Reengineering the Corporation: A Manifesto for Business Revolution* (HarperBusiness: New York, 1993), p. 38.

44. Rifkin, p. 103.

45. Ibid., pp. 6–7.

46. Hammer and Champy distinguish reengineering from downsizing which is considered just a fancy term "for reducing capacity to meet current, lower demand" (p. 48). For them, reengineering means "doing **more** with less." Michael J. Piore in *Beyond Individualism*

(Harvard University Press: Cambridge, 1995) makes a highly similar distinction that indicates at the same time the high stakes involved:

> One strategy is to create new, more flexible organizational and productive structures and use them to move up-market with more customized products, competing on the basis of quality and variety. . . . The other faction, however, would compete on the basis of cost alone, preserving much of the old organizational structure and many of the practices associated with it, but driving down cost through increased pressure on workers and suppliers and the squeezing of wages, commissions, and sub-contractor mark-ups. . . . Quality versus cost: the high road and the low road. (p. 78)

47. *New York Times*, ibid.

48. Rifkin, p. 7.

49. Handy, pp. 149–50.

50. Rifkin, p. 7.

51. Ibid., p. 101.

52. Handy, p. 136.

53. All quotes from ibid., p. 158.

54. Ibid., p. 159. For such an American example, the *New York Times* series pointed to Chase Manhattan: "Chase, in the lingo of human resources, no longer wants to be a parent to its employees. It wants to be their best friend." (Monday, March 4, 1996, p. A8)

55. Jaffe, Scott, and Tobe, p. 15.

56. Ibid., p. 36.

57. Ibid.

58. The *New York Times* states that in "step with other large companies, Chase has replaced a paternalistic organization that guaranteed a job and a raise and a pension with one that tries to assist the employee by sharpening skills that will enhance career success, but will not guarantee anything." (ibid.)

59. Ibid., p. 38.

60. Ibid.

Chapter 6

1. Rifkin, p. 96.

2. Ibid.

3. James Womack, Daniel Jones, and Daniel Roos, *The Machine that Changed the World* (Macmillan: New York, 1990), quoted in Rifkin, p. 96.

4. Handy, pp. 32–33.

5. Ibid., p. 52.

6. Womack, Jones, and Roos; quoted in Rifkin, p. 96.

7. Handy, p. 51.

8. Ibid. p. 90; emphasis added.

9. Ibid., pp. 90–91.

10. Ibid., pp. 156–57.

11. Drucker, p. 133.

12. Peter Drucker, *Post-Capitalist Society* (Harperbusiness: New York, 1993), p. 73.

13. Martin Kenney and Richard Florid, *Beyond Mass Production: The Japanese System and Its Transfer to the United States* (Oxford University Press: New York, 1993), quoted in Rifkin, p. 100.

14. Ibid., p. 97.

15. Drucker, p. 89.

16. Rifkin, p. 97.

17. Ibid., p. 98.

18. Ibid., p. 99.

19. Quoted in Rifkin, p. 98.

20. Drucker, p. 92.

21. "Jobs and skills under the lifelong nenko employment practice," *The Transformation of Work*, pp. 116, 120.

22. Quoted in ibid., p. 124.

23. Ibid., p. 121.

24. Rifkin, p. 146.

25. Ibid., p. 147.

26. Ibid.

27. Quoted in ibid., p. 148.

28. Ibid., p. 149.

29. Ibid.

30. Buchmann, p. 49.

31. Ibid., p. 50.

32. Ibid., p. 51.

33. Ibid.

34. Ibid., p. 50.

35. Ibid.

36. Ibid.

37. Ibid., p. 51.

38. Handy, p. 173.

39. Ibid., p. 114.

40. Ibid., p. 45.

41. Ibid., p. 46.

42. Ibid., p. 48.

43. Ibid., p. 114.

44. Ibid., p. 172.

45. Ibid.

Chapter 7

1. Handy, p. 47. Handy's second book, *The Age of Paradox*, appears to admit that 45 hours/week could be a decided undercalculation.

2. Ibid., p. 48.

3. Ibid., p. 91.

4. Drucker, *Managing for the Future*, p. 197.

5. Drucker, *Post-Capitalist Society*, p. 95.

6. Ibid., p. 23.

7. Hammer and Champy, p. 43.

8. Ibid.

9. Handy, p. 96.

10. Rifkin, p. 192.

11. Handy, p. 92.

12. Ibid.

13. Drucker, p. 276.

14. Handy, p. 93.

15. Ibid., p. 96.

16. Ibid., p. 99.

17. Ibid., pp. 98–99.

18. Ibid., p. 93.

19. Ibid.

20. Ibid.

21. Rifkin, p. 191.

22. Quoted in ibid.

23. Handy, pp. 54, 53.

24. Rifkin, p. 192.

25. Handy, p. 98.

26. Handy, *The Age of Paradox, p. 29.*

27. Rifkin, p. 193.

28. *New York Times,* Sunday, March 3, 1996, p. 16.

29. Beck, p. 144.

30. Handy, *The Age of Unreason,* p. 171.

31. Buchmann, p. 48.

32. Ibid., p. 66

33. Handy, p. 27.

34. Rifkin, p. 194.

35. Kotre and Hall, p. 289.

36. Handy, p. 177.

Chapter 8

1. Barbara R. Bergmann, *The Economic Emergence of Women* (Basic Books: New York, 1986), p. 10.

2. The family wage was also an underpinning for the corporate loyalty as well, as Barbara Ehrenreich explains in *The Hearts of Men:*

American Dreams and the Flight from Commitment (Anchor: Garden City, N.Y., 1983): "Men who were the sole support of their families could be counted on to be loyal, or at least, fearful employees." (173)

3. Kathleen Gerson, *Hard Choices: How Women Decide about Work, Career, and Motherhood* (University of California Press: Berkeley, 1985), pp. 204–7.

4. Bergmann, ibid.

5. On the issue of the traditional cultural norm, Beck and Beck-Gernsheim claim that "Anyone seeking to force women out of jobs and back to the kitchen ought to acknowledge that in the face of the rising number of divorces this means reserving the gaps in the social security system for women." They then argue that this "contravenes legal positions in modern democratic society which offer equal rights irrespective of gender and make success dependent on personal achievement" (p. 143). The same issue as well as the further issue of how well the social security system serves the needs of woman have been obvious topics of much feminist scholarship. For an overview of some of the most important contributions of feminist scholarship on the welfare state until 1990, see in particular the essay, "The New Feminist Scholarship on the Welfare State," by Linda Gordon as well as the other essays collected in *Women, the State, and Welfare*, ed. Linda Gordon (The University of Wisconsin Press: Madison, 1990). See also by Linda Gordon, *Pitied But Not Entitled: Single Mothers and the History of Welfare* (The Free Press: New York, 1994) and Part 3 of *Unruly Practices* by Nancy Fraser.

6. Bergmann, p. 11.

7. Ibid., p. 201.

8. Ibid., p. 217.

9. Ibid., pp. 51–2.

10. Quoted in Katherine S. Newman, *Declining Fortunes: The Withering of the American Dream* (Basic Books: New York, 1993), p. 107.

11. Isabel V. Sawhill, "Developing Normative Standards for Child-Support Payments," in *The Parental Child Support Obligation*, ed. Judith Cassetty (Lexington Books: Lexington, Mass., 1983), pp. 91–2.

12. Beck, p. 114.

13. For clarification of the broad meaning of this concept, see note 3 in the preface.

14. Ibid., p. 117.

15. Bergmann, p. 237.

16. Ulrich Beck, *Ecological Enlightenment: Essays on the Politics of the Risk Society*, tr. Mark A. Ritter (Humanities Press: New Jersey, 1995), p. 43.

17. Beck, *Risk Society*, pp. 122–23.

18. Ruth Sidel, *On Her Own: Growing Up in the Shadow of the American Dream* (Viking: New York, 1990), p. 27.

19. Ibid., p. 23.

20. Ibid., pp. 16, 20.

21. Ibid., p. 32.

22. Ibid., p. 15.

23. Ibid.

24. Judith K. Sprankle, *Working It Out: The Domestic Double Standard* (Walker and Company: New York, 1986).

25. Bergmann, p. 272.

26. Ibid.

27. Ibid., pp. 269–70.

28. Ibid., p. 270.

29. Arlie Hochschild, *The Second Shift: Working Parents and the Revolution at Home* (Viking: New York, 1989).

30. Bergmann, p. 270.

31. Aasta S. Lubin, *Managing Success: High-Echelon Careers and Motherhood* (Columbia University Press: New York, 1987), p. 51.

32. Ibid., p. 116.

33. Ibid., p. 128.

34. Ibid., pp. 127–28.

35. Ibid., P. 156.

36. Ibid.

37. Ibid., p. 51.

38. Ibid., p. 123.

39. Sidel, p. 225.

40. Ibid., p. 226.

41. Ehrenreich, p. 180.

42. Ibid., pp. 180–81.

43. Sidel, pp. 169–70.

44. Ehrenreich, pp. 172–73.

45. Ibid., p. 175.

46. Ibid., p. 176.

Chapter 9

1. Quoted in William Bridges, *Jobshift: How to Prosper in a Workplace without Jobs* (Addison-Wesley Publishing Company: Reading, Mass., 1994), p. 100.

2. Peter Wagner, *A Sociology of Modernity: Liberty and Discipline* (Routledge: London 1994), p. 164.

3. Bridges, pp. 50–1.

4. Ibid., pp. 58–9.

5. Ibid., p. 128.

6. Ibid., p. 63.

7. Ibid.

8. Ibid., p. 104.

9. Ibid.

10. Ibid., p. 105.

11. Ibid., p. 167.

12. Ibid., p. 112.

13. Piore, p. 182.

14. Ibid.

15. Ibid., p. 190.

16. Bridges, p. 112.

17. Ibid.

18. Ibid., p. 113.

19. Handy, p. 171.

20. Ibid., p. 180.

21. Handy, *The Age of Paradox*, p. 76.

22. Handy, *The Age of Unreason*, p. 185.

23. Ibid., p. 186.

24. Ibid., p. 188.

25. Ibid.

26. Ibid., p. 189.

27. Ibid., pp. 160–61.

28. Ibid., p. 204.

29. Ibid., p. 205.

30. Handy, *The Age of Paradox*, p. 85.

31. Handy, *The Age of Unreason*, p. 206.

32. Ibid., p. 177.

33. Ibid.

34. Ibid., p. 114.

Chapter 10

1. Drucker, *Managing for the Future*, p. 181.

2. Ibid.

3. Ibid.

4. Ibid., pp. 180–81.

5. Ibid., p. 181–82.

6. Drucker, *Post-Capitalist Society*, p. 60.

7. Ibid.

8. Ibid., p. 59; punctuation is changed in final sentence.

9. Ibid., p. 57.

10. Ibid., p. 60.

11. Handy, *The Age of Paradox*, p. 50.

12. Ibid.

13. Jaffe, Scott, and Tobe, pp. 104–5.

14. Handy, p. 51.

15. Ibid., p. 53.

16. Ibid., p. 57.

17. Ibid., p. 58.

18. Ibid., p. 57.

19. Ibid., p. 54.

20. Ibid., p. 57.

21. Ibid., p. 63.

22. Ibid.

23. Drucker, p. 57.

24. Ibid.

25. Zygmunt Bauman, *Life in Fragments: Essays in Postmodern Morality* (Blackwell: Oxford, 1995), p. 114.

26. The term "juggernaut" is used by Anthony Giddens in his phenomenological description of modernity in *The Consequences of Modernity* to describe a "runaway engine of enormous power which, collectively as human beings, we can drive to some extent but which also threatens to rush out of our control and which could rend itself asunder" (p. 139). I consider the image to be a very powerful and apt one and wish to emphasize the pace of the runaway engine more than the capacity to veer which Giddens highlights. Both elements are present in the image of an accelerating, reaping and destroying machine which appears at both the beginning and the end of William Greider's *One World, Ready or Not: The Manic Logic of Global Capitalism* (Simon & Schuster: New York, 1997).

27. Bauman, p. 265.

28. Ibid., p. 89.

29. Ibid., p. 266.

30. Ibid.

31. Ibid., p. 89.

32. Ibid., p. 266.

33. Ibid., p. 265.

34. Ibid.

35. Ibid. p. 266.

36. Ibid. p. 76.

37. Ibid., p. 88.

38. Ibid.

39. Ibid., p. 89.

40. Ibid.

41. Ibid., p. 267.

42. Ibid. p. 81.

Chapter 11

1. Ibid., p. 153.

2. Compare this comparison on the level of technologies of the self with the comparison Bauman draws between the modern pilgrim and the postmodern tourist, pp. 268–69.

3. Ibid., p. 154.

4. Newman, p. 57.

5. Ibid., p. 212.

6. Chapter sixteen of Nicholas Rose's *Governing the Soul* (Routledge: London, 1989), is entitled "obliged to be free."

7. Compare the reactions of one Steven Holthausen, "loan officer turned tourist guide," to the loss of his former employment:

> His high-velocity slide has caused him to go into his soul with calipers. He is suffused with anger, much of it toward himself. Why, he berates himself over and over, did he give so many evenings and weekends to his employer? Why didn't he see that his job was doomed? . . . . (*New York Times*, ibid.)

8. Zygmunt Bauman, *Postmodern Ethics* (Blackwell: Oxford, 1993), p. 98.

9. Ibid.

10. Bauman, p. 154n. Bauman makes this distinction in a very different context of discussing the replacement of psychotherapy by sexual therapy.

Chapter 12

1. Newman, p. 216.

2. Ibid.

3. Bauman, p. 271.

4. Ibid.

5. Ibid., p. 272.

6. Ibid., pp. 271–72.

7. Ibid., p. 272.

8. Ibid., p. 274.

9. Ibid., p. 271.

10. Skocpol, p. 258.

11. Ibid.

12. Ibid., 32.

13. Skocpol follows Hugh Heclo in arguing that Social Security is "helping the poor by not talking about them" (p. 265).

14. Ibid., p. 5.

15. Ibid., p. 268.

16. Ibid.

17. Ibid., p. 267.

18. Ibid., p. 268.

19. Ibid., p. 269.

Appendix

1. Rifkin, p. 236.

2. Philippe Van Parijs, "Competing Justifications of Basic Income," *Arguing for Basic Income*, p. 3. The basic income would not have to be granted on an individual basis, but could be paid to households. A major argument for individual payment concerns the economic and social situation of women: "on the one hand, the labor market crisis makes maintenance through wage labor precarious and discontinuous; and, on the other, it coincides with already existing societal trends toward individualization and the individual grounding of choices. . . . **neither** on the **labor market** with its falling capacity to absorb continuous wage labor and the claim to a living wage—**nor** through **marriage** are women able to earn enough to secure a livelihood." (From Claus Offe, *Modernity and the State* (MIT Press: Cambridge, Mass., 1996), p. 206.

3. Ibid.

4. Ibid., p. 7.

5. Esping-Anderson, p. 37. See also footnote 38 (p. 34) of the Van Parijs essay for other quotations from other sources which express this same idea.

6. Ibid., p. 46.

7. Phlippe Van Parijs, "The Second Marriage of Justice and Efficiency," *Arguing for Basic Income*, p. 232.

8. Standing, p. 59.

9. Ibid.

10. Ibid.

11. Beck and Beck-Gernsheim, p. 162.

12. Claus Offe, "A Non-Productivist Design for Social Policies," *Arguing for Basic Income*, p. 76.

13. Ibid., p. 77.

14. Offe, p. 73.

15. Ibid., p. 74.

16. A.B. Atkinson, "Beveridge, the national minimum and its future in a European context," *Incomes and the Welfare State* (Cambridge University Press: Cambridge, 1995), p. 301.

17. Ibid., p. 303. The higher level of participation income would depend on raising the English tax rate from 25 percent to 35 percent and the higher rate to 50 percent. For a similar discussion of costs and benefits involved in the implementation of a basic income, see Chapter 13 of *Capitalism with a Human Face*, Samuel Brittan (Edward Elgar: Hants, 1995), pp. 242–262.

18. Bridges, p. 190.

19. Ibid.

20. Ibid., p. 189. In this quotation, Bridges means by "jobless" not having what has been termed an "occupation" here. The transition from occupation to job here parallels his transition from job to the newly "dejobbed" world.

21. Ibid.

22. Ibid.

23. Ibid., p. 190.

24. Ibid., p. 189.

25. Daniel Moynihan, *The Politics of a Guaranteed Income* (Random House: New York, 1973), quoted in Allan Sheahen, *Guaranteed Income: The Right To Economic Security* (Gain Publications: Los Angeles, 1983), p. 111.

26. Ibid.

27. Van Parijs, p. 8.

Bibliography

Aronowitz, Stanley and William DiFazio. *The Jobless Future: Sci-Tech and the Dogma of Work*. Minneapolis: University of Minnesota Press, 1994.

Atkinson, A. B. *Incomes and the Welfare State*. Cambridge: Cambridge University Press, 1995.

———. *Public Economies in Action: The Basic Income/Flat Tax Proposal*. Oxford: Clarendon Press, 1995.

Bauman, Zygmunt. *Intimations of Postmodernity*. London: Routledge, 1992.

———. *Life in Fragments: Essays in Postmodern Morality*. Oxford: Basil Blackwell, 1995.

———. *Modernity and Ambivalence*. Ithaca, NY: Cornell University Press, 1992.

———. *Modernity and the Holocaust*. Ithaca, NY: Cornell University Press, 1989.

———. *Postmodern Ethics*. Oxford: Basil Blackwell, 1993.

Beck, Ulrich. *Ecological Enlightenment: Essays on the Politics of the Risk Society*. Tr. Mark A. Ritter. New Jersey: Humanities Press, 1995.

———. *Risk Society: Towards a New Modernity*. London: Sage, 1992.

———. and Elisabeth Beck-Gernsheim. *The Normal Chaos of Love*. Cambridge: Polity, 1994.

————, Anthony Giddens and Scott Lash. *Reflexive Modernization: Politics, Tradition and Aesthetics in the Modern Social Order.* Stanford: Stanford University Press, 1994.

Bergmann, Barbara. *The Economic Emergence of Women.* New York: Basic Books, 1986.

Beveridge, W.H. *The Pillars of Security.* London: Allen and Unwin, 1943.

Bridges, William. *Jobshift: How to Prosper in a Workplace without Jobs.* Reading, Mass.: Addison-Wesley Publishing Company, 1994.

Brittan, Samuel. *Capitalism with a Human Face.* Hants, Eng.: Edward Elgar, 1995.

Buchmann, Marlis. *The Script of Life in Modern Society: Entry into Adulthood in a Changing World.* Chicago: The University of Chicago Press, 1989.

Burchell, Graham, Colin Gordon, and Peter Miller, eds. *The Foucault Effect.* Chicago: The University of Chicago Press, 1991.

Craib, Ian. *The Importance of Disappointment.* London, Routledge, 1994.

Defert, Daniel. "'Popular Life' and Insurance Technology." *The Foucault Effect.* Graham Burchell et al., eds. Chicago: The University of Chicago Press, 1991. 211–34.

Dreyfus, Hubert and Paul Rabinow. *Michel Foucault: Beyond Structuralism and Hermeneutics.* Second Edition. Chicago: University of Chicago Press, 1983.

Drucker, Peter. *Managing the Future: The 1990s and Beyond.* New York: Truman Talley Books/Plume, 1993.

————. *Post-Capitalist Society.* New York: HarperBusiness, 1993.

Dworkin, Gerald. "Paternalism." In *Morality and the Law.* Richard Wasserstrom, ed. Belmont: Wadsworth, 1971. 107–26.

Edwards, Richard. *Contested Terrain: The Transformation of the Workplace in the Twentieth Century.* New York: Basic Books, 1979.

Ehrenreich, Barbara. *The Hearts of Men: American Dreams and the Flight from Commitment.* Garden City, NY: Anchor, 1983.

————. *The Fear of Falling: The Inner Life of the Middle Class.* New York: Pantheon Books, 1989.

Esping-Andersen, Gøsta. *The Three Worlds of Welfare Capitalism.* Princeton: Princeton University Press, 1990.

Ewald, François. "Insurance and Risk." *The Foucault Effect.* Graham Burchell et al., eds. Chicago: The University of Chicago Press, 1991. 197–210.

——. *L'Etat providence.* Paris: Editions Bernard Grasset, 1986.

Falkingham, Jane and John Hills, eds. *The Dynamic of Welfare: The Welfare State and the Life Cycle.* Hertfordshire: Prentice Hall/Harvester Wheatsheaf, 1995.

Fornäs, Johan. *Cultural Theory and Late Modernity.* London: Sage, 1995.

Michel Foucault. *Discipline and Punish.* Alan Sheridan, trans. New York: Pantheon, 1979.

——. "Foucault at the Collège de France I: A Course Summary." James Bernauer, trans. *Philosophy and Social Criticism* VIII, 2 (summer 1981). 235–42.

——. "Foucault at the Collège de France II: A Course Summary." James Bernauer, trans. *Philosophy and Social Criticism* VIII, 3 (fall 1981). 349–59.

——. "Governmentality." Colin Gordon, rev. In *The Foucault Effect.* Burchell et al., eds. 87–104.

——. *The History of Sexuality.* Robert Hurley, trans. New York: Vintage, 1980.

——. "Is it really important to think?" an interview with michel foucault." Thomas Keenan, trans. *Philosophy and Social Criticism* IX, 1 (spring 1982). 29–40.

——. *Michel Foucault: Politics, Philosophy, Culture: Interviews and Other Writings 1977–84.* Lawrence D. Kritzman, ed. Oxford: Blackwell, 1988.

——. "Omnes et Singulatim: Towards a Criticism of Political Reason." *The Tanner Lectures on Human Values.* Salt Lake City: University of Utah Press, 1981. 223–54.

——. *Power/Knowledge: Selected Interviews and Other Writings.* Colin Gordon, ed. New York: Pantheon, 1980.

——. "The Subject and Power." In Dreyfus and Rabinow, 208–226.

——. *Technologies of the Self: A Seminar with Michel Foucault.* L.H. Martin, et al., eds. Amherst: University of Massachusetts Press, 1988.

Fraser, Nancy. *Justice Interruptus: Critical Reflecting on the "Post-socialist" Condition.* New York: Routledge, 1997.

——. *Unruly Practices.* Minneapolis: University of Minnesota Press, 1989.

Freeden, Michael. *The New Liberalism: An Ideology of Social Reform.* Oxford: Clarendon Press, 1978.

Gauthier, Anne Hélène. *The State and the Family: A Comparative Analysis of Family Policies in Industrialized Countries*. Oxford: Clarendon Press, 1996.

Gerson, Kathleen. *Hard Choices: How Women Decide about Work, Career, and Motherhood*. Berkeley: University of California Press, 1985.

Giddens, Anthony. *Beyond Left and Right: The Future of Radical Politics*. Stanford: Stanford University Press, 1994.

———. *The Consequences of Modernity*. Stanford: Stanford University Press, 1990.

———. *Modernity and Self-Identity: Self and Society in the Late Modern Age*. Stanford: Stanford University Press, 1991.

Gigerenzer, Gerd et al., eds. *The Empire of Chance*. Cambridge: Cambridge University Press, 1989.

Goodin, Robert E. *Reasons for Welfare: The Political Theory of the Welfare State*. Princeton: Princeton University Press, 1989.

Gordon, Colin. "Afterword." In *Power/Knowledge: Selected Interviews and Other Writings*. 229–259.

———. "Governmental Rationality: An Introduction." In *The Foucault Effect*. 1–52.

Gordon, Linda. *Pitied but Not Entitled: Single Mothers and the History of Welfare*. New York: Free Press, 1994.

———, ed. *Women, the State, and Welfare*. Madison: University of Wisconsin Press, 1990.

Gorz, André. *Critique of Economic Reason*. London: Verso, 1989.

Greider, William. *One World, Ready or Not: The Manic Logic of Global Capitalism*. New York, Simon & Schuster, 1997.

Haber, William and Wilbur J. Cohen, eds. *Readings in Social Security*. New York: Prentice-Hall, Inc., 1948.

Hacking, Ian. *The Taming of Chance*. Cambridge: Cambridge University Press, 1990.

Hammer, Michael and James Champy. *Reengineering the Corporation: A Manifesto for Business Revolution*. New York: HarperBusiness, 1993.

Handy, Charles. *The Age of Paradox*. Boston: Harvard Business School Press, 1994.

———. *The Age of Unreason*. Boston: Harvard Business School Press, 1990.

———. *Beyond Certainty: The Changing World of Organizations.* Boston: Harvard Business School, 1996.

Harvey, David, *The Condition of Postmodernity: An Enquiry into the Origins of Cultural Change.* Oxford: Blackwell, 1989.

Held, Thomas. "Institutionalization and De-Institutionalization of the Life Course." *Human Development* 29. Martin Kohli and John W. Meyer, eds. 157–62.

Hewitt, Patricia. *About Time: The Revolution in Work and Family Life.* London: Rivers Oram, 1993.

Hirschman, Albert O. *The Passions and the Interests: Political Arguments for Capitalism before its Triumph.* Princeton: Princeton University Press, 1977.

Hochschild, Arlie. "The Fractured Family." *The American Prospect* 6 (summer 1991). 106–115.

———. *The Second Shift: Working Parents and the Revolution at Home.* New York: Viking, 1989.

Jaffe, Dennis, Cynthia D. Scott, and Glenn R. Tobe. *Rekindling Commitment.* San Francisco: Jossey-Bass Publishers, 1994.

Kenney, Martin and Richard Florida. *Beyond Mass Production: The Japanese System and Its Transfer to the United States.* New York: Oxford University Press, 1993.

Kohli, Martin. "Die Institutionalisierung des Lebenslaufes." *Kölner Zeitschrift für Soziologie and Sozialpsychologie.* 37: 1–29.

———. "The World We Forgot: A Historical Review of the Life Course." In *Later Life: The Social Psychology of Aging.* Victor W. Marshall, ed. Beverly Hills: Sage, 1985. 271–303.

———. and John W. Meyer. "Social Structure and the Construction of Life Stages." *Human Development* 29. Kohli, and Meyer, eds. *Social Struture and Social Construction of Life Stages.* 145–49.

Kotre, John and Elizabeth Hall. *Seasons of Life: Our Dramatic Journey from Birth to Death.* Boston: Little, Brown and Company, 1990.

Lubin, Aasta S. *Managing Success: High-Echelon Careers and Motherhood.* New York: Columbia University Press, 1987.

Lubove, Roy. *The Struggle for Social Security.* Cambridge: Harvard University Press, 1968.

Madrick, Jeffrey. *The End of Affluence: The Cause and Consequences of America's Economic Dilemma.* New York: Random House, 1995.

Mayer, Karl-Ulrich. "Structural Constraints on the Life Course." *Human Development* 29. Martin Kohli and John W. Meyer, eds. 163–70.

———. and Walter Müller. "The State and the Structure of the Life Course." *Human Development and the Life Course: Multidisciplinary Perspectives.* Aage Sorensen, L. Sherrod, and F. Weinert, eds. Hillsdale, N.J.: Erlbaum, 1986. 217–45.

McNay, Lois. *Foucault: A Critical Introduciton.* New York: Continuum, 1994.

Meyer, John W. "Self and the Life Course: Institutionalization and Its Effects." *Human Development and the Life Course: Multidisciplinary Perspectives.* Aage Sorensen, L. Sherrod, and F. Weinert, eds. Hillsdale, N.J.: Erlbaum, 1986. 199–216.

Moynihan, Daniel. *The Politics of a Guaranteed Income.* New York: Random House, 1973.

Myles, John. *Old Age in the Welfare State: The Political Economy of Public Pensions.* Lawrence: University Press of Kansas, 1989.

Neugarten, Bernice L. *Middle Age and Aging.* Chicago: University of Chicago Press, 1968.

———. and Gunhild O. Hagestad. "Aging and the Life Course." *Handbook of Aging and the Social Sciences.* Robert H. Binstock and Ethel Shanas, eds. New York: Van Nostrand Reinhold, 1976.

Newman, Katherine S. *Declining Fortunes: The Withering of the American Dream.* New York: Basic Books, 1993

———. *Falling from Grace: The Experience of Downward Mobility in the American Middle Class.* New York: Free Press, 1988.

New York Times. "The Downsizing of America." Seven article series: "The price of jobs lost: a national heartache"; "The company: one happy family, no longer; "The community: pulled apart, scrambling to regroup"; "The family: holes where the dignity used to be"; "The college class: 25 years later, success and anxiety"; "Politics: a struggle to find the right sell"; "Is there a better way? The search for answers." March 3–9, 1996.

Oestreich, Gerhard. *Neostoicism and the Early Modern State.* Brigitta Oestreich and H.G. Hoenigsberger, eds. David McLintock, trans. Cambridge: Cambridge University Press, 1982.

Offe, Claus. "Arbeit as Schlüsselkategorie?" *Krise der Arbeitsgesellschaft?* Joachim Mathes, ed. Frankfurt: Campus, 1982.

———. *Arbeitsgesellschaft: Strukturprobleme und Zukunftsperspektiven.* Frankfurt: Campus, 1984.

———. *Contradictions of the Welfare State.* Cambridge, Mass.: MIT Press, 1984.

———. *Disorganized Capitalism: Contemporary Transformations of Work and Politics.* Cambridge, Mass.: MIT Press, 1985.

———. "A Non-Productivist Design for Social Policies." *Arguing for Basic Income.* Phillipe Van Paris, ed. London: Verso, 1992. 61–78.

———, Karl Hinrichs, and Helmut Wiesenthal, eds. *Arbeitszeitpolitik: Formen und Folgen einer Neuverteilung der Arbeitszeit.* 2nd ed. Frankfurt: Campus, 1983.

Piore, Michael J. *Beyond Individualism.* Cambridge: Harvard University Press, 1995.

Reich, Robert B. *The Work of Nations: Preparing Ourselves for 21st Century Capitalism.* New York: Alfred A. Knopf, 1991.

Rifkin, Jeremy. *The End of Work: The Decline of the Global Labor Force and the Dawn of the Post-Market Era.* New York: G.P. Putnam's Sons, 1995.

Ritter, Gerhard A. *Social Welfare in Germany and Britain: Origins and Development.* Kim Traynor, trans. Leamington Spa: Berg, 1986.

Rose, Nicholas. *Governing the Soul.* London: Routledge, 1989.

Rowntree, B.S. *Poverty: A Study of Town Life.* London: Macmillan and Co., 1902.

———. *Poverty and Progress.* London: Longmans, Green, and Co., 1941.

Rubinow, I.M. *Social Insurance.* New York: Henry Holt and Company, 1916.

Sawhill, Isabel V. "Developing Normative Standards for Child-Support Payments." *The Parental Child Support Obligation.* Lexington, Mass.: Lexington Books, 1983.

Sheahen, Allan. *The Politics of a Guaranteed Income.* New York: Random House, 1973.

Sidel, Ruth. *On Her Own: Growing Up in the Shadow of the American Dream.* New York: Viking, 1990.

Skocpol, Theda. *Protecting Soldiers and Mothers: The Political Origins of Social Policy in the United States.* Cambridge: The Belknap Press of Harvard University Press, 1992.

———. *Social Policy in the United States.* Princeton: Princeton University Press, 1995.

———. "Sustainable Social Policy." *The American Prospect* 1 (2) (summer 1990). 58–70.

———. with Edwin Amenta. "Redefining the New Deal: World War II and the Development of Social Provision in the United States." *Social Policy in the United States.* 167–208.

Sprankle, Judith K. *Working It Out: The Domestic Double Standard.* New York: Walker and Company, 1986.

Stack, Maurice. "The Meaning of Social Security." *Readings in Social Security.* William Haber and Wilbur J. Cohen, eds. New York: Prentice-Hall, Inc., 1948.

Standing, Guy. "The Need For a New Social Consensus." *Arguing for Basic Income: Ethical Foundations for a Radical Reform.* London: Verso, 1992. 47–60.

———. *Unemployment and Labour Market Flexibility: The United Kingdom.* Geneva: International Labour Office, 1986.

Tough, Paul, Ronald Blackwell, Albert Dunlap, George Gilder, Edward Luttwak, Robert Reich. "Does America Still Work? On the turbulent energies of the new capitalism." *Harper's Magazine* May 1996. 35–47.

Van Parijs, Philippe. *Arguing for Basic Income: Ethical Foundations for a Radical Reform.* London: Verso, 1992.

———. "Competing Justifications of Basic Income." In *Arguing for Basic Income.* London: Verso, 1992. 3–43.

———. *Real Freedom for All: What (If Anything) Can Justify Capitalism?* Oxford: Clarendon Press, 1995.

Wagner, Peter. *A Sociology of Modernity: Liberty and Discipline.* London: Routledge, 1994.

Womack, James, Daniel Jones, and Daniel Roos. *The Machine that Changed the World.* New York: Macmillan, 1990.

Wood, Stephen, ed. *The Transformation of Work.* Boston: Unwyn Hyman, 1989.

Index

231